POLISH ROBBIN' HOODS

The Inside Story
of the Panczko Brothers,
The World's Busiest Burglars

Ed Baumann
and
John O'Brien

Bonus Books, Inc. Chicago

96 95 94 93 92   5 4 3 2 1

Library of Congress Catalog Card Number: 92-74152

International Standard Book Number: 0-929387-85-6

Bonus Books, Inc.
160 East Illinois Street
Chicago, Illinois 60611

Printed in the United States of America

To Peanuts and Pops

Talking to us might have been the
only honest ting dey ever did.

CONTENTS

Foreword By Mike Royko / vii

1. Shopping at the "Mersh" / 1
2. A Day in the Life of / 9
3. Masters of Innovation / 19
4. One Burglar's Family / 27
5. Serving Uncle Sam—Sort of / 45
6. Getting Down to Business / 57
7. Waiting in the Wings / 71
8. Making a Name for Himself / 93
9. Letting George Do It / 105
10. Pops Stops Another Slug / 115
11. The Parker Pen Caper / 119
12. The Nashville Diamond Heist / 131
13. Bullets Busting Out All Over / 137
14. A Shakedown Backfires / 147
15. Tennessee State Prison / 153
16. Butch Takes Over / 165
17. The Road to Mandel-Lear / 175
18. Pops Gets Buckshot of the Brain / 183
19. Something Fishy at 26th and Cal / 195

20. One Screwdrive, Hold the Onions / 205

21. Peanuts Comes Home; Pops Goes Bye-Bye / 221

22. Peanuts Goes Hollywood / 233

23. Go East, Young Man, Go East / 249

24. The Pompano Beach Boys / 257

25. Hey, Mister, Your Keys / 267

26. King Solomon's Mines / 275

27. And So, to Jail / 283

28. Peanuts on Ice; Butch Dies / 293

29. Pops' Last Hurrah / 303

30. Advice for Jewelry Salesmen / 309

31. Anti-Crime Tips from One Who Knows / 315

32. Keep Your Nose Clean / 319

33. Epilogue / 323

FOREWORD

I'm sitting in this lawyer's office. We're waiting for Pops.

Pops is his client. Joseph (Pops) Panczko, Chicago's best-known professional thief, politicians aside.

The lawyer is excited. I'm going to write a book about Pops. My publisher has promised a big hard-cover advance. There will be paperback royalties and maybe a movie.

So we're talking about serious money. Pops' split would be more than he could make stealing in a year or two. And all he'd have to do is talk into a tape recorder for a week and ride around town recreating some of his most spectacularly stupid crimes.

The more we talk, the happier the lawyer becomes. If Pops makes a lot of money, he can pay the lawyer what he owes. Then the lawyer, an enthusiastic horse-bettor, can pay his bookie.

While waiting, we swap a few Pops stories. I had a lot of them because we're from the same Humboldt Park neighborhood. We loitered in some of the same bars and restaurants, although the cops never stopped in to shake me down for meal money, as they did with Pops. A couple of my boyhood pals had become part of Pops' burglary gang. And as a reporter, I had covered parts of his dippy career.

The lawyer, of course, knew even more because he had been keeping Pops out of jail.

He tells me about Pops being nailed on a federal rap for using slugs to make long distance phone calls.

See? That's why I wanted to write a book about him. Here is a man who, in his more serious moments, is one of America's most accomplished burglars, but he gets himself pinched by the Feds for using slugs in a phone.

"We're in court on the slug case," the lawyer says. "There's a recess and we go out in the hall and I want to check in with my office but I don't have any change for the phone. I ask Pops if he has any coins. He says: 'Here, this will work.' And he hands me a slug. Right there in the court house where he's on trial for using slugs."

So I tell the lawyer about the time I'm in a barber shop in my old neighborhood where my mother still lived. Pops comes into the shop, one of his hangouts. He riffles through the stack of old newspapers and says: "I wanna show you something."

It's a front-page picture of a couple of dead men, lying on a floor with guns in their hands. They had broken into a store late at night. The police had been tipped and were waiting. The thieves opened fire. The police shot back and killed them.

Or so the newspaper story said. Pops has a different version.

"Look close at the picture and tell me what you see."

I tell him I see two thieves who shouldn't have been carrying guns because a smart burglar is never armed. A gun is damning evidence. I also see two guys who would have been wiser to drop their guns and put their hands up.

"What hands are the guns in?" Pops asked.

The guns are in their right hands.

Pops jabbed a finger at one of the dead men. "He was a pure lefty. Did everything lefty. So why would a lefty use a gun righty? You figure it out."

A throw gun: an untraceable weapon that some police carry in the event they shoot someone who turns out to be unarmed so they can put it in his hand and make it justifiable. It is not in any dictionary, but it's part of the street language.

"See, one of them had this wife. But she got a boyfriend. So she wants to get rid of the husband. She tells the cops she'll make a deal. She'll tip them where they're going to pull the job if they make sure she gets out of the marriage."

So the cops became heroes, she was spared the cost of hiring a lawyer, and the divorce rate was reduced.

"And people wonder why I never got married," Pops says.

The law office door finally opens and Pops enters, dressed like the building janitor. Maybe not as good. He has about ten leather brief cases under his arms. He tosses one at me and dumps the others on the desk. "Here, you can pass 'em around."

Now, where does one suddenly acquire ten leather briefcases?

He shrugs. "There was this delivery van down stairs by an office store. The driver left his van door open and when he drove away they must've fell out of his truck."

We have the meeting. At one point, I ask what time it is. Pops says: "You don't have a watch?"

He pulls back his jacket sleeve. There are a dozen fine watches on his arm. "Go on, have one."

I select a spiffy French model and don't ask where he got them. Maybe a jeweler left his door open and they fell out of his store.

We discuss the book deal. Pops is agreeable, the lawyer is elated, and we set a date for our first interview session.

The next day, the phone rings. The lawyer is distraught. The deal is off. Pops' sister says it will ruin the family name. I tell him that is ridiculous, since everybody knows the Panczkos aren't candidates for the Social Register.

He says he'll try again. But he calls back and says it is more serious than that. The sister fears Pops will be bumped off if he reveals trade secrets.

No problem. We'll leave out anything that could get him bumped off. Besides, Pops is not a member of the Mafia. He's just a blue collar thief. Unlike his brother, Peanuts, Pops never used a gun. He didn't hurt people. All he did was steal something every day. If anything, The Mob would be amused.

I also told him that I intended to mention Peanuts only briefly. Mugs who use guns aren't amusing. Bad seed, that lad.

But the sister was adamant. And it was no go.

Years passed. One day the phone rang and it was the lawyer. But now he was a judge.

Sounding a bit sheepish, he said he was doing a pro-bono favor for an old client who is having some legal and financial difficulties. Was I still interested in doing a book on Pops?

Consider that. A black-robed judge acting, in effect, as literary agent for a professional thief. What a town Chicago is.

The idea still had appeal, but I was tied up with other projects and had to take a pass. And I felt bad because I believed Pops' story was well worth telling.

So I'm glad that it's finally been done in amazingly meticulous detail by two veteran Chicago newsmen.

And maybe it will be made into a movie. My choice to play Pops would be Chicago's own Bill Murray, of Saturday Night Live fame. Sure, he's a comic. But who else but a natural-born comic runs around with a dozen watches on his arm?

Mike Royko
September 1992

ACKNOWLEDGEMENT

This book could not have been written without the cooperation of Joseph and Paul Panczko and their long-suffering sister, Louise, and the authors are eternally grateful to Mary Lou Frank for bringing us together.

"Never break into a building more than one story tall, in case the cops start shooting, 'cause if the bullets don't kill you, the fall will."

—Joseph "Pops" Panczko

"I tell you, if there's a legit cop who hasn't got his hand out, he hasn't caught me yet, so I've never met him."

—Paul "Peanuts" Panczko

The authors apologize to anyone who might be offended by the occasional use of profanity or ethnic commentary that appear in these pages. The characters in this book are not priests or Sunday School teachers, but real-life Chicago street bozos who have lived by their wits in a nether world beyond the ken of law abiding citizens. To clean up their conversations or launder their verbiage would not be giving the reader an honest portrayal of a way of life that exists in our cities today, and probably always will.

Ed Baumann and
John O'Brien
Chicago, 1992

CHAPTER 1

![black bar]

SHOPPING AT THE "MERSH"

It was a balmy April afternoon along the brackish Chicago River's north bank and the western sun reflected brightly off the side of the sprawling Merchandise Mart. The Mart, 97 acres of floor space along seven and a half miles of corridors, all owned by *the* Kennedy family, had been the world's largest building under one roof for twenty years until the Pentagon came along.

Inside the eighteen-story Mart is the world of tomorrow, the latest in furniture, furs, fashions, chinaware, cutlery, crystal—just about anything a factory representative might want to show to a wholesaler—including diamonds and the finest of jewels.

As busy salesmen, clerks and customers hurried in and out of the Mart's revolving brass doors, the lonely figure of an old man shuffled aimlessly along the sidewalk.

He wore dark work trousers, a sports shirt open at the neck, and a soiled windbreaker. His wrinkled, scarred face and hawk nose bore the marks of long-ago violence. White socks showed beneath his pantlegs, and he walked like his feet hurt.

1

The old man slowed to admire a bronze colored Cadillac, with a well known dealer insignia on the trunk, parked near the head of the alley behind the Mart. "Da Mersh," he called the place. Lots of dirt and road dust on the Caddy. Probably belonged to a salesman just back from making the rounds of the big cities.

There were fingermarks on the dusty trunk lid, a sure sign that the sales guy carried his wares locked in the storage space, safely out of sight—like jewelry, for instance.

The old man leaned against the building and gazed wistfully at the car, as if he wished for all the world that he could afford a boat like that. He pondered the Caddy for more than an hour, from a discreet distance of course, until at last his patience was rewarded.

A well-dressed man in his late forties emerged from the Mart carrying a matched pair of jewelry sample cases. He looked both ways, then walked briskly over to the Cadillac. Glancing cautiously around once more, as if to make sure no one was creeping up on him, he unlocked the trunk, raised the dusty lid, and quickly thrust his fortune in wares inside and slammed it shut.

As the old man watched the car pull away and lose itself in traffic bound for the expressway, an 18th District police car from the East Chicago Avenue station, a few blocks away, screeched to a halt in the middle of Orleans Street.

"Hey, you fuckin' Polack! Yass you! What the hell are you doing around here?" the middle-aged officer behind the wheel bellowed out the half-open squad window.

"Huh?"

"You heard me, Pops," the uniformed officer growled, easing his potbelly out of the car and swaggering over to the curb. "Just what the fuck are you up to anyhow?"

The old man, appearing somewhat bewildered, blinked at the officer's brass name tag: Scarpelli.

"I was lookin' for Greaseballs," he explained, unveiling a broad, toothy grin.

"Yer what?"

2

"Din'tcha see? I was just sniffin' da trunk of dat Caddy to see if maybe it had a Dago in dere."

"I didn't know you Polacks were clowns, too," the cop said sarcastically.

"Naw, honest. Ain't ya ever noticed?" the old man persisted. "Every time dey find a stiff in da trunk of a car it's a Dago. The niggers kill 'em on street corners and da sheenies leave 'em in parking lots, but it's always Dagos in da trunks of cars."

"That's enough, you peckerhead," the law interrupted, caressing his nightstick. "You're liable to end up over on Milwaukee Avenue with your noggin split open."

"Don'tcha know the Eye-talian word for mausoleum?" the old man asked, pushing his luck to excruciating limits. "Trunkofacar! Haw, haw. Get it, Scarpelli? Trunk-of-a-car. Haw, haw, haw!"

"That's all. You've had it, you mother-f . . . . ." Scarpelli advanced on the stoop-shouldered old man. "You're goin' for a ride, and I don't care if I do have to fumigate the fuckin' squad car afterwards."

"No, no. Wait a minute, officer," the old man protested, holding up his hands protectively as if to fend off Scarpelli's biting words. "I'm goin'. Honest, I'm goin'. Just lemme go over to dat pay phone dere and call my sister, Lou, and tell her I'm on da way home. She might want me to pick up somethin' for supper."

The cop glowered menacingly. It was getting near quitting time, and running the old fool in would be more trouble than it was worth. He'd have to type out papers and all kinds of crap. "OK, make your lousy call, but I'm gonna be sitting right here in the car watchin' so don't try to pull nothin' or I'll drag you in by the kielbasa. Got it?"

"Tanks, officer," the old timer bowed with his best senior citizen humility, as he hobbled over to the pay phone under the Mart's protective canopy.

Dropping a quarter in the slot, his gnarled index finger punched out the number of the Illinois Secretary of State's

3

office over in the Loop, which he knew from long years of practice. "Gimme records," he said when a state employee answered on the fourth ring.

With the stub of a pencil he had jotted down the license number of the bronze Cadillac while appearing to admire it. He held the scrap of paper up against the telephone coin box as he waited until his party came on the line.

"Hello, records?" he said authoritatively, affecting a remarkable change in the tired old voice he had used on the policeman. "Yeah, this is Sergeant Murphy over at the eleventh district. Say, our computer's down again, and I need a fast make on a car we have under surveillance. It could be involved in a felony. It's an '85 Cadillac Eldorado, Illinois license number 36–507W. Yeah, I'll hang on."

A few moments later the voice from records came back on the line: "Okay, officer. Your Eldorado, license 36–507W is listed to an Irving Goldstein in Skokie. The address listed is . . . ."

"Yeah, yeah, got it. Thanks pally," the old man said snappily, almost salivating as he wrote down the jewelry salesman's home address.

Deftly, under the watchful eyes of Patrolman Scarpelli and his rookie partner, Tim Reilly, he flipped open the pages of a small, well-worn address book in which he kept the phone numbers of Chicago area auto dealers.

"H . . . H . . . where da fuck is H?" he mumbled under his breath. "Ah, here it is. Hanley Dawson. Yeah, dat's dem."

From the angle at which the two police officers were eye-balling the old geezer, it appeared that he had never hung up the phone, but was just fidgeting as he carried on a conversation with his sister. "Come on, Pops. Wrap it up!" Scarpelli yelled through the window of the squad car.

"Yeah, yeah. Just anudder minute. My sister's yellin' at her old man again," he pleaded, as he punched out the number of the well known Cadillac agency.

"Hello, Cadillac? Let me speak to the little lady in customer service, please," he said, sounding just a bit anxious.

He could hear his party being paged on line two over the mood music in the background. Then customer service came on the line.

"Can I help you?"

"Hi. This is the Ace Key Shop on Wells Street. I got a fellow here who claims he's one of your customers. Locked himself out of his car. Ha, ha."

"Oh, oh. That happens."

"Yeah, ha, ha. I know what you mean. Listen, just to be on the safe side, can you check your sales records and confirm that an Irv Goldstein bought an '85 Eldorado from you? Make that Irving Goldstein. I can give you his address in Skokie if that'll help any." (Short pause.) "Yeah, that's him, all right. Good. Okay, I just need the serial number of the key for his door lock. Uh . . 5–D–1–9? Right, got it. That'll open his trunk, too, right? Fine. Oh, hey, you might as well give me the number of his ignition key, too. I'll pop out an extra one for him free in case he loses that, haw, haw. Wait a sec . . . 8–A–5–7. Got it. Thanks, honey. Have a nice day."

Gleefully jotting down the serial numbers of Irv Goldstein's car keys, the old man hung up the phone.

"That's it, Polack! You made your fuckin' call. Now let's see you move your ass out of here fast," Scarpelli threatened.

"Okay, okay, tanks for standing by, officer."

The old man tossed a friendly wave in the direction of the squad car as he shuffled north on Orleans Street. Scarpelli, at the wheel of the patrol car, crawled along slowly behind him, making sure he kept his promise. At the corner of Kinzie Street the old man got into a battered green Plymouth with oil dripping from the crankcase, started her up, and sputtered off down the street in a cloud of suffocating smoke and fumes.

"And don't come back or I'll run your Polack ass in for keeps," Scarpelli yelled after him.

"What the hell was that all about, Tony?" the rookie patrolman asked the jaded veteran. "The old fart wasn't bothering anybody. Why'd you give him such a rough time?"

"That old fart wasn't bothering anybody," Scarpelli whined, mimicking the rookie. "Jesus, Mary and Joseph! Don't you know who the fuck that was?"

"No."

"Well, for your information, junior. That poor old fart, as you call him, was none other than Pops Panczko."

"That was Panczko?"

"Yer fuckin'-A, buster. He's loony now, the old coot. Whippy as a radio antenna. His elevator don't stop at the top floor, if you know what I mean. A copper shot him right in the face once and blew part of his fuckin' brains out. That's why he's so ugly.

"I like to ride his ass, just to keep in practice. Makes up for all the grief him and his Polack brothers caused us all those years when they were operating big. Let's stop at Ed Debevic's for a quick coffee before we check out."

Heading toward his sister's house on West School Street, Joseph "Pops" Panzcko, the 67-year-old burglar emeritus of Chicago's best known clan of thieves, was more than pleased with himself. "Hey, Daddy. I wanna diamond ring . . ." he sang along with the golden oldies radio station he kept the dial set at when he wasn't tuned in to police calls.

As soon as he got home he'd get his key-making machine out from under the bed, set it to the serial numbers the customer service lady gave him, and punch out a set of keys for Goldstein's Cadillac from a couple of official General Motors Unican blanks.

After supper he'd pop open a can of Old Style and take a little nap. Then, around midnight or so, he'd pick up a pal and they'd drive out to Goldstein's house in Skokie. Panczko would unlock the Cadillac with his own set of keys, start the son-of-a-bitch up and drive away, with his buddy following in the tail-car.

Back in Chicago they'd unlock the trunk and take out the jewelry cases. Then they'd abandon the Cadillac near one of the black housing projects to make it look like some nigger kid stole it. By the time it was found the tires, wheels, battery, stereo, seats, and maybe even the doors would be gone.

He could turn the car in to one of the syndicate chop-shops and make an extra grand or so, but that meant getting involved with someone else. Pops liked to keep his operation as simple as possible. Why be greedy? Leave the car for the "jigs" to strip. That was his contribution to the economy of society's underclass.

"Dat guinea bastard," the old man laughed, shaking his battle-scarred head from side to side.

He just remembered where he'd seen that Scarpelli before. That was one of the coppers who bled him for protection money. Scarpelli had caught him in the middle of the night in the alley behind Walgreen's with the store's padlock in his hand. It cost him a hunnert bucks to get a pass. No way was that greaseball going to run him in this afternoon. He was just showing off for the rookie.

As the battered Plymouth rattled to a stop for the traffic signal at North Avenue, a Checker Cab whizzed by heading west. The burly driver gave Pops a short beep of his horn and raised a beefy left hand in recognition, but didn't take his eyes off traffic.

It was Pops' kid brother, Paul, known in the burglar clan as "Peanuts."

Wheeling his leased Checker through traffic like a man possessed, 62-year-old Peanuts Panczko was a man to contend with. A physical culturist, he was a powerful, bull-like man—happy-go-lucky much of the time, but he could get mean as a bear if he thought anyone was trying to cross him.

As far as the world at large was concerned Peanuts, freshly out on parole, had turned over a new leaf and was eking out a living on the streets at the first honest job he had ever held in his life.

Pops knew different. Peanuts was hauling customers for his latest girlfriend, Dolly Fischer, a north suburban madam who ran the city's most sophisticated credit-card sex operation, Fantasies Unlimited.

Pops thought Peanuts was nuts, driving pussy-hungry conventioneers around day and night.

Peanuts thought Pops was nuts, period.

Pops could hardly wait to get his mitts on Goldstein's sample cases.

CHAPTER 2

A DAY IN THE LIFE OF

On days when he is not working his "route," Pops usually sleeps until 3 a.m., when the whine of the family's black cat tells him it's time to roll out of the sack. "C'mon, ya black son-of-a-bitch," he mumbles, as Cat obediently follows the old man to its bowl in the kitchen. "Eatcher breakfast and den ya kin go out an' look for broads." Cat is fed and let out. Pops then shaves his wrinkled, leathery face, pulls on his clothes, slips out of the house shortly before 4 a.m. and rattles off in his old green beater.

The first stop on his agenda is a neighborhood all-night gas station, where he breaks a ten-dollar bill. "Gimme six bucks in change and four singles," he instructs the attendant. "I gotta get me some rolls at da bakery, and da guy ain't got change dis early in da mornin'."

"I know, Pops, I know. I ain't fukkin' stupid, you know. You come in here three-four times a week for the same thing, and never buy any fukkin' gas."

"Maybe I'm just casing da joint. Ha, ha," Pops laughs. "I'm wit' da syndicate, ya know."

"Syndicate my ass," the attendant scoffs, handing Panczko his change. "You ain't got the right last name."

"Tell yer boss ya took care o' Pops, an' I won't knock da joint over tonight," Panczko smiles appreciatively, patting the gas station guy on the shoulder. "Ya got my pertection. Haw, haw."

Pops is in a good mood as he drives off in a cloud of oil smoke and radiator steam. As a matter of fact, he's always in a good mood. A lot of people don't know it, but his brain occasionally thinks great thoughts.

It was Pops Panczko who invented the lock-puller, a tool no modern-day burglar would be without. In the old days, if you wanted to "make" a joint in the middle of the night, and it had a pick-proof lock, you had to jimmy open a window, or maybe break the front glass and set off the burglar alarm. Pops invented this device that you press against the door, tighten onto the lock, exert some leverage, and pull the sucker clean out by the roots. Then you just open the door, go in with your sacks, and clean the place out.

Panczko was also indirectly responsible for those safes and vaults you see firmly imbedded in the concrete floors of service stations, currency exchanges and convenience stores. He and his brothers hauled off so many safes full of dough in their halcyon years that the insurance industry came up with the idea of encasing them in wet cement, which would harden and hold them securely on the premises forever.

They thought! Haw, haw!

They hadn't reckoned with Panczko, who adeptly perfected a glorified lock-puller mounted on a winch that pulled the damned things right out of the concrete floor. You could do the same thing with a stout tow truck, if you could get it through the doorway.

Alas, if only Joseph Panczko had gone legit, he might have been another Thomas Edison, and squandered his riches on patent attorneys instead of defense lawyers.

From the gas station where he got change for a ten-spot, Pops drives over to the White Castle on Milwaukee Avenue, where he gets three coffees to go, in styrofoam cups.

Then, with the coffee bumping along in a sack on the passenger seat, he heads for the bakery at Montrose and Kedzie Avenues. The place doesn't open for business until 6 a.m., but the side door is unlocked and he lets himself in.

The bakers look up from their ovens as Pops wobbles into the room on his perpetually-aching feet, a Santa Claus grin on his face. "Coffee man," he sings out. "Get it while it's hot."

"Thanks, Pops," one of them says, wiping his hands on his apron. He hands Panczko two bags of assorted rolls. "I got 'em all ready for you." It's part of a regular routine.

"I need some bread, too."

"Help yourself."

Panczko goes behind the counter and stuffs six loaves of freshly baked bread into a couple of paper sacks. He lays the exact change on the counter. A man of principle, he never steals from friends.

"See ya later," he waves as he lets himself out.

From the bakery Pops returns to his sister Lou's, to drop off the rolls for her and her husband, Frank, for breakfast.

Then the old green Plymouth rumbles back downtown to Mister Grand's, a sandwich stand run by Nick the Greek on the southwest corner of Grand Avenue and Orleans Street, in the shadow of the Merchandise Mart. Before going in Pops drops a quarter in the slot of the newspaper honor box on the corner, flips down the lid, and helps himself to a handful of Tribunes.

"Hey, here comes the Crime Syndicate," the Greek beams, holding up a complimentary paper cup of coffee and bag of sweet rolls as Pops enters the restaurant and distributes free newspapers along the counter for breakfast customers to enjoy.

"I tink I'll have me a fried egg samwich on white," Pops says as he eases his rump onto a worn stool.

"You got it, Pops."

Truck drivers and office workers start their day at Mister Grand's. They eat at the long 'L' shaped counter, their backs to cooks who fry everything. Illinois Lottery signs on the walls

11

invite diners to "haul away one million dollars." They show pictures of money-laden armored cars and the happy faces of lottery winners.

"I kin tink of a lot easier ways to get a million bucks," Pops mumbles, recalling his historic past. While he's waiting for his sandwich he obligingly refills the sugar bowls and creamers on the counter.

The morning rush hour is in full swing. Pops watches the traffic sliding into the city. He points to an unmarked car waiting at the red light, with two plainclothes cops in the front seat. "See-Eye-You," he enunciates, meaning that the vehicle is from the police Central Intelligence Unit.

"How do you know that, Pops?"

"Dint'cha see da silver wheels?"

"Silver wheels?"

"Yeah. All da cops' cars got silver wheels. Soon as dey get a new car dey paint da wheels silver at da motor pool. Dat way if dey ever bring it in wit a flat tire, dey can take a wheel off anudder car and it matches."

"I didn't know that, Pops."

"Yeah. So if yer ever out on a job an ya see silver wheels goin' by, ya keep on walkin'. Know what I mean?"

"I'm glad you warned me about that, Pops," the Greek winks, setting the egg sandwich in front of him, next to the unopened sack of rolls.

As Panczko idly munches his sandwich he puts on his bi-focals and scans the morning paper. This is the one he paid for. The other customers are leafing through the freebies. Most of them turn directly to the sports pages. One is agonizing over the crossword puzzle. Pops looks for crime stories.

"Anything going on?" the Greek asks. "I don't have time to read the paper, myself."

"Ahh, somebody made a clothing salesman at Milwaukee and Ashland," Pops says, running his finger down the local page. "An a shoe store got knocked off over on Broadway. Hah! Now I know where to stay away from for a coupla days. Da cops'll have da neighborhoods staked out. Dey'll run me in if dey see me drivin' down da fukkin' street."

"Speaking of shoes, mine are killing me," the Greek complains. "Standing on my feet twelve hours a day. I got to get me a new pair next time I get a day off."

"Oh, yeah? What size ya wear, anyhow?"

"Ten and a half."

"Me too," Pops grins, as he pushes the empty plate away, folds the newspaper and arranges it in the middle of the counter. He reaches for his wallet to pay for the egg sandwich, but the Greek waves him off. "Get outa here."

"Tanks," Pops salutes, picking up the bag of rolls and the coffee. "See ya later."

"You got some egg on your tie, Pops."

Panczko gives the red necktie a quick brush with the side of his hand, knocking off the egg and leaving a dark stain. "It's gotta eat, too. Haw, haw, haw."

Then it's off to a nearby gas station, where Pops is the first customer of the day, arriving shortly after 6 a.m. to replenish the fuel tank, crank case and radiator. He exchanges the rolls, a pound cake and the free coffee for gas, oil and coolant.

"Hey, that radiator hose needs replacing," says Jimmy, the attendant, noting the steam hissing out from under the front end of the car.

"Naw, dat don't need no fixin'," Pops insists. "Fuck it."

"I'm tellin' ya, Pops. It's gonna blow."

"No it ain't. Don't worry about it."

The hose blows as Pops is rounding the corner a block from home, sending up a steaming geyser and showering the street with bright green antifreeze.

Pops coasts into the corner gas station—the one he didn't buy gas from earlier—and eases to a stop in front of the garage door. "Hey, pally, take a look under my hood, will ya? It's runnin' kinda funny."

The guy lifts the gaping hood, holds it aloft with one hand, and waves the steam away with the other. "Your hose is fuckin' busted, Pops."

"Honest to God? Kin ya fix it?"

"What year's this here shitbox?"

"It's a '74."

"Lemme see what we got hangin' on the wall in there."

He comes out a minute later, waving a dusty black rubber tube that looks like the end of an elephant's trunk. "You're in luck, Pops."

"How much?"

"Twenty-eight bucks."

"Twenty-eight bucks? I coulda made a auto parts store on da way over here and got one for nuttin'."

"That includes replacing your anti-freeze, which is laying all over the driveway here and out in the road. Do you want it or not?"

"Yeah. What da fuck. Put it on."

Hose replaced, coolant replenished, and his billfold twenty-eight dollars lighter, Pops drives back home to pick up his forty-year-old nephew, Richie, to drive him to the methadone clinic for his 7:30 appointment. Richie damn near fried his brains awhile back, like on those TV commercials. Pops takes him downtown to the clinic near the Merchandise Mart every other day. "Whatcha got in the bag, Uncle Joey?" the nephew asks, noting the paper sack Pops placed on the seat between them.

"It's sumpthin' for the Greek."

Sometimes, while Richie is in the clinic getting his fix, Pops just sits in the car and watches the girls go by, especially on hot days when they don't wear coats, and you can see right through their skirts if the sun is behind them at just the right angle. On other days he puts the time to better use, prowling the precincts of "da Mersh," scouting future business opportunities. Or, maybe he'll just wander back to the Greek's for another cup of coffee and chew the rag once the morning rush has died down.

"Watcha got in the bag?" the Greek inquires, as he sets a fresh cup of coffee down in front of the old man.

"Here," Pops says, handing the sack across the counter.

The Greek reaches into the bag and pulls out a brand new pair of shiny black shoes. "Well, I'll be damned! Size ten and a half!"

"Dere yours," Pops beams benevolently, lighting up a Lucky Strike and snuffing out the match in the ash tray.

"I'll be damned," the Greek repeats, kicking the worn, greasy shoes off his feet and stepping into the new ones. "These are perfect. They feel like a million bucks. Uh, where'd you get 'em?"

"Yeah, well, I had 'em at home, see, an I can't wear dem pointy toes. Dey hurt my feet. Dey look good on you, Nick."

"Thanks, Pops," he says, tossing his old ones into the garbage can. "I like the pointy toe style. I'm tickled to death."

"Ferget it."

Pops drains the cup of coffee and has a refill. He smiles modestly and blows a long puff of cigarette smoke across the counter as the Greek models his new shoes for some of the other regulars. When it's time to go, there is no tab. Instead the Greek hands him a Po-Boy sandwich, wrapped in cellophane. "Take this home with you, Pops. Have it for lunch."

"Gee, Nick. Ya don't have to do dat."

"G'wan. Get outa here."

"See ya later!"

"Get yourself a new tie!" the Greek yells as Pops lurches out the door.

Pops picks up Richie at the clinic and they head home together. Richie holds the giant Po-Boy on his lap while Pops drives.

Panczko never married. He lives with his sister, Louise, and her husband, Frank Grygiel, along with their ex-convict son, Richie, in the Grygiels' modest bungalow at 4323 West School Street on the Northwest Side. The only honest job of record he ever held was driving a soda pop truck in the 1940s. It earned him a neighborhood nickname, "The Pop Man," later shortened to "Pops"—and a Social Security card, number 320–18–8114A.

Since Social Security is based on one's most recent declared income, Pops now finds himself at the bottom of the benefit ladder, getting less than $200 on the third of every month, plus $30 in state welfare payments. Lou doesn't charge him rent unless he's got the money.

Lou's husband is retired. He spends much of his days "junking" in neighborhood alleys. Pops does his part by visiting an old crony, Gerald Tomasczek, who is married to the daughter of a former Rush Street belly dancer.

Tomasczek greets each day with a can of beer, followed by another, and another, and another. Pops drops by every afternoon and fishes all the empties out of Tomasczek's waste basket.

The two have been pals as long as anyone can remember. In 1983, when the cops impounded Panczko's Chevrolet after finding a jewelry salesman's grip containing $80,000 worth of diamond rings in the back seat, Tomasczek told him, "Pops, you can use my Caddy any time you need to go out on a job."

The cops never did give Panczko's car back, contending it had been used in the commission of a felony. Pops drove Tomasczek's faded old green Cadillac for two years until one day Jerry told him he could keep the goddam thing as a gift. Some gift. By that time the car, which had outrun the cops more than once, was leaking two quarts of oil and two quarts of radiator coolant a day.

Even Pops was able to deduce that the car wouldn't be able to save his ass many more times, so he bought himself the dark green Plymouth and returned the Caddy's keys to Tomasczek, who had thought he was rid of the damned thing.

On this particular afternoon, when Pops comes home from Tomasczek's, he's got a whole trash bag full of empty aluminum cans in the trunk for Frank's collection.

Frank nods in appreciation, but doesn't say anything. Aside from being married to one of them, Frank has as little to do as possible with the Panczko clan—especially the burglar who makes his home under his own roof between prison terms.

Pops goes to his room, sits on the edge of the bed, and unwraps the Po-Boy sandwich the Greek had given him for the pointy-toed shoes. Then he watches the 6 o'clock news on TV to see whether any of his pals have been arrested, and goes to bed.

Tomorrow will be a busy day. He's got three different theft cases pending before Judge E.C. Johnson in Criminal Court out at 26th and California.

CHAPTER 3

MASTERS OF INNOVATION

From their mischievously delinquent childhoods to their felonious adult years, the Panczko brothers, Joseph, Edward and Paul—AKA Pops, Butch and Peanuts—broke the mold. They symbolized crime, so good were they at being bad. Not only in their hometown of Chicago, or elsewhere in the Midwest, but in Miami, Boston, Los Angeles and other cities across the country, big and small. Sometimes, it seemed, the brothers could be active everywhere at once.

Woe to the jewelry salesman who crossed Peanuts Panczko's path, particularly in the months of May or June. He had robbed several of them in Ohio, for example, for he was acutely aware of the fortunes "June brides" could bring during this traditional time of matrimony. The grips and sample cases of of the salesmen could be hefty indeed, carrying gold rings aplenty.

Police bullets were only temporary impediments to the Panczkos.

Like the steel bars of prison, gunshot wounds were endured until the pain went away or, in the case of prisons, it was time for parole.

Pops Panczko bears the scars of four shootings, two by policemen, one by a victimized merchant, and another by a security guard who fired from ambush inside a fur truck. Pops recovered, even though three of the four wounds were potentially fatal ones, inflicted at virtual point-blank range.

Pops and Butch Panczko, both older then baby Peanuts, amounted to your basic stay-at-home, garden variety thieves and burglars. All three distinguished themselves by their ability to survive jail and anything and everything the law could throw at them.

While the older two specialized in domestic crime, swiping everything from precious stones to men's underwear and socks, often humorously, Peanuts had discovered America. Beyond Milwaukee Avenue, focal point of the brothers' hectic lives in Chicago, he found a land of milk and honey waiting just for him.

Pops and Peanuts Panczko spent a total of 46 years in prison, with Peanuts doing the most time of the two, 26 years. His longest stint behind bars stemmed from the robbery of a jewelry salesman in Nashville in the 1950s.

By the time Peanuts got out, jet airplane travel had become routine and affordable, and he wasted no time becoming a frequent flier to once distant cities. Outside Chicago he wasn't known. Thus, his handiwork generally bore the signature of success. Peanuts' plunder went into the millions.

Whether a laborious gem heist at the King Solomon Mines jewelry store in the Bahamas, forcibly extracting a diamond ring from a rich matron's finger in Beverly Hills, or smashing a jeweler's window with a gift-wrapped brick (the festive wrapping allowed him to openly carry it under his arm), Peanuts ever found new ways for career expansion.

An airplane ride became as much a part of his modus operandi as the pry bar, screwdriver and revolver.

To tell the Panczko brothers' story is to tell what life was like for three uncommon thieves, in Chicago for openers, during their combined century of crime, beginning in the 1930s. Their story also is one of growing up in grinding poverty and making do without welfare checks, food stamps or any of the other government handouts so familiar today.

But shed no tears for the Panczkos, unless they be from laughter. For these crooks were jokes onto themselves.

A close examination of their swag and what happened to the "profits" clearly shows most were gobbled up and spent by people not Polish at all. Corrupt police officers, lawyers and even judges were more like it.

The Panczkos were cash cows who falsely believed they were having the last laugh. Often the real beneficiaries of their crimes were corrupt lawman and swank, double-talking "officers of the court." They fed off the brothers, sucking away much of their hard-earned ill-gotten gains, all in the name of law and order.

"Every week I used to give half a hunnert dollars to a copper," Pops said. He named the now deceased officer, saying the money bought free passage on the streets to drive his car, usually loaded with stolen merchandise. Over the years many other hands were outstretched in his direction as well.

Indeed, from the information contained in this book, it may be confusing at times for the reader to fathom who the real criminals were—the Panczkos or the police of their time?

In the Panczkos' heyday, it was not uncommon for the brothers to be threatened with injury or death by some police officers who loathed their pilfering ways—if they were carried out in their districts—and who took the law into their own hands when the courts failed.

A new Oldsmobile belonging to Pops was peppered with police gunfire and all four tires flattened, he recalled of the 1950s incident. That happened after someone poured sugar into the gas tank, he added.

The venerable thief also tells of how he was once threatened with death at the hands of frustrated detectives at Police Headquarters. They pushed him toward an open window on an upper floor, he claims, threatening to throw him out if he didn't stop burglarizing downtown businesses.

When the State of Illinois revoked his driver's license for 13 years, Pops simply drove without one until word got around and the police began routinely stopping him, knowing full well he couldn't take a pinch and would pay. Tired of handing over as much as $100 per stop, Pops found a crooked payroller and forked over $1,800 in bribe money to get back his license and the cops off his back.

Easy come, easy go. A lock in the hands of Pops Panczko was like a basketball in the hands of Michael Jordan. A score was inevitable.

While Pops might open the door of a safe by picking the combination, Peanuts would simply walk away with it in his beefy arms. Crime was all so easy for them.

One of them is gone now, and the other two claim to steal no more. But the Panczko brothers' crimes, even by today's battered dollar value, continue to be impressive. Forget the exotic stuff of gems, furs and designer clothing. Yes, even cash. You'd expect that in the crawl of a good thief.

Think instead of these examples:

• A hot load of real sponges, impossible to get legally during World War II, when the brothers stole theirs.

• Or the twenty-to-thirty shotguns lifted from the gun racks of a closed department store.

• Enough gold-tipped Parker Pens removed from the company's Wisconsin warehouse to fill the trunk and back seat of Peanuts' car.

• Four shopping bags full of silk neckties from the old Stevens Hotel in Chicago.

• A truckload of Alberto VO-5 hair cream.

• Enough cases of liquor and cigarettes to fill a warehouse.

• More than 36,000 nickels ($1,800) from a telephone company truck collecting coins from pay phones.

Only twice did their stealing business go to the dogs— literally. Pops dog-napped them, a poodle and a cocker spaniel. One by accident, the other by design.

The cocker spaniel happened to be in a car that belonged to a salesman of women's dresses when Pops swiped the car, taking the pup in the process. The pet was later returned, left tied to a tree, after the salesman went on the radio pleading for the animal's welfare. A dog lover himself, Pops could understand the salesman's pain, and called and told him where the pooch was tied.

The theft of the poodle, also from a parked car, was an out-and-out dognapping for profit. A lawyer for the Panczkos, they claim, had solicited the poodle's theft to replace one that a friend of the attorney's seemed to have lost. What Pops wouldn't do to please!

While Pops has been credited with inventing the lock puller and the more glorified safe remover, Peanuts, known as the brightest and boldest of the trio, claims responsibility for a number of innovations in the security industry.

• Crash gates. Peanuts and his gang robbed so many liquor stores during the World War II shortage of good booze, that the merchants devised the so-called scissors gates, that came down and protected the front of the store. So, Peanuts and the boys simply went around to the back. Mounting a log on the front of the car, like a battering ram, they would knock the heavy steel door off its hinges. They found it worked equally well at currency exchanges.

• Tank traps. Today, if you were to go around the back of many currency exchanges, you would see concrete pillars, not unlike those used to stop tanks during wartime. Only these were installed to stop Panczko's battering-ram car.

• Steel shutters. Finding himself unable to get past the concrete pillars out back, Peanuts decided to use the front entrance. He would walk into a currency exchange carrying a brown paper bag containing a heavy sledge hammer with the handle sawed off. Fishing the sledge out of the bag, he would start banging for all he was worth at the bullet-proof glass surrounding the cashier's cage. After four or five good hits, even the bullet-proof glass would begin to shatter. Then one of Panczko's accomplices, "a skinny little guy," would jump through the hole in the glass and grab the money.

Today if you hit the bullet-proof window a steel shutter drops down to shield it.

• Steel plate walls. With the advent of the steel shutter, Butch and his boys decided they would have to make their own door into the currency exchange offices. They would pick an exchange next to a vacant store. They would break into the empty store at night, then cut a hole in the inner plaster wall adjacent to the currency exchange, and saw out the two-by-fours. When the Brinks armored car guards brought a fresh supply of money the next day, they would knock out the remaining veneer of plaster, leap into the office—behind the bullet-proof glass, and grab the cash. Today currency exchanges are protected by steel walls, all around.

• Plastic face masks. Peanuts claims to have been the first bandit to wear a clear plastic Halloween mask to disguise his features. He bought the mask at a novelty store, and used some nail polish remover to take off the rouge and facial coloring.

Then he went into the shop with the mask over his face, giving him a natural look, but still distorting his features enough to make him unrecognizable.

Once the cops got onto the fact that he was the "Plastic Mask Bandit," they began to lean on him every time there was a stick-up. Peanuts solved that by telling members of rival gangs, "Hey, you want a good way to go into a place without being identified? Go buy a plastic mask. It looks real, but makes your face look different so nobody'll know ya."

It sounded like a good idea, and other gangs tried it out. As a result there were suddenly "plastic mask" holdups all over town. Realizing that Peanuts couldn't be everywhere at once, the police were forced to let up their pressure on him— although they still thought he knew more than he was telling.

There are some who even credit Peanuts Panczko with perfecting the van, as we know it today.

If he couldn't crack a safe in an office he was burglarizing, he'd take the whole safe with him and bust the door off in the security of his old neighborhood.

Of course, he couldn't get an office safe in an ordinary car, so Peanuts improvised. He welded the rear door shut on the driver's side of an old jalopy, took out the seats and installed overload springs. Then he altered the center post on the right side so he could snap it out and open the front and back seat doors wide enough to accommodate the safe. Seated behind the wheel on an orange crate, he'd speed off into the night with his treasure.

It was, indeed, a forerunner of the modern van. With the proper guidance Paul Panczko might have become another Lee Iacocca.

While Peanuts is generally acknowledged as being the brainier of the brothers (Pops lost part of his in a shootout), it is Pops, without a doubt, who enjoys the more perverse sense of humor. Streak of devilment, perhaps, might be a better way of describing it.

Early on a Sunday morning, before the Jewish merchants have opened their shops for the day, the old man might be seen shuffling aimlessly along Maxwell Street on Chicago's near Southwest Side, peering casually over his shoulder from time to time to make sure no cops are around.

Pops edges into a doorway of a men's clothing store and eyes the case-hardened steel padlock protecting the front door. Series M10, manufactured by the American Lock Company. It's the kind you can't cut with a hacksaw. Not to worry. Pops slips a ten-cent nail file out of his pocket, inserts it into the key slot, gives it a practiced twist, and the loose padlock is in his hands in a matter of seconds.

Looking around again to make sure he isn't being observed, he saunters across the street—open padlock in hand—to a ladies fur shop. The furrier, too, has protected his store with a case-hardened steel padlock. With a flick of the nail file, it snaps open with a muffled click.

The wrinkled, bullet-scarred face breaks out into a mischievous grin. Pops slips the clothing store's padlock onto the fur shop door and snaps it shut. Then he strolls back across the street and locks the clothing store with the furrier's lock.

"Haw, haw!" he laughs to himself. "When da Jew comes to work he won't be able to unlock his store—and da guy across the street, he'll say, 'I can't open my fuckin' lock either.' Haw, haw!"

A variation of the lock trick is to pop the padlock open with his nail file, and just drop it in the doorway and casually walk away.

"Den, when da Jew guy comes to work in da mornin' he'll see da lock on da ground and say, 'Jesus Christ, I been robbed!' An' he'll call da cops an' spend half a day doin' inventory, and dey won't find nuttin missing. Drives 'em nuts! Haw, haw, haw!"

Brother Butch has gone to that great unlocked store in Paradise. He died at the top of his game. Peanuts is in the federal government's witness protection program, living like a feudal lord at an undisclosed location under an assumed name ("Walnuts" perhaps?). Pops still roams the streets of Chicago, pointing out his favorite landmarks.

"See dat furniture store over dere? I 'made' it in 1949. Went back again in '60. Haw! Dey still don't know it was me."

But today is a new day. Both Pops and Peanuts say they're through with stealing forever, "Honest to God!"

But it was one hell of a ride while it lasted.

By his own estimate, Peanuts figures he stole somewhere between $5 million and $20 million worth of goodies during the half of his adult life that was not spent behind bars. The score depends on whether you figure the wholesale or retail value, or what Peanuts was able to fence it for.

Pops, never one to keep records, "couldn't even guess" how many millions he stole.

"Just give us a boxcar figure," he was urged.

"Hey, I never stole no boxcars," he guffawed. "Just about everyting else, maybe, but no boxcars!"

It's hard to believe that three such innovative rogues as the Panczko brothers evolved from the humble beginnings that they did.

CHAPTER 4

ONE BURGLAR'S FAMILY

Peter and Eva Panczko came to America from a small town near Warsaw around the turn of the century. Both settled in the Polish community on Chicago's near Northwest Side, where they were married by a Polish speaking priest in Holy Innocents Roman Catholic Church on Armour Street. In order to make ends meet, the newlyweds got a job baling rags and newspapers for a Jewish rag man in the Humboldt Park neighborhood.

A total of eight children were born of their union. The first two, both boys, died in infancy—a tragedy that was not uncommon in those days preceding World War I. Louise, the only girl, was the third born, and the first to survive. She entered the world on September 28, 1913. Brothers John, Edward, Joseph, Frank and Paul followed in that order.

Joseph, who would grow up to become Pops, was born on August 30, 1918. Paul, whose sister and brothers dubbed him "Peanuts" because he was the runt of the litter, came on June 28, 1923. Edward, known as "Butch," a gentle tough guy who would rather fish than work, would one day join brothers Peanuts and Pops as a career burglar.

Little more will be said in these pages about Frank and John. They proved to be a mortal embarrassment to their three thieving brothers because, to quote Pops, "Dey turned legit. Ya know, dey worked for a livin'. Butch and Peanuts and me, we didn't want nuttin' to do wit 'em. We called John 'Lily White' and Frank, everybody just called him 'Fats'."

As the Roaring Twenties drew to a rock 'em-sock 'em close the country found itself in the midst of a blossoming depression, and the Panczko family—in their own unorthodox way—was trying to make the best of it.

They lived near Grand and Ogden in the heart of the Bad Lands, a concentration of pimps, prostitutes, pickpockets, thieves, and all manner of underworld creatures who could hold their own with their brethren in Little Cheyenne, the Black Hole, Bed Bug Row, Hell's Half Acre and the infamous Levee on the southern fringe of the Loop. It was not a place for sissies.

It was also no place for Santa Claus, who never visited the Panczko home. The family never exchanged gifts, and Christmas, for the most part, was just another day spent scrounging for food. There wasn't a Christmas tree, because they couldn't afford one. They did have a wreath one year, thanks to Joey. "I found it in somebody's window," he proudly explained in Polish to his mother. Most years he was also lucky enough to "find" a chicken for Christmas dinner.

Birthdays were the same. Nobody took any notice. You just turned a year older and kept right on scrounging.

Next to putting food on the table, the family's biggest problem was keeping clean—since their modest home did not come complete with bath. Their sanitary needs were provided for by a hole in the back yard. Once a week on Saturday night Ma, Pa, and the six kids trooped over to Nobel Park fieldhouse with their towels and soap. More than once somebody ran off with their clothes while they were in the shower.

Heat was another consideration, and supplying coal for the stove became a family adventure. In one of his sober moments Old man Panczko had slapped together a homemade wagon out of some scrap wood and a set of junk wheels.

He pulled it down to the Milwaukee Road railyard every morning while the kids trailed along and scavenged for coal that sometimes fell out onto the roadbed from the hopper cars.

If there wasn't enough on the ground to fill the wagon, the boys shinnied up the iron rungs on the sides of the coal cars and onto the pile, quickly tossing as many lumps over the side as they could before the railroad dick came along and shagged the whole tribe off the property.

Keeping food from spoiling during the summer months was also a challenge, since the Panczko's had no ice box. The ice man slogged down the muddy alley twice a day, dropping off a quarter's worth of ice, which was put into a pail along with whatever perishables were on hand. The trick, of course, was to shop for only what was needed on a day to day basis. That chore often fell to young Joey who, even at that early age, was proving himself a master of resourcefulness.

"Get up and get dressed, Joey. Time for breakfast," Ma Panczko called, rousing her young son before the crack of dawn. Joey obediently pulled on his clothes and took to the streets. "Be back in a little while, Ma," he shouted over his shoulder as he headed for the neighborhood business district. There he knew just what to do.

The bakery delivery man would stack neatly wrapped loaves of bread, cakes, pies and rolls on the sidewalk in the doorways of groceries and restaurants that weren't yet open for the day's business. Hot on the delivery man's heels, Joey helped himself to enough sweet rolls for his family's breakfast, and perhaps a loaf of bread or two for lunch and supper. He "shopped" at a different store every morning, so no one would get overly suspicious.

Most of the time the shop owner would just call the bakery and say, "What the hell's goin' on? You shorted me a dozen sweet roles this morning."

"Didn't I leave 'em off? Gee, I could'a sworn I did."

The family never sat down to the dinner table together. At mealtime it was everyone for himself.

After breakfast Joey was off to the Fulton Street Market, where one of the merchants might unwittingly oblige him by leaving several dressed chickens unattended. The Panczkos would feast tonight! His foray was so successful that he zipped through the market the following morning, proudly bringing home another chicken.

"Joey, we can't eat all these chickens, and we don't have no ice box to put them in," Ma Panczko protested. "You gotta get rid of this one here, or it'll stink up the place." Reluctantly, Joey picked up one of the dead chickens by the legs and headed down the alley, trying to figure out how to dispose of it without attracting too much attention."

"Hey, Kid. How much ya want for the chicken?" It was old man Kaczynski, leaning over the back fence.

"A dollar," Joey said, holding it up for the neighbor to inspect.

"I'll give ya half a buck."

"Well, okay. I was gonna trow it away, anyhow."

Mr. Kazcynski fished two quarters out of his pants pocket and slipped them into one of Joey's eager hands, as the boy forked over the chicken with the other. Mr. Kaczynski held it up to the sunlight to admire it.

"Oh, my. Where'd you get the nice bird, Mr. Kaczynski?" It was old lady Pulawski, the next door neighbor.

"From Joey, the Panczko kid," he said, holding it aloft for her to see. "Half a buck."

Joey was getting ready to run when old lady Pulawski hollered, "Joey, can you get me one of those?" "Yeah," he replied. "A friend of mine, he raises dem."

And so a new business was born.

Every morning after downing a few purloined sweet rolls Joey headed for the Fulton Street Market, where he lifted spring chickens and delivered them to the neighborhood—three for $1, or heavy soup chickens for $1 apiece—guaranteed fresh.

Easy pickings were too good to last, however. Or maybe Joey got a little bit careless. He was making his first pick-up one morning when he felt a huge hand clamp over his skinny wrist. "Caught ya red-handed, ya little peckerhead!" It was the chicken man himself.

There was only one thing to do. Joey handed him the chicken and turned on the tears. "Please, mister," he bawled. "I didn't do nuttin'. Honest. I was just lookin' at 'em. I gotta get home. My ma's sick and my pa's outa work, an . . ."

"Don't pull that malarkey on me. I seen ya around here before, ya little thief. I'm calling the cops."

"No! No! No! Please don't lock me up," Joey pleaded through the tears gushing down his face. "Gimme a break, mister. Pleeeze. I'll never come back here no more."

But the chicken man was not in a forgiving mood. Somebody had been ripping him off for a couple of weeks, and the time had come to set an example.

The old blue patrol wagon rolled up with its bell clanging, and two burly cops gave Joey a free ride to the juvenile home, across town on Roosevelt Road.

Would they send him to Joliet? Joey was so scared he damn near wet his pants. Then his ma would be really mad at him. He was still bawling like a wounded heifer when a bewildered Peter and Eva Panczko called at the detention home that afternoon at the request of authorities. They brought Joey a couple of oranges and an apple, and asked a juvenile official, in halting English, what was going to become of their son:

"We'll keep the little guy over night. Teach him a lesson," the official explained, nodding sagely as he folded his hands across his belly. "You've got to nip this kind of stuff in the bud. Throw a damn good scare into the kid and he'll never do it again, I can guarantee you that. You can pick him up in the morning."

At the time Joey was the family's sole means of support. Despite the fact that Prohibition was in full swing, Peter Panczko had managed to become a confirmed alcoholic. In an effort to try to keep the old man sober, Ma would send Joey to church with his father, admonishing, "Make sure your Pa throws the quarter I gave him into the basket."

After the sermon, when the ushers passed the collection plates, Joey obediently dropped in his dime, while Pa sat looking straight ahead. The usher paused and rattled the basket in front of the Old Man for a full ten seconds, but Pa Panczko ignored him to the point of embarrassment.

"Don't come here no more," the usher growled under his breath.

On the way home from church Joey and his father stopped off at a neighborhood speakeasy, where Pa bought a half pint of Capone whiskey for his two bits.

On the day after Joey was arrested for stealing the chickens, his pa picked him up at the appointed time and they took the streetcar home. "Don't get caught stealing no more," the old man admonished, cuffing him playfully on the side of the head.

By the time they got home Joey was starved, but there was nothing to eat except a half a loaf of hard bread. The whole family might have starved to death if he'd been kept in jail, Joey told himself. He found an empty potato sack and hurried off to market.

Joey gave a wide berth to the produce store where he'd been nabbed the previous day, grabbed an apple off a fruit peddler's stand, and took a healthy bite as he looked around for newer pastures. The Fulton Street Market, an olio of fruits, vegetables, meat, fish and fowl, was the forerunner of today's Farmers Market. Housewives, restaurateurs, deli operators, grocers and bargain hunters alike converged on the area at the crack of dawn to buy fresh food from wholesalers, or right off the back ends of farmers' trucks and wagons.

For a grade school kid like Joey Panczko, whose belly button felt like it was rubbing against his backbone a good part of the time, this was indeed a preview of Paradise. He took another juicy bite out of the apple.

He had already solved the problem of spoilage. He simply wouldn't lift no more dead chickens. You'd think he had radar, the way the young boy in high button shoes and knickers followed the sound of clucking and cackling straight to a wire cage filled with spring chickens waiting for the pan. The cage was setting on the bricks, behind one of the drays, and the driver was busy haggling with a customer over some lettuce.

Joey slipped the nail on the end of a chain out of the loop that held the cage shut, reached in, and deftly stuffed one . . . two . . . three . . . four . . . five . . . six pullets into his pack. Their terrified squawking alerted the farmer, however. "Hey, you little son of a bitch," he bellowed, moving in for the grab. He was wearing heavy boots, however, and was no match for the light-footed 11-year-old who took off through the crowd with his shirttail flapping in a cloud of feathers.

The chickens went over big at home, and Joey made several trips back to the market to help supply the hungry neighborhood—"tree fer a dollar." Some neighbors, in fact, began placing orders with the young entrepreneur.

Business was so good that Joey got careless again, blatantly picking up pullets and walking off as though he had paid for them. It was only a matter of time before he was back in the juvenile detention center, and his pa had to spend his whiskey money to ride down on the streetcar and bring him home. "No more stealing chickens, Joey. Understand?"

"Yeah, Pa. I won't take no more chickens," he promised.

Joey even went to confession, and told the priest, "Father, I wanna confess my sins. I stoled some chickens, an I sweared, an I . . ."

"Get out of here," interrupted the priest. "Say a hundred Hail Marys and get lost."

Joey obediently said one hundred Hail Marys and, true to his word, he stopped stealing chickens. Of course, nobody said anything about eggs.

The next day, after the family had made the afternoon coal run, Joey borrowed his father's wagon and pulled it over to the market, which by then was closed for the day.

Casting around for a vulnerable store, he found a produce mart that even a kid could get into. Letting himself in through an unlocked window, he did his shopping in the rear of the store so nobody could see him if they happened to peer through the locked front door.

Joey had a taste for eggs, and there just happened to be lots of them back there, so he helped himself to two cases.

He could have had more, but two cases were all the small wagon could safely hold. He laboriously pulled the cart home, and for the next two weeks the Panczkos dined on eggs—poached, scrambled, sunny side up, hard boiled, omelettes—just about any way Ma could think of to fix them.

Not long afterward 11-year-old Joey skipped happily home from school on a wintry day all decked out in a new leather jacket.

"Oh, my, Joey. Where in the world did you get that?" his mother said, caressing the leather. It looks so expensive."

"I got it from a Jew kid at school, Ma."

"He stole it, Ma!"

"Johnnie! How could you say that about your little brother? You didn't take some Jew kid's jacket away from him, did you?"

"No, Ma. I took it off da hook in da cloak room."

"Well, where's your old jacket. The one with the holes in it?"

"I left it dere for da Jew kid."

"See, Johnnie? They traded."

The Panczkos held members of the Jewish community in envy, if not outright awe. Envy, because it seemed as though they had everything the Panczkos had not, and awe because of how hard they worked to get it. In his own way, Joey had managed to penetrate the system.

One of Joey's favorite "shopping" areas was the Jewish market along Maxwell Street on the near West Side. He and his 12-year-old buddy, Walter Kupinski, would take the streetcar over there on Sunday mornings. Innocently carrying a shopping bag, Joey wandered aimlessly among the stalls, casually slipping a pair of socks or some trousers into the sack when no one was looking. If one of the merchants spotted him, Wally would clumsily manage to get into the way of the pursuer while Joey lost himself in the crowd.

"Geez, Joey, you run like a snake," Wally said admiringly as they rode the streetcar home after one such close call.

Back in the bosom of the Bad Lands, they would divvy up the loot, and deck themselves out in new finery.

"Joey, do you know where a person might get some cheese? I'll pay a good price for it." It was old lady Pulawski again.

"Gee, I dunno. I'll see if I can find any for ya."

The next day was Sunday, and nothing was open at 7 o'clock in the morning. It was the perfect time to shop for a youngster of Joey's talents. It was bitter cold, and snowing, which meant few people would be out on the streets. Joey went over to his friend Walter Kupinski's house and banged on the door. "Ya wanna go to da store wit' me?"

Wally pulled on his worn woolen coat and put on his galoshes. "Where we goin'?"

"Fulton Street," Joey explained. "Ya remember dat lady what bought the chickens off me in da alley? She needs some cheese."

The two kids cased the street and quickly found a shop specializing in cheese.

They went around to the back, broke a window in the door, and reached in to unlatch it. The door was one of those that locked with a key on either side, and they couldn't open it, so Joey shinnied through the broken window, with Wally right on his heels.

Just to the side of the back door was a small office. The boys hastily rifled the desk drawers, but found nothing of value. As they were heading into the store Joey spotted something and said, "Just a minute." As Wally stood by, Joey ripped a pay phone off the wall, smashed it onto the floor, and scooped up $2.50 worth of nickels. His pockets bulging, they proceeded into the store.

"Joey, lookit all the fuckin' cheese!" Wally gasped.

"Yeah. We gotta get somethin' to carry it in," Joey acknowledged.

Looking around, they spotted several sacks of walnuts. Just the thing. Opening two of the sacks, the boy burglars poured the walnuts out onto the floor, and stuffed four ten-pound bricks of imported Italian cheese into each bag.

When it came time to leave they discovered that the sacks were too big to stuff through the broken window. They tried to pull open the door, but it wouldn't budge. "It's no use," Joey said. "We ain't got no tools."

"What're we gonna do, Joey?"

"Let's go upstairs. Dere's big windows up dere."

They lugged the two forty-pound sacks up to the second story, raised a large window, and dropped their booty into a snowdrift in the alley below. Then they scampered down the stairs, climbed back out through the broken window, hefted the sacks onto their shoulders, and struck off through the snow for the twenty-block walk home.

They were about half way there, having just crossed the railroad tracks, and were approaching the intersection of Racine Avenue and Hubbard Streets when a dark blue Cadillac touring car with a black canvass top pulled alongside them. The open car had a large silver gong mounted on the outside of the driver's door, and a star painted on the rear door under the word POLICE. There were two large men wearing heavy gray overcoats in the front seat and one in the rear. Detectives.

"What have you kids got in the sacks?"

"Some old stinky cheese," Joey said apprehensively.

"Yeah? Where'd you get it?"

"Found it in a alley."

The big cop in the back seat got out, took the two sacks and put them into the car, told the boys to get in, and said, "Show us."

Driving slowly down Racine Avenue, the detectives followed the boys' tracks through the snow, right into the alley behind the cheese store.

"Dat's where we found 'em," Joey said, pointing to the snowbank.

The cops looked around and spotted the open window directly overhead, and the broken glass in the back door. They took the youngsters to the Racine Avenue station, booked them as juveniles, and held them for their parents. This time there would be a court hearing.

"So, where did you get the cheese?" the judge asked.

"In a cheese store," Joey answered in all honesty.

"Yes, but the store was locked, so how did you get eighty pounds of cheese out of there?" the judge pressed.

"We trew it outa the upstairs window," Joey explained.

"One year in St. Charles," said the judge.

Then, turning to the trembling Wally, the judge put the same question to him. "Where did you get the cheese."

"I found it in the alley," Wally stammered.

"Discharged," said the judge. "You can go home."

It was another lesson in honesty. For telling the truth Joey was whisked off to the Illinois Correctional Institute for boys at St. Charles, where he was placed in Harding Cottage. His daily assignment was to polish the floors. As soon as the weather turned warm, he was moved outside and handed a shovel. He dug holes and planted saplings. Sixty years later he would drive past the institution and discover a healthy stand of sturdy trees.

"I planted dem fuckers," he would smile in satisfaction.

After his release from St. Charles, Joey returned home, completed seven and a half years at Lafayette elementary school, and dropped out of organized education forever.

His most vivid memory of grade school was of an eighth-grade teacher who used to squeeze her handkerchief between her thighs, and then sniff at it, when she thought the pupils had their noses buried in their books.

"Haw! Didja see dat?" Joey erupted, turning around at his desk and snickering. "Didja see what da teacher's doin' wit her hankie?"

"Joseph, what seems to be so amusing?"

"Ah, nuttin', Miss Brown."

"Well, you seem to be giggling at something. Would you care to share what you think is so funny with the rest of the class?"

Joey's face reddened. He had already shared it with the kids nearest him. But what could he say to the teacher?

"It ain't nuttin', honest. I was just thinkin' of somethin', I guess."

"Go down to the office and remain there until the bell rings."

Joey had excellent penmanship, and was good at arithmetic and spelling, but his attendance was abominable. Plus the fact that Miss Brown didn't appreciate his classroom attitude. Shortly after the handkerchief incident she had a long talk with the principal, and they agreed to give Joey his diploma at the age of fifteen without making him finish the rest of the semester.

For the rest of his life his school would be the streets and alleys of the city.

Standing on the corner with two of his buddies one balmy evening, the trio got to discussing what nice weather it was for a bicycle ride.

" 'cept we don't have no bikes," one of them moaned.

"We kin get some bikes," Joey suggested.

"Where we gonna get some bikes?" the third chimed in.

"We could go over to Nort' Avenue around Devon," Joey speculated. "Lotsa rich Jews live around dere. All da Jew kids got bikes."

"Good idea."

A short time later the trio was prowling the North Side alley, where they spotted a pair of bicycles leaning against the side of a garage while their owners were inside having supper. The other two boys grabbed the bikes, hopped onto them, and pedaled away like bats out of hell, leaving Joey to fend for himself. He walked a little farther, spotted another bike, and put the grab on it. Gripping firmly onto the handlebars, he got a flying start, hopped onto the seat, did a fast set of zig-zags and fell on his ass.

Only then did it dawn on him that he had never learned to ride a two-wheeler.

So Joey took off down the alley on foot, steering the bike as he ran alongside, until he came to a streetcar line. When the streetcar came along he clambered aboard with his bike, put seven cents into the fare box, and stood in the aisle with his newly acquired possession.

"Why in the hell don't you ride your bike?" the annoyed motorman asked, clanging the bell.

"'cause its got a flat tire," Joey explained.

When he got home he proudly displayed his new bike to his two pals, who were slightly out of breath from their long pedal.

"How'd ya get home so fast?" one of them asked.

"I took da streetcar," Joey grinned.

After a series of skinned elbows and banged up knees he eventually mastered the bike, and was cruising down an alley with Wally one day when they came upon several cars parked behind a small flour mill. Checking around for something to steal, they opened the unlocked rumble trunk of a 1928 Model T Ford, and discovered a 50-pound sack of flour.

It wasn't easy, but Joey managed to balance the bag on the handlebars while he rode triumphantly home and presented the flour to his mother. Ma Panczko was so happy she baked seven loaves of bread the next day. When they were gone, she baked more, until the supply ran out.

No problem. Joey and his pal pedaled back to the same factory, spotted the same old Model T, and found another sack of flour in the trunk. It lasted two weeks, while Ma Panzcko kept busy in the kitchen. When it was gone, Joey made a third foray to replenish the supply.

"Stop, or I'll shoot!" a voice yelled from on high as Joey hefted the heavy flour sack out of the trunk. Looking up, he saw a man with a shotgun leaning out of a third floor window.

Dropping the flour, Joey and his pal jumped on their bikes and took off like big-assed birds as the gun boomed overhead.

"Jeez, I'm sweatin' like a pig," Joey panted, once they were safely back in the neighborhood. "My back's soakin' wet."

"That ain't sweat. Your shirt's fulla blood," Wally said.

"I must be shot! What should I do?"

"Go home and tell your ma."

Ma Panczko was out baling rags when Joey ran panicky into the house. His teen-aged sister, Lou, took one look at him, ran down to the pay phone on the corner, and called a doctor. The doctor came to the house—which they did in those days—picked the buckshot out of Joey's back, and gave him a tetanus shot in the buttocks.

"You're going to be okay," the doctor advised, as he packed his instruments into his black leather bag. "By the way, I'm required by law to make out a gunshot report for the police."

The cops, who had already been alerted by the flour man, came by in response to the physician's call and took Joey and his pal to the now familiar Juvenile Detention Center.

When the matter came up in court the next day the flour man told the judge, "Oh, Jeez. I didn't know it was just a couple of kids. I wouldn't shoot a kid."

"Do you wish to press charges, or don't you?" the judge inquired.

"No, your honor. I didn't know they were just kids. I never . . ."

"Case dismissed!"

Joey was free once more. The sores on his back were healing like magic. Ain't life wunnerful?

Not long afterward the Panczkos found a flat on Iowa Street with a bath tub, and the familiar procession to the Nobel Park fieldhouse became a thing of the past.

Unfortunately the apartment had no hot water, and a new Saturday night ritual was developed that was something to behold. Ma would heat buckets of water on the coal stove, pouring them into the tub until it was deep enough to soak in. Then Pa would climb in and scrub himself clean. Next was Ma's turn. Then each of the children piled in, in order of seniority, until you didn't have to look at that water twice to know that the entire family had bathed in it before Ma finally pulled the plug.

With the new neighborhood came new victims, Stanley Sterczek in particular. He got it both front and back.

Joey and his pals reveled in filching Polish sausage from Sterczek's grocery and butcher shop at 1430 N. Rockwell Street. Hardly a day would go by that Sterczek wouldn't laud his son, Walter, who was the same age as Joey, saying, "I'm glad you're not a thief like those Panczko kids."

When not swiping sausage from the meat counters, Joey and his confederates would go around to the rear of the shop and steal pie tins. Then—brazenly claiming they had "found" the tins—they would bring them in through the front door and ask old man Sterczek for refunds.

As soon as he was sixteen Joey got a job with Peter Fox & Sons at May and Fulton Streets, in the heart of the Fulton Market, starting at 5:30 a.m..

It was like turning the fox loose in the hen house.

He worked the loading docks and elevator, hauling tubs of butter, and crates of chickens and turkeys. Before long he had earned enough to buy himself a battered 1929 Chevrolet, so he no longer had to take the streetcar to work.

One afternoon Pete, the foreman, called him aside. "Joe, I left my key in the restaurant. Would you run over there and pick it up for me? I gotta get these trucks unloaded."

"Sure, Pete. Be right back."

Joey raced all the way to the restaurant. There was no time to lose. Retrieving his foreman's key, he headed back to Fox & Sons, making only one brief stop along the way—at a key shop. He stayed just long enough to have the key duplicated. Then he returned to the loading dock and gave the foreman the original.

"Thanks, kid. Take the rest of the afternoon off."

Joey arrived at Fox & Sons at 4 o'clock the next morning, a full hour and a half before his regular starting time. The place was still locked, but he quietly let himself in with his own key.

Knowing just what he wanted, he went straight to the poultry department and filled a sack with capons. Next he visited the egg department, and helped himself to several cartons of the best white eggs. Finally he buzzed through the butter department, loading up with as many pounds of Grade-A butter that he could carry.

Quickly he carried the goods out to his Chevy, where he packed everything away out of sight.

Then he patiently waited for 5:30 and reported for work. At the end of the day he drove home with enough chicken, butter and eggs to keep the Panczko family fed for a month.

Eva Panczko quickly spread the word that Joey had a good job at the Fulton Market where he could get food wholesale. In no time at all neighbors were stopping by the house and placing orders. Joey soon found himself in the butter and egg business.

"I'll give you a quarter a pound for all the butter you can bring me," the neighborhood grocer said. He couldn't get it that cheap from his own sources. The next day Joey brought him twenty cases.

Joey was able to steal more than he could unload among his neighbors. He made a deal with a well-known fence, Arthur "Fish" Johnson, who promised him twenty cents a pound for all the butter he could steal.

One blistering hot afternoon Pete, the foreman, said, "Joe, we got a couple of truckloads of goods coming in late. I need you to work overtime."

Joey looked at the thermometer on the side of the building. It registered 90 degrees in the shade. His Chevy, parked under a tree around the corner, was loaded to the gills with butter for Fish Johnson. "Jeez, Pete, I wish I could, but I gotta take my ma to the doctor. In fact, I was gonna ask if I could take off a little early."

"Okay, get the hell out of here. See you in the morning."

A half hour later Joey delivered eighteen cases of melted butter to Fish, who had to put it in the freezer and mold it back into shape before he could resell it at a nickel a pound profit.

Among the errands Joey was called upon to perform for his foreman was the daily whiskey run, picking up a half pint of Cream of Kentucky for fifty cents. It wasn't part of his job, but he did it willingly to keep the boss happy. It entailed a lot of unnecessary running around, however, so Joey purchased an entire case of 48 half-pint bottles and put it in the trunk of his car.

Each morning when he punched in he'd hand the fat, ruddy-faced foreman a half pint of Cream of Kentucky and say, "Here, I picked it up on my way in." The boss paid him a half-dollar, which he pocketed at a fair profit.

Temptation was everywhere at the Fulton Street Market. In Joey's mind it spelled opportunity. He swiped a bill of lading one day, and passed it on to a friend in a restaurant at Grand and Racine.

"You get a truck and back up to da loading dock and give 'em dis bill of lading," Joey explained. "Da guy on da dock'll give you a whole skid of turkeys."

The operation went off without a hitch. But when the real truck showed up, the turkeys were long gone. Joey was called on the carpet by the foreman, who had followed him to the restaurant earlier. "What were you doing in that restaurant?" the boss demanded.

"Nuttin!"

"I saw you hand that fellow a piece of paper, Joe. What's this all about?"

"I don't know what yer talkin' about."

"Here's your check, Joe. You're through."

"Trough?"

"You're fired. Things have been disappearing around here for a long time, and I think I know where they've been going."

Joey studied his final paycheck, but only for a second. Pete snatched it back out of his hands. "On second thought, we'll keep that check to pay for the turkeys," he snapped.

As Joey turned to leave the office two detectives walked up and put the arm on him. "You're not only fired, you thieving son-of-a-bitch—you're going to jail," Pete yelled as the dicks clamped handcuffs on his wrists and marched him out the door.

Joey was held for four hours at the Desplaines Street Station, but nobody showed up to sign a complaint against him. When their shift ended, the arresting officers didn't feel like hanging around so they opened the cell door and turned him loose. "Get the fuck out of here, and don't let us ever catch you near that joint again," they warned him.

Back at Peter Fox & Sons the bookkeepers were amazed at how much their inventory rose after Joey's abrupt departure.

Without a steady job, Joey was able to devote more of his time to petty thievery around the neighborhood, honing his skills for adulthood.

Late that fall Peanuts, who admired big brother Joey as a role model, came home from school wearing a new jacket.

"My, oh my. Where did you get the new coat, Peanuts?" his mother asked. "It looks so expensive."

"I took it off a Jew kid in Humboldt Park," he beamed proudly.

Peanuts was starting to get the idea.

CHAPTER 5

**SERVING UNCLE
SAM—SORT OF**

As soon as he looked old enough Joey joined the Civilian Conservation Corps. The CCCs, as it was called, was one of Franklin D. Roosevelt's programs for helping to keep idle young men like him off the streets until they could find gainful employment.

Old man Panczko was already holding down a government job. He toiled as a laborer with the Works Progress Administration (WPA), leaning on a shovel for $30 a week.

In the Chicago area the CCC boys, who engaged mostly in forestry projects, were busy beautifying Fort Sheridan, a military base twenty-five miles north of the Loop.

In the same manner in which he would do things for most of his life, Joey more or less got in through the back door.

It was actually the two older brothers, John and Eddie, who joined the conservation corps. John couldn't find a job and Eddie, whom everyone knew as Butch, figured his position at the neighborhood junkyard had gone down the toilet the day he lost his temper and pounded the hell out of Sam, the owner. When Butch didn't show up for work the next day Sam came around the Panczko house sporting a magnificent black eye.

"Hey, Sam, where'd ya get the fuckin' shiner?" Joey guffawed, pointing at the junk man's battered face.

"That crazy Butch," Sam complained, as if Joey didn't know. "The son-of-a-bitch is always hitting me."

"Well, ya won't have to worry about Butch hittin' ya no more," Joey assured him. "He' goin' into da Cs."

"He can't do that to me," Sam protested. Turning to Eva with his arms outstretched, he pleaded, "Joey, tell your ma to make Butchie come back to work. I need him at the junkyard. He ain't ever gonna make the eighteen bucks a week that I pay him in no CCCs."

"What d'ya want him back for if he beat ya up?" Joey pressed.

"So he beat me up, I don't give a rat's ass. Butch, he does the work of three guys. Tell him he ain't fired. All is forgiven. Remember, not too many guys are making eighteen bucks a week in these troubled times."

Joey explained the situation to his mother in Polish. Ma Panczko went into the bedroom where Butch and his older brother were throwing some clothes into a couple of cardboard boxes tied with rope. "You can't go, Butchie," she asserted. "Mr. Sam, he needs you."

"Ma, I gotta go to the Cs," Butch tried to explain. "I signed up."

"We can use the eighteen dollars a week from Mr. Sam, Butchie."

"I signed the paper, Ma. That means I gotta go with John. Three years."

Ma Panczko turned and ran her eyes up and down Joey, who was a year younger than Butch. "Ma, I'll go," he piped up.

"Joey will go," she ordained.

"The kid's just seventeen," Butch protested. "We don't even know if they'll take him. Besides, I already signed up. Don't you understand? I have to go."

Eva Panczko examined the CCC papers. Then she handed them to Joey. "You be Edward," she declared. "Butchie, get back to Mr. Sam's."

So John and Joey hiked to the El station with their makeshift suitcases and took the North Shore electric train to Highwood. A half hour later they got off with a bunch of other apprehensive young men, walked across Sheridan Road to Fort Sheridan, and reported for duty. Joey was given a big footlocker to keep his gear in, with the name **EDWARD PANCZKO** stenciled across the top. The guys in the barracks all called him Ed.

For the next three years the two Panczko brothers helped hew out the Skokie Lagoons, a man-made nature area just inside the Lake-Cook County line, on the east side of U.S. Hwy. 41 near Glencoe. It was all pick-and-shovel work. No heavy machinery. For this each was paid a grand total of thirty dollars a month—twenty-five of which the government sent home to their parents, while each CCC boy got to keep the other five for spending money.

It was good, healthy, back-breaking labor and, for the most part, kept Joey out of trouble. At the end of their three years, John put his arm around his younger brother's shoulders and said, "What do you say we sign on for three more, kid? Where else can we have so much fun making thirty bucks a month?"

"Okay wit me," Joey agreed. "I will if you will."

Before they went home that weekend to tell their parents, Joey snuck over to the R.O.T.C. summer encampment, slipped into a tent at 5 o'clock in the morning, and stole a cadet officer's shirt, so he'd have a more impressive uniform to impress the girls with.

"You shouldn't have taken the guy's shirt," John admonished him as they rode the train home.

"I wanted it real bad," Joey salivated. "Besides, I didn't take his wallet. It was right dere, in his pants, but I didn't take it. The Army'll give him anudder shirt."

Joey was the peacock of the neighborhood that weekend. When it came time to return to Fort Sheridan Sunday night he had to remind his older brother, "Better get your ass in gear, John, or we're gonna miss da last train."

"Uh, you go without me, Joey. I meant to say something earlier but I didn't get a chance. I, uh, didn't sign up again."

"What the . . ."

"I got a real job, Joey, helping to build the subway. No more thirty bucks a month. I'm gonna be a sandhog, for a hundred bucks a day, digging tunnels under the Chicago River. Better get goin' now. You miss the North Shore, it's a long fucking walk."

Twenty-year-old Joey rode the midnight train back to Highwood alone. He was depressed and he was steaming. He was no dummy. John had tricked him, figuring three more years would keep him out of trouble.

With Joey safely tucked away at Fort Sheridan, John turned his attention to his youngest brother, Peanuts. He'd already been in trouble with the law several times, and John hoped he could set him straight before it was too late.

It already was, but John didn't know it.

When he was twelve years old, Peanuts decided he needed a new wardrobe, so he went to the neighborhood dime store and stole a penknife. Then he went over to Humboldt Park and picked out a well-dressed kid who was just his size.

"Get dat jacket off," Peanuts ordered, waving the knife in the boy's face. "Gimme your watch, too."

As Peanuts made off with his latest acquisitions, the young victim screamed bloody murder, and several bystanders took off after the pint-sized thief. Peanuts could run almost as fast as Joey, but his pursuers caught up with him when he slowed down for traffic at California Avenue. They held him until the police arrived. "I ain't done nuttin'," he protested, as the cops hustled him off to the juvenile detention home.

As he had done with Joey a few years earlier, Peter Panczko took the streetcar over to the Home on Roosevelt Road to retrieve his youngest son, with unexpected results.

"This was his first offense, so he probably won't be charged. The judge just wants to put a little scare into him," the man at the desk explained. "Come back tomorrow and you can take him home."

The next day the old man spent some of his valuable beer money on another streetcar ride to the detention center. "I come take my boy, Paulie," he explained in halting English.

"We're sorry, Mr. Panczko, but Paulie can't go home with you. Has to stay here."

"But you told me . . ."

"I know, but something dreadful has happened. Several of the youngsters have come down with the measles. The whole place has been quarantined."

"What means quarantined?"

"It means nobody comes in and nobody goes out. Health department orders."

It was nearly four interminably long weeks before the measles epidemic subsided and Peanuts, who never came down with the disease, was marched before Judge Frank H. Bicek in Juvenile Court.

"You gotta watch out for old Bicek, he's a Polack judge," the other kids in the detention home had warned ahead of time (actually Bicek was Bohemian). "He's got this glass of water in front of him all the time, see? If he don't take a drink, that mean's he's gonna let you go. But if old Bicek picks up that glass of water, bye-bye. You're goin' to St. Charles."

Peanuts was apprehensive when he made his first appearance, ever, in a court of law. Sure enough, there was that ominous glass of water on the bench, right in front of the judge. John took the day off from his sandhog job to stand at his kid brother's side.

The arresting officers related how Peanuts had taken the other youngster's jacket and watch at knifepoint. Judge Bicek listened intently, then slowly reached for the glass of water. He wrapped his fingers around the glass and stared at the young prisoner. It seemed like a couple of years as the judge sat there glaring, and fingering that glass. The glass was starting to fog up from his hot hand. His eyes drilled through the terrified boy-thief who stood before the bench.

"Time served!" he snapped. That meant Peanuts could go home, because old Bicek figured the time he spent in the juvenile home during the measles epidemic was punishment enough. For a change, he was only too glad to get back to school.

After graduating from Lafayette grammar school on Augusta Boulevard, Peanuts spent two and a half years at Crane Technical High School. John monitored his report cards to make sure he wasn't playing hookey. What John didn't know, was that Peanuts had gone to school early one day and filched a pad of absence slips, and was regularly excusing himself from study.

Peanuts skipped school more often than he had slips to cover himself with, however, and whenever John caught him he'd take his kid brother's shoes away so he couldn't go out of the house.

After John left for his tunnel digging job, the elder Panczkos gave Peanuts his shoes and told him, "Here. Go out and play."

Peanuts' idea of playing was not "Red Rover" or "Pin the Tail on the Donkey." He busied himself stealing cars, swiping tires, and breaking into groceries and butcher shops.

Big sister Louise, meanwhile, was trying to find a life of her own, and it wasn't easy. Most of her spare time was spent washing, ironing and folding her brothers' clothing.

It wasn't enough that Lou worked full time in a laundry. Ma Panczko made her do wash for Frank, John, Butch and Peanuts. And Joey could be relied on to bring a big barracks bag full of dirty clothes home with him every weekend.

"Do it for your brothers," Ma said, every time Lou complained.

Lou rarely had a date, but one of the few she did enjoy ended up being memorable. Not happy-memorable, but the kind that a person never forgets.

Lou met Frank Grygiel, a print shop worker from Chicago's South Side, in the spring of 1938. On their first date he kept her out until midnight. Eva Panczko was sitting on the concrete porch in front of the Iowa Street apartment, waiting up for her. Joey, who was home for the weekend, drove up in his '29 Chevrolet and parked at the curb.

"Hey, Ma. Whatcha doin' out here dis time of night?"

"Lou, she ain't home yet," Eva Panczko explained in Polish. "I'm worried sick. I don't know where she might be."

"Ma, she's twenty-five years old."

"Joey, she's your sister."

As they argued a car pulled around the corner and eased to a stop behind Joey's Chevy. There were three young couples in it, two in the back seat and one in the front.

"Joey, Joey. Tell Lou to come upstairs," Ma said, slipping into the house so her presence wouldn't be noticed.

Joey walked over to the car as the back door swung open. A dark haired young man got out, turned, and politely helped Lou out of the back seat. So engrossed in his chivalrous act was he that he barely heard the wind whistle as Joey's fist landed with a sickening splat right in the middle of his face.

The young swain went down, and Joey was on top of him before he could get to his feet, pummeling and cursing him as they rolled in the dirt. Lou had her hands up to her face and was screaming to high Heaven. The other two couples in the car sat petrified as the young man staggered to his feet and Joey sent him reeling with another well-aimed punch.

Neighbors, awakened by Lou's piercing screams, went to their windows or came out onto their porches to watch the battle, as Joey belted the young man all over Iowa Street. As he lay on the ground bleeding, and Joey's chest heaved as he tried to get his breath, Lou finally got a word in edgewise.

"Joey, you dumb shit, he didn't do nothin'," she screamed. "He's my boyfriend."

"Jeez, Lou, I'm sorry," Joey said, bending over to help the other man to his feet. "I thought he was a Dago."

That was Frank Grygiel's introduction to the Panczko clan. Only slightly daunted, he continued his courtship of Louise, but on future dates they met in secret, three blocks away. Six months later, on October 15, 1938, they were married. Joey was an usher.

The church wedding was followed by a full-scale Polish reception in a rented hall on Noble Street. Joey and Butch worked as bartenders. Frank and John mingled with the crowd, glad-handing the guests. Peanuts, who was 15, looked on in wonderment.

"These guys are drinkin' like pigs. I'm afraid we might have some trouble here," Joey confided to Butch and John, as Grygiel's South Side buddies assaulted the bar. Chicago's North Side-South Side rivalry could always be relied upon to produce a battered nose or two.

"What're we gonna do?" Butch mumbled.

"Don't worry. Lemme take care of it," Joey winked.

As unfinished drinks were being brought back to the bar, Joey had been tossing their contents into a mop bucket before he washed the glasses. The pail soon contained a festering mixture of stale beer, whiskey, gin, rum, wine, lemon peels and cigarette butts.

"Gimme a shot and a beer," one of the burly South Siders ordered, banging a hefty fist on the bar.

"Comin' right up, sir," Joey smiled as he bent over and scooped a glass of high-octane swill out of the slop bucket. Holding it under the beer tap, he put a fresh head on it and slid it over to the customer.

"Hey, pal. Gimme one of them, too," another South Sider demanded.

"Comin' right up, sir."

By the end of the evening, the would-be South Side trouble makers had all either passed out or were hunched over the toilet bowl puking their guts out. There wasn't a serious fight in the hall, Lou and Frank left in good spirits, and more than one South-Sider awoke the next morning with a four-alarm headache. Joey went back to camp the next day satisfied that, for once in his life, he had done something for Lou.

Peanuts dropped out of Crane Tech in his third year, much to big brother John's consternation. "Listen, kid. Somebody in this family's got to get an education. You stay in school, go on to college and I'll pay for it."

"Thanks, John, but I don't wanna go to school no more. I'm gonna join the CCCs like Joey."

Instead of joining his brother like he figured, Peanuts was sent to an Army base at Camp McCoy, near Sparta, in west-central Wisconsin. After the standard indoctrination program he was outfitted with an olive drab uniform and shipped to a CCC camp at Shoshone, Idaho, about 60 miles from Sun Valley.

For awhile he hauled rocks and worked on road improvements, but farmers throughout the area had been losing their crops to hordes of hungry rabbits, and were pleading with the government to do something about it.

Peanuts and his companions were trucked out to the prairie, handed shovels, and put to work digging a long trench, six feet deep. Then, wielding clubs and yipping like wild Indians, the CCC boys charged through the sagebrush, stampeding thousands of terrified jackrabbits before them until they plunged headlong into the pit like cattle going over a cliff. The dirt was then shoveled back in on top of the unfortunate rabbits. The process was repeated across the prairieland until there weren't enough rabbits left to endanger the farmers' crops.

"This job stinks," Peanuts complained. "I thought I was gonna be plantin' trees or building roads. Instead I'm chasing fucking rabbits while my brother, Joey, sits on his ass at Fort Sheridan."

It was Peanuts' first time away from home, and his first taste of travel. That part of it he liked. It was a pleasure he would enjoy in later years as he burgled jewelry stores or cracked safes from coast to coast.

Back at Fort Sheridan, without his older brother looking over his shoulder, Joey eventually drifted back into difficulty. He had a chip on his shoulder, and on one of his weekends home he got into a bloody fistfight in a neighborhood candy store where he'd gone to play cards. His jaw was fractured, and he spent the better part of a month in the hospital with his teeth wired together while the bone mended.

When he got back to camp he was reassigned to the warehouse. Fort Sheridan was the supply center for CCC camps throughout the Middle West and beyond. Instead of digging ditches in the Skokie Lagoons, Joey now spent his days loading boxcars.

He piled in cartons of string beans by the thousands, apple sauce, canned corn, sacks of sugar and bundles of clothing destined for other camps, including the one in Idaho where Peanuts chased rabbits.

Joey's industrious work habits eventually got him a job in the kitchen as a cook's helper. This was considered the best duty, because the kitchen help ate like generals.

With the approach of Thanksgiving, Joey surreptitiously slipped two fat turkeys into the ice machine. When he got his pass to go home for the holiday, he stuffed the turkeys into a shopping bag under his dirty laundry, hiked to the Highwood station, and took the train to Chicago.

"Hey, Ma! Lookit what Joey's got," he said proudly as he walked into the apartment on Iowa Street. Just like old times! It was one of the most bountiful Thanksgivings the Panczko family ever enjoyed. They all gave thanks to Joey.

When it was time to head back to camp Ma Panczko slipped him two bucks, because she knew his five-dollar allowance for the month was long gone. He didn't have to be back until 1 a.m., but feeling flush, he took the 4 o'clock train so he'd get back in time for the Sunday afternoon poker game. It took him exactly five minutes to get rid of every cent he had.

"Sorry, Ed, you're out," his buddies told him, still thinking that he was his brother, Butch.

Few of the guys in the barracks overlooking Lake Michigan had anything of value in their footlockers but Sy, the man in charge of making coffee in the mess hall, kept a combination padlock on his. His bunk was right across the aisle from Joey's. The lock was a challenge.

"Whatcha got in dere, Coffee Guy? Gold or somethin'? Haw-haw."

"None of your business, Ed," the coffee man smirked.

The next time Sy bent secretively over the lock Joey got up and nonchalantly headed for the latrine, noting as he passed that Sy had spun the dial to number fifteen. A few days later Joey sauntered by at the precise moment Sy was turning to the second number—five. The next morning, while Sy was getting his shaving kit out, Joey timed his stroll so he would pass just as the lock opened, and noted that it was set on number nine.

The combination to that prick's lock was fifteen-five-nine!

That afternoon, while the kitchen crew was taking a break, Joey slipped into the barracks, opened the Coffee Man's footlocker, and grabbed his wallet. Naturally he replaced the lock and spun the combination before ducking out. The Coffee Man never did figure out what happened. He thought he must have lost his billfold at a movie or something.

The next day "Ed" was able to get back into the poker game. "My ma sent me a couple of bucks," he grinned through a mouthful of irregular teeth.

By the time Joey finished his second hitch in the CCCs, war clouds were gathering over Europe. He and his childhood buddy, Wally Kupinski, decided to sign up for military service.

"We'll join da Marines," Joey chortled as they took the El downtown to the recruiting office. "White hats, and blue uniforms wit' red stripes on the pants. Shiny black shoes dat you can see yerself in."

"Fuckin-A," agreed Wally. "We ain't wearin' none of them dumb-ass brown uniforms like the Army's got or those sissy sailor pants with all the buttons."

"From da halls of Montezuma, to da shores of Tripoli!" they sang as the El train clickety-clacked its way downtown to the Loop.

"Here we come," Wally laughed.

"Yeah," Joey agreed.

Unfortunately, the Marine Corps physicians did not share Joey's enthusiasm for serving his country. "Your jaw's crooked and your teeth don't line up evenly," the doc told him.

"Tough luck, feller. The Marines can't use you."

"I busted it once, but it's okay now," Joey pleaded, flashing a warped grin.

"Sorry. Why don't you try the Army? Maybe they'll . . ."

"Fuck it!" Joey said, picking his clothes up off the bench. It was the biggest disappointment of Joseph Panczko's life.

"If you don't go, I don't go," Wally declared, picking up his clothes too.

Rejected and dejected, the two would-be Leathernecks silently rode the rumbling El back to the North Side. The snappy blue uniform with the white hat a shattered dream, Joey commenced working on his police record in earnest.

CHAPTER 6

GETTING DOWN TO BUSINESS

The Chicago press first took notice of Joseph Panczko on January 17, 1940. The fledgling thief, who would one day command page one headlines as "dean" of all Windy City burglars, rated just one lousy paragraph on an inside page over an ad for kosher meat balls. It was what newspaper people call a filler item:

SEIZE 2 FLEEING BURGLARS
Two young burglars, trying to flee from a drug store at 3645 Division Street early yesterday, were seized by Park Policemen Lester Walsh and Herbert Vansclow. They identified themselves as Joseph Panczko, 2648 Iowa Street, and Adolph Starzyk, 1500 North Washtenaw Avenue.

"Hey, Adolph, whatcha doin' tonight?"

"Nothin', Joey. What you doin'?"

"I was wonderin' if ya maybe wanna go to dat drug store over on Division wit' me."

"Yeah, I'll go wit' ya. What time do they close?"

"Nine o'clock. Da owner, he messes around in dere for anudder half hour, turnin' out da lights and stuff."

"When d'ya wanna go?"

"How 'bout midnight?"

The two of them drove over in Joey's car. The store was a snap to get into, even though the front door was securely locked. They went around to the alley and simply pushed in the wooden back door.

"There ain't nothin' in the cash register, Joey. The Jew guy must of cleaned it out when he closed."

"Dere's a safe in da back room, Adolph. I'll betcha he put all his dough in dere."

The young burglars made several attempts to work the combination, but it was beyond their limited talents.

"Dis is gonna take time," Joey observed. "Maybe we oughta take it home wit' us and go to work on it wit' sledge hammers."

"Jeez, it's a heavy son-of-a-bitch," Adolph complained as they started wrestling the metal safe toward the back door.

"Push!" Joey grunted. "I can't do it all by myself for Chrissake!"

"I am pushing, Joey. How we gonna get this fucker into the car?"

"I dunno yet. I tink if we kinda maybe tip it in sideways," Joey huffed.

The inexperienced young burglars were so engrossed in struggling with the ponderous safe that they forgot it was the middle of the night. The noise of their laborious effort woke the neighbors. Spotting the back door to the drug store ajar, one of them telephoned the police. Suddenly the druggist's back room was illuminated by a beam of light.

"Hold it right there!" There was no mistaking the silhouette in the back door. It was a cop with a flashlight.

Hold it, hell! Unhanding the safe, Panczko and Starzyk bolted for the front door, but the sucker was locked. Starzyk grabbed a bucket of something in the dark and hurled it through the plate glass window with a crash.

"C'mon, Joey. Run for it! Hold it! Don't run!"

Just as they were about to leap through the broken window they spotted a cop waiting for them on the front sidewalk with a shotgun. Then two more cops pulled up in a squad car. The night was a disaster.

After slapping the handcuffs on Joey and Adolph, two of the coppers stood guard over them in the store while the other officers brought the Jewish pharmacist and his wife down to take a quick inventory to determine whether anything was missing.

After the inventory the woman glared angrily at the two chagrined burglars, cocked her right arm back over her shoulder, and startled Joey with a resounding slap across the face with her open hand. "You goddam Polack!" she screamed. "You thought there was money in my husband's safe, didn't you!"

"Naw, I had a headache, and we was lookin' for some aspirins," Joey mumbled, wishing he could rub his flaming cheek.

He and Starzyk were booked for attempted burglary and burglary. The racket they had made trying to get the heavy safe out of the building earned them six months in the House of Correction.

The Bridewell, as it was also known, situated a block south of the gray stone Criminal Courts Building at 26th Street and California Boulevard, made St. Charles look like a summer camp.

After surrendering his street clothes to a potato sack, Joey was handed a blue denim jail uniform with a big white "HC" stenciled on the back of the shirt and assigned to a cell he would have to share with a thriving community of bedbugs. There were no blankets, despite the fact it was the coldest time of winter. Every night before calling it a day he had to light old newspapers under the springs of his bunk to burn off the reddish-brown, blood-sucking bugs.

The House of Correction was not young Starzyk's cup of tea, either. He slipped a guard ten dollars and got himself transferred to a work farm out in the county. Joey, who didn't have ten bucks, did not see his partner again until both were back out on the streets the following summer.

He was assigned as an orderly in the jail hospital, ministering to Skid Row bums who had been brought in to dry out. A black prisoner, who held the position of barn boss, explained Joey's duties to him.

"Those two rows are yours. Just bring 'em water when they ask for it, and kind of take care of them. If one of your guys dies, you have to stuff his butt up, tie his pecker and plug his ears. Then you get a sheet out of the closet over there and wrap him up and bring him to the elevator. That's all you have to do."

Joey went up and down the aisles, pretending he was a doctor, checking his patients. When he got to bed 14 he discovered one of the patients assigned to him had, indeed, expired. He got a clean sheet out of the closet and told the barn boss, "The old geezer in number 14 croaked."

"Okay, I'll show you what to do."

While Joey watched, the barn boss "stuffed" the dead man and tied him up in the sheet. "You take his legs, I'll get the arms," the black man told him.

They lifted the dead man off the soiled mattress and carried him down the hall to the elevator. Joey gently lowered his end of the sheet to the floor, but his partner casually dropped the other end from the waist. The corpse's head bounced with a loud thud as it hit the tile floor.

"What da fuck did ya do dat for?" Joey demanded.

"He didn't feel nothin'. He daid!" the black man grinned.

Joey did not like playing nursemaid and undertaker to winos, and beefed to one of the guards that it was a lousy job. The guards, who wore street clothes and fedoras instead of uniforms, were mostly Capone era holdovers, strategically placed in county penal institutions to take care of their own.

"You don't like wiping winos' butts?" the guard smirked.

"Naw. I'd rather be a runner. I'd make a good runner. I'm a real dependable person."

The guard, who had taken a liking to the affable Panczko, took him off the hospital detail and made him a runner. As a jailhouse errand boy, Joey's job was to tell inmates when they had visitors, and to escort them to the visitors' room. He pretty much had the run of the place. His only trouble was that he wouldn't take any crap from anybody, and several days into his new job he got into a fistfight with another prisoner.

Joey was thrown into the "hole," a pitch-dark, window-less cell whose only furniture consisted of a metal "shit bucket." The only way he could tell one day from the next was that every morning he was given his daily ration of two slices of bread and a cup of water.

At night, with the aroma of steaks frying in the guards' quarters wafting under his door, he curled up on the concrete floor next to the bucket and tried to sleep. On the fourth day, weak, hungry, his bones aching and sorely in need of a bath, he was let out of the hole, given a shower, and put to work making cement bricks out in the yard.

"Well, Joe, how d'ya like your new job?" a guard asked, stopping by his cell while making the rounds one evening.

"Ya can stick it in yer ass," Panczko explained, rubbing his raw hands.

"That guy you had the fight with, he's a trouble maker. You got a bum rap. Listen, Joe, the nigger who takes care of the big shots' cars is going home. They're looking for somebody to take his place."

"Yeah? What's he do?"

"Washes and waxes the cars, cleans the floor mats. You know how to shine a car?"

"Yeah!" The friendly guard suddenly had Joey's attention.

"Do you want me to see if I can put in a word for you?"

"Okay. You take care of Joey, and I'll remember ya."

The guard pulled the right chain, and for the rest of his stretch in the Bridewell Joey washed and waxed cars for the hoods who ran the jail. At the end of his six months he fished his reeking, wrinkled clothes out of the potato sack that contained the clothing of everyone who went in the same day he did, put them on, and took the streetcar home.

He stunk like a woodpecker. He looked like a common bum. And he knew it.

The first thing Joey did when he got home was toss his clothes in the laundry and soak in the bathtub. Then he started plotting ways to make up for lost time.

Working with one crony or another—he still wasn't fully organized—Joey began making regular daytime forays along Division Street, stealing whatever was left unattended in salesmen's cars. At night he and his associates would return and burgle the stores.

Every once in awhile he'd be arrested, but the police could never make the charges stick. The worst that happened was a fine of $100 and costs for attempted burglary in the suburb of Oak Park.

Off hours were spent in a pool hall at Noble and Erie Streets, where there was always a dice game in progress. Whatever money Joey had, he lost shooting craps before the day was done. As soon as night fell he took a crowbar and set out to get some more. A crowbar, in Joe Panczko's hands, became the key to any door.

He became one of Fish Johnson's regular suppliers, bearing offerings of jewelry, furs, men's clothing, meat, dairy goods or anything else he could midnight requisition from the Division Street merchants. "Fish, I like dealing wit' ya," Joey beamed as Johnson counted out a fistfull of bills. "Ya pay every day. No installment plan."

"Cash, that's the Bohemian credit plan," Fish quipped.

Johnson, a one-time contact man for bank robber John Dillinger, worked out of a clothing store in the rear of a confectionery and delicatessen at 2838 Armitage Avenue. After he became comfortable working with Joey, he began placing orders with him. "Joe, my stock is getting low. I'll pay top dollar for a good load of furs."

What Fish had in mind was nice minks, sables and chinchillas, right off the rack, that he could wholesale to shady furriers.

But to Panczko's untutored eye, a fur was a fur. He "made" a fur storage warehouse, and brought Johnson a truckload of coats that Gold Coast women had placed in summer storage. Many of the plush coats, jackets and stoles had their wealthy owners' names sewn into the lining. Removing the identification made a lot of extra work for Fish before he could pass them on.

Fish gave Joey only $3,500 for the entire lot.

While waiting for Fish to come out of his office and inspect the load, Joey wandered about the store and, when he thought no one was looking, slipped into a nice sports jacket. He was wearing it, as though it was his own, as Fish counted out the money.

What Joey didn't know was that Johnson's clerk, Elmer "Whitey" Madsen, had seen him filch the jacket off the rack. As Panczko was smugly leaving the store, thinking he'd put one over on Fish, Whitey poked him in the ribs and whispered, "Joe, take the fucking tags off."

By not fingering Joey, Whitey had made a friend for life. Unfortunately for Whitey, it was destined to be a short and violent one.

Joey and his cohorts, meanwhile, were hitting Division Street with such regularity that the merchants combined resources and hired the famed Pinkerton Detective Agency to protect their shops.

Only Joey's acute presence of mind averted disaster a few weeks later when he, Adolph Starzyk and Chester Kaczmarek made a men's clothing store on Division near Kedzie Avenue. "I already cased da joint, Adolph. It ain't got no burglar alarm or nuttin'," Joey said self assuredly. "We just walk in and clean da joint out. Da stuff is in dere waitin' for us."

They drove around to the alley, where Joey popped the back door open with his crowbar. Then, just to be on the safe side, he returned to his car to monitor police calls on the radio while Starzyk and his accomplice went inside to clean off the racks.

There hadn't been a peep out of the radio, but the same did not hold true for Starzyk and Kaczmarek. The trio hadn't been separated two minutes when the would-be burglars ran up to the darkened car, jumped in and slammed the doors behind them.

Startled, Joey turned his ear away from the radio and said, "What the f . . ."

"Joey!" Starzyk interrupted. "There's a big fuckin' dog in there!"

"A dog?"

"Yeah. Some casing job you did. We could've been eaten alive."

"Aw, Jeez," said Joey, shaking his head. Every member of the Panczko clan was an animal lover, and the prospect of a watchdog causing harm to anyone never entered his head. Easing himself out of the car he said, "You guys stay here and listen to da radio. I'll go talk to da dog."

The German shepherd was growling suspiciously as Panczko edged into the darkened store, but he went right up to the animal, stooped down and faced him off.

"Hiya, pooch. Whatsa matter, those mean people lock you in dis here store all by yerself? Awww. C'mere, doggie. Come to Joey. Come on. Joey'll let ya go outside and play. You like dat?"

The trained watchdog cautiously approached and sniffed his hand, as Panczko reached out and scratched his ears.

"C'mere. Don't be afraid. Joey won't hurt ya." Then, taking a firm grip on the scruff of the animal's neck, Joey led him out of the store, escorted him across the alley, and locked him in a neighbor's fenced-in yard.

While the dog was sniffing out his new surroundings, Joey yanked open the door and told his companions, "C'mon. We ain't got much time."

The three of them moved through the store with lightning precision, swiftly sweeping coats, pants, suits and jackets off the racks and stacking them neatly in the back seat and trunk of the car.

"That's about it," Starzyk observed, scanning the empty racks.

"Just a minute," Joey said, leaping into the front display window where three well dressed mannequins stood staring blankly out through the plate glass. He was unbuttoning the jacket of one of the mannequins when a car pulled up in front of the store. It was the Pinkerton detective, making his hourly rounds.

Joey, who was standing between two of the mannequins, took a deep breath and froze. The Pinkerton man got out of his car and swept the window with his flashlight. Joey stared blankly out through the plate glass. The Pinkerton man admired the window display for a moment, rattled the front door to make sure it was locked, and went back to his car. He would try a few more doors down the block, then loop back through the alley.

Joey quickly pulled the clothes off the mannequins, leaving them naked as he dashed through the store and joined his companions in the car. "Let's get outa here," he said. "Da Pinkerton guy's on his way."

As they sped off into the night, Joey started to chuckle.

"What's so funny, Joey?"

"Da Pinkerton guy," he laughed. "He shined his light right on me. I was da fourth dummy in da window, an he didn't know it. Haw!"

By now the cops had a pretty good line on who was master-minding the neighborhood crime wave, but they couldn't prove it. They decided to keep an eye on Panczko to see if they could catch him in the act.

On the night of December 11, 1941, just four days after Pearl Harbor, Joe Panczko, 23, Frank Forst, 21, and Sam Leoto, also 21, were out cruising in Leoto's car. Joey was behind the wheel. They were on the way to a score. As they crossed the intersection of Milwaukee and Western Avenues, they were spotted by Detectives Dwight Webb and Raymond Berg.

"There goes the son-of-a-bitch now," Berg declared. "Let's pull them over and see what the hell they're up to."

The detectives drove up behind Leoto's auto in an unmarked car, flashed their spotlight on the occupants, and hit the siren.

Joey hit the gas. A blue haze spread out over the pavement as the rear tires spun and the car lurched forward and sped off at sixty miles an hour, the police car in pursuit. The chase went on for two miles, hitting speeds of eighty miles an hour on the Northwest Side streets, until a produce truck pulled into Panczko's path at Rockwell and Walton Streets.

Joey hit the brakes. The car spun into the truck, slamming it broadside, and knocking it over. It happened so quickly that 18-year-old Marvin Malitz, who was walking nearby, was unable to get out of the way. The produce truck heeled over on top of the youth and crushed him to death.

Frank Forst and Morris Portman, the 18-year-old truck driver, were seriously injured. Portman, who would be partly paralyzed for the rest of his life, was rushed to Norwegian-American Hospital. Forst was taken to the Bridewell Hospital. Panczko and Leoto, who were only shaken up in the crash, were roughly handcuffed and hustled off to the Racine Avenue police station.

Leoto was taken into one upstairs room, where police used him for a punching bag, while detectives worked up a winter sweat pummeling Panczko in another. Finally one of the detectives said, "Let's throw the son of a bitch out the window." Somebody raised the window, and two dicks took Joey, whose hands were cuffed behind his back, and rammed him head first through the opening.

The next thing he knew he was hanging upside down in the cold night air, and someone had hold of his ankles. "Tell us what you were up to tonight or we'll drop you, you fuckin' Polack," a voice threatened.

Another voice cautioned, "Jesus, don't drop the son of a bitch. The heat's still on over that nigger who fell out the window last week."

"Go ahead and drop me," Joey yelled. "I ain't telling you fuckers nothin'. Drop me. I'd rather be dead than go to the pen."

After several terrifying minutes, Joey was hauled back in through the window and thrown into a cell to lick his wounds.

An inquest into the pedestrian's death was held in the Racine Avenue Police Court a week later. Joey was out on bond, thanks to his sister, Lou, who also hired him a lawyer.

"It'll take eighteen bills," the attorney told him.

Joey gave his counsel eighteen hundred dollars, and the lawyer went backstage to file what was known in criminal circles as a "motion to fix."

Fifteen minutes later the coroner's jury returned a verdict of accidental death. As a result, a manslaughter charge pending before Judge Charles S. Dougherty in Criminal Court was dropped. And Joey went home free.

Up to now Joey never had much time to dedicate to members of the opposite sex, but he was particularly attracted to a blonde haired young woman who had been maid of honor at his sister's wedding. Afterward Joey, standing ramrod straight in his rented tux, had posed for a picture with the bridesmaid, holding her bouquet.

It took a long time before he finally conjured up the courage to ask her for a date, and he was flabbergasted when she said yes. She was, in the vernacular of the neighborhood, "a nice girl."

Joey had great plans that star-filled evening. The night of March 22, 1942, could be, he thought, the turning point of his life. As a matter of fact it was, but not the way he had figured.

He and his date had just started out for their very special evening together in a neighborhood restaurant when they encountered one of the guards from the Bridewell. Recognizing Panczko, he called him aside and whispered, "Joe, I've got something that might interest you. There's this stationery store and printing plant at Elston and Milwaukee—Severinghaus, Weiler and Heager—and they keep a ton of money in their safe."

"Why are ya tellin' me dis?"

"Because I need a man of your talents to open it."

"You wanna work wit' me?"

"We'd be partners on this score."

"When d'ya wanna go dere?"

"Tonight. It's got to be tonight."

Joey mulled the prospect over in his mind, but not too long. He pulled out his billfold and handed his date a few dollars. "Take da streetcar home," he said. "I gotta go to work."

It was one of those nights when nothing went right. As Joey and the Bridewell guard were forcing the door of the printing plant, a pane of glass broke. A woman who lived upstairs heard the shattering of glass and called the police. Joey was working intently on the combination of the safe when squad cars started pulling in from every direction.

The cops searched the premise and found the two intruders hiding near a stairway. They were taken to the 34th District station, where police threw the book at them.

The Cook County Grand Jury subsequently indicted Joey and his unlikely partner on a charge of "feloniously, burglariously, wilfully, maliciously and forcibly" breaking into the printing plant "with intent to steal."

Lou hired Harry J. Busch, one of the most respected criminal lawyers in Chicago, to defend her brother, but not even Busch could work his magic on this one. Three weeks later a Criminal Court jury found Joey guilty.

Judge Julius H. Miner—known in legal circles as "Julius the Just"—sentenced him to the Illinois State Penitentiary for a term of two to five years.

Joey went off to Joliet on May 29, 1942, but the battle to spring him was far from over.

For the next nine months Busch pelted the courts with motions, and on February 8, 1943, he won a reversal from the Illinois Supreme Court, which ruled that Joseph Panczko had not been properly sentenced.

This did not change the guilty verdict, only the sentencing. Joey was brought back from Joliet in chains, and arraigned before Judge John Sbarbaro in Criminal Court.

Sbarbaro, it should be noted, had been gangland's favorite funeral director before becoming an assistant Cook County state's attorney, and eventually rising to the bench. In fact, when Capone mobster Hymie Weiss was cut down by bullets in front of Holy Name Cathedral in 1926, it was Sbarbaro who embalmed the body. And as the gangster's funeral cortege made its way through the streets of the city, many of the mourners' automobiles dislplayed placards proclaiming "JOHN SBARBARO FOR MUNICIPAL JUDGE."

It should also be noted that Joey had never been popular with the "Mob," as the local crime syndicate was known. Thieves who were not directly associated with the Mob had long been expected to pay a "street tax," or tribute to the Mafia, in exchange for being permitted to do business unmolested. The "tax" usually consisted of a percentage of their loot. The hoods were shaking down the hoods.

Panczko, who had acquired an abiding distrust for Italians because of unrelenting pressure put on him by the local Mafia, refused to pay the tax and operated as a loose cannon. He was not going to let "a bunch of Dagos" tell him what to do.

He now found himself standing humbly before the very judge that they had helped put into office.

The gray haired Sbarbaro glared down at the defendant, vacated the original sentence of two to five, and imposed the new one:

"One year to life."

CHAPTER 7

![black bar]

WAITING IN THE WINGS

Old Gypsy Proverb:
Always help brothers;
Never harm brothers;
Always pay when you owe,
although not necessarily money;
And Never be afraid.

Twenty-year-old Paul "Peanuts" Panczko was sitting in court as a spectator the day Judge Sbarbaro gave Joey the works. He pushed himself back in his seat, stunned. "Jeeeeezus Christ!" he whistled under his breath. "One to life! Joey's never gonna get out. I'm gonna have to take over for him."

If it is indeed true that great minds run in the same channel, an historic example was about to unfold. Peanuts no sooner got back to the old neighborhood than one of Joey's partners, Walter Marko, looked him up. "Why don't you stop by the pool hall at Noble and Erie Streets tomorrow afternoon? We gotta talk."

"Yeah, yeah, okay," Peanuts grunted.

Unlike Joey, who had started out on the scrawny side, Peanuts was built like a Brahman bull. He had discovered the joy of gormandizing and, at a solid 190 pounds, was hardly the kind of person to mess around with.

Rejected for military service because of a bad right eye, he had landed a defense job running a lathe at the Crane Company. It was hard work, but honest, and he no longer had to steal. After Joey got slapped with one to life, however, Peanuts felt obliged to uphold the family honor.

"I'll see ya after work."

Peanuts kept the appointment, showing up at the crowded pool hall with a good idea of why Marko had wanted to talk. Marko introduced him to two older men, Marty Gariti and James "Snuffy Ryan" Cartin.

"How'd you like to come in with us?" he was asked. "We can teach you a little bit."

"Yeah, sure," he agreed. "What have I got to lose?"

Peanuts proved to be a fast learner. His first classroom was a West Side liquor store at Cicero Avenue and Madison Street. His teacher was Walter Marko.

"You got a lotta balls, kid. You get up on the roof there, knock a hole through the ceiling, drop in and shut off the alarm. I'll stay in the car and listen to police calls, so we'll know if anyone's coming."

It worked like a charm. After disabling the alarm system, Peanuts unlocked the door and motioned Marko into the store. They casually loaded fifty cases of Canadian Club and top shelf Scotch whiskey into their Ford panel truck, drove over to Grand and Ogden, where they stashed it in a garage, and went back for more.

The next day they delivered the booze to a fence. Peanuts' share of the profit for one night's work came to $7,000, which was a hell of a lot more than his "legit" job paid in an entire year.

In addition to liquor stores, he and Marko, along with other members of the pool hall bunch, began targeting ration board offices throughout the city and suburbs. Meat and gasoline were rationed during World War II, and consumers had to present stamps with each purchase, to make sure nobody was getting more than his fair share.

The ambitious burglars were making off with as much as $25,000 to $30,000 worth of stamps a night from ration board safes. Peanuts would peddle the stamps on the black market—the meat stamps to butchers and the gas stamps to service station owners—getting fifty to sixty cents on the dollar.

When things started heating up in Chicago the gang hit the highways, knocking over more than twenty ration board offices in suburban communities ringing the city. They had stolen a batch of dealer license plates, which they put on their cars when they went on the road, so they could not be traced in case anyone spotted them.

Before Paul Walter "Peanuts" Panczko turned twenty-one he had $100,000 salted away in a cash box, was driving a Cadillac and paraded around in tailor made clothes.

Panczko's activities did not escape official notice. Chicago police knew he and his cohorts were up to something, but if they were unable to pin anything on them, it wasn't because they didn't try.

In a period of less than a year he was picked up nine times for "investigation," but each time he was released without being charged. Of course, each time he was picked up he had to "make the drop."

"It's costing me a hundred bucks every time a copper stops me," he complained to Marko.

"I know what you mean," Marko sympathized. "Ain't nobody legit any more?"

"You ask me if there's any coppers who are legitimate? I can't name you a fuckin' one," Peanuts scoffed. "Everybody got their mitts out. I'm taking care of the politicians, too. I thought *we* were supposed to be the crooks."

What didn't go to pay off the police and the pols went to gamblers. An ardent Cubs fan, Peanuts thought he saw a way of increasing his nest egg by putting money on his favorite baseball team. After placing as much as $5,000 to $10,000 on a single game with a bookie at Clark and Lake Streets, he went to Wrigley Field to watch his money disappear.

"I'm curious. How the fuck do you pick a team to win?" one of his new found friends, Guy "Lover Boy" Mendola, queried one summer afternoon. Unlike Joey, Peanuts had no problem working with Italians.

"What?" said Peanuts, waving his hand. "I don't know a pitcher from a catcher. I just bet on the Cubs, period. They're my team, ya know."

"Yeah, but you've never had a winner. Right?"

"Yeah, well, I'd say I lose maybe eighty percent of the time," Peanuts admitted.

"You lose eighty percent of the time?"

"The Cubs can't win shit."

"Why don't you try the White Sox?"

"The Sout' Side? Are you fuckin' nuts?" Peanuts asked incredulously.

Mendola, a die hard Sox fan, coaxed his partner into driving across town to take in a ball game at Comiskey Park. "It'll do ya good to see some guys win for a change," Mendola laughed.

Peanuts agreed to go and watch the White Sox play ball, but he'd be damned if he'd put money on the South Siders. Of course, he couldn't resist the betting impulse—only this time he bet *against* the home team. On the way to the ballpark, he stopped off at Clark and Lake and put $10,000 on the Washington Senators.

Mendola, who normally was not a betting man, made a side wager with Peanuts for $5.

On that day the Sox could do no wrong. By the end of the fourth inning they were leading, 11–0. Lover Boy was screaming hysterically. He had five dollars riding on the home team, and you'd think he'd bet his life. Peanuts saw his ten grand going down the toilet.

"I'm goin' down to get a hot dog," he told his wildly cheering companion. "Ya want anything?"

"Nah. I don't wanna miss a minute of this."

"I'll see ya later."

"Don't forget. You owe me five bucks!" Mendola jeered.

Peanuts elbowed his way up to the refreshment counter under the stands and bought a hot dog. He took one bite out of it, and thought about the ten grand. Plus the fin he was losing to Mendola, which made him even madder.

"Aw, fuck it!" he said, flinging the rest of the sandwich at the garbage can. Peanuts stormed down the ramp, out the gate and into the parking lot, got into his car and drove home, leaving Lover Boy to fend for himself.

That night Peanuts and another up-and-coming thief, Steve Tomaras, broke into a men's clothing store and made off with one hundred suits.

"Now, here's what we do, Steve," Peanuts suggested, as they drove up to the store in a souped-up 1940 Ford getaway car. "If the alarm goes off, let the fucker go. It'll take the cops maybe five minutes to get here. We both run in and grab as many suits off the rack as we can carry, and toss 'em into the car—maybe twenty, twenty-five apiece. Then I'll hop behind the wheel and start her up. You run in and grab two more armloads. Boom! We're gone! And they'll never catch this car."

The job went off like clockwork. Peanuts was elated the next day to read in the press that police were calling the thieves the "Three Minute Gang" because of the speed at which they were in and out.

He and Steve took the carload of suits to a fence, who gave them $3,000 for the lot.

Peanuts was now forming the nucleus of his own gang, and Tomaras fit in like a well worn glove. He was first arrested in 1938 at the age of seventeen for robbing a Loop jewelry store. Although he protested, "I ain't done nothing," a $349 diamond ring, with the price tag still attached, was found in his pocket.

The clothing store formula proved so successful that Panczko and Tomaras began knocking over shops throughout the city, the South Side one night, the North Side the next.

"Lookit this, Steve," Peanuts chortled, holding up the newspaper.

3 MINUTE GANG
STRIKES AGAIN

"Jeezus Christ! We're famous!"

So heady was Peanuts with his newfound success that he let Mendola talk him into taking in another White Sox game.

They were playing a double-header against the Boston Red Sox. Peanuts put $9,000 on the Red Sox, a powerful team, led by Ted Williams, who had hit 37 home runs in 1941 and 36 in 1942.

It was a gusty day. The Red Sox, behind Williams' bat, should have been ahead by ten runs, according to Peanuts' careful calculations. Instead, at the end of eight and a half innings, game one was all tied up. In the last of the ninth some stupid asshole from the White Sox that Peanuts had never heard of popped the ball so high into the air that the wind carried it into the right field stands for a home run.

"Didja see that?" Mendola screamed. The crowd was going wild.

"Yeah. I seen it. I just seen nine tousand bucks go over the fuckin' wall," Peanuts scowled.

"You gonna go home mad again?" Mendola asked.

"Hell, no! I'm gonna double up and get my dough back. I'm puttin' twelve grand on Boston in game two. It was just that freaky wind that beat 'em. Hold my seat while I make a phone call."

Sure as Satan, that "freaky wind" came up at just the right time again, and blew the White Sox to victory, giving them both games of the double header. And Peanuts was out $21,000.

"I can't belieeeeve it!" he carped at Mendola, as he cursed his way back to the car. "There's no way in your lifetime that you're ever gonna see the Red Sox lose two fucking games to the White Sox with Ted Williams and that crew they got there."

"So, how come you bet on baseball, anyway? Why don'tcha put your money on the nags?" Mendola suggested.

"Aw, shit!" Peanuts exclaimed. "If I can't pick one out of two baseball teams, how the fuck am I ever gonna pick one out of eight horse races?"

"So, whaddya gonna do now?"

"What else? I'm goin' back to stealin'. I gotta stick wit somethin' I know."

Nylons and chewing gum were as good as gold during the wartime years, and Peanuts knew where to get his hands on plenty of both.

Shortly before 5 o'clock in the afternoon, minutes before closing time, two burly men in work clothes slouched into the building at Adams and Franklin Streets, in the heart of the garment district. Nobody paid any attention to them. They might have been movers as they got on the creaky freight elevator and rode up to the eighteenth floor.

The hosiery warehouse was closed for the day, so it became necessary to pull the lock out of the door. The "movers" quickly moved as many cartons of nylons as they could handle into the elevator, rode back to the ground floor, and carried the loot out to their car in full view of workers going home for the day.

Peanuts drove directly over to Fish Johnson's, where he fenced the entire load for a fast $20,000.

Genuine sponges were also hard to come by during the war, but Peanuts discovered a mother lode of them in a store at Western Avenue and Division Street. One dark night he and three of his boys backed a panel truck up to the place, broke in, and cleaned out the entire stock. Next stop: Fish Johnson's warehouse under the elevated tracks at Fullerton and Milwaukee Avenues.

"Well, what've you boys got for me today? Some more furs, maybe?"

"You'll never guess, Fish?"

"So, don't keep me in suspense."

"Sponges!"

"You got sponges?"

"Fish, we got tousands of fuckin' sponges. Maybe half a million of 'em."

"So, show me."

Fish was impressed. He could turn them at a tidy profit. Possibly even sell them back to the store they were stolen from. Johnson paid the burglars $20,000 each.

When the war wound down, and the ration boards closed their doors, the gang shifted their attention to the huge 3,800-gallon tank trucks that hauled gasoline from distribution points to the corner service stations. Peanuts and other members of the group took turns tailing the trucks for an entire day, noting that they would make as many as five stops, collecting for the gas at each place they unloaded. By quitting time the drivers were carrying $18,000 to $20,000 in their pouches.

Peanuts and his pals relieved them of these burdens.

In 1946 he traded in the Caddy for a flashy Mercury convertible. Tooling down the street with the top down, he figured no broad in her right mind could resist him. The Merc was put to the test at 9 o'clock that night, when he pulled alongside a gorgeous brunette in bobby-socks, walking down the sidewalk.

"Get in," he smiled.

She ignored him and started walking faster. "I'll call the cops," she said.

The girl was a knockout. Peanuts couldn't get her out of his mind. He cruised the neighborhood again the next day until he spotted her. This time he pulled ahead, got out of the car, and properly introduced himself. "Hi. I'm Paul. I live over on Iowa Street."

"I'm Lauretta," she said. She was eighteen, and Polish.

"I was wonderin'. Would you like to go to a drive-in movie?"

"I'll have to ask my folks."

Lauretta got permission, and Peanuts drove to a drive-in theater he had recently robbed. It was 10 p.m. and the show had already started. He drove around to the exit gate and headed in.

"Hey, where do you think you're going?" a white cover-alled attendant yelled.

"Here's a fin," Peanuts said, tossing a five-dollar bill in his direction. "We're goin' to the movie."

Later Lauretta took Paul home to meet her folks. "Momma wants to know what kind of work you do," she told him.

"Work? Oh, I'm a car dealer. Yeah. Didn't you see the dealer plates on my car? I sell cars."

Lauretta's mother had heard something about the Panczkos. She was afraid her daughter might be getting mixed up with an unsavory character.

"Oh, that's my brother, Joey," Peanuts said, sadly shaking his head. "Poor fellah. He's payin' his debt to society right now. Yes he is. Broke my mother's heart, it did."

Paul and Lauretta were married in St. Hedwig's Church on North Hoyne Avenue. They had a big reception in the hall on Milwaukee Avenue, near Ogden, with two Polish bands.

Once they were settled down, Lauretta began to suspect that her husband kept pretty strange hours for a car salesman.

Most of the police officers in the district knew Peanuts on sight, and curbed his car whenever they saw him, hoping to find a load of furs, men's suits or cigarettes. Peanuts routinely carried a $1,000-bill in his money clip to deal with such eventualities.

After a men's clothing store at Milwaukee and Ashland Avenues was cleaned out, he and Walter Jednyak were brought in to the district police station for questioning. When Lou heard her brother had been arrested, she went down to the station with some coffee and sandwiches, in case he was going to be there awhile. She walked into the interrogation room just as Detective Roland Hayes punched Peanuts in the face, opening a cut over his left eye.

Lou went home and told Butch what had happened. "That fuckin' Hayes. I know the son-of-a-bitch," Butch snarled, putting on his jacket.

"Don't go down there," Lou pleaded. "You'll only get in trouble."

"Nah, I know better than that. I'm just going out for a couple of beers."

Later that evening Hayes unwittingly walked into the same bar where Butch was drinking. He had just enough under his belt by this time to throw caution to the wind. Recognizing the detective, Butch sailed into him with both fists.

The saloon owner called the police, but Butch was gone by the time they arrived. When the bloodied Hayes related what had happened, an order went out to shoot Edward "Butch" Panczko on sight.

Surmising that the law would be out for revenge, Butch stopped to pick up a girlfriend, and wasted no time getting out of town. The fugitive couple drove to Fox Lake, where they checked into a motel. Butch slept uneasily that night, with a .45 caliber pistol under his pillow.

The next day, after his release from custody, Peanuts called on Hayes and offered the detective one thousand dollars to forget the whole thing. "After what your brother did to me? Not on your life," Hayes told him.

Peanuts knew what made Chicago work. If a man wanted to be a police officer, he paid off his alderman. If he wanted to be promoted, he made another drop. It cost $5,000 to become a lieutenant, and $10,000 to get promoted to a captaincy.

Peanuts paid a call on the detective's alderman/sponsor and explained the situation. "Hayes says he's gonna testify against my brother for beating him up. Now, we don't want no trouble, so I'd like to know if there's anything I can do to kind of smooth this thing over."

"Okay. It'll cost you a grand," the alderman said.

Notified that the fix was in, Butch returned to Chicago, where police arrested him for assaulting an officer. When the matter came up in court, Hayes buttonholed Peanuts in the corridor and told him, "I changed my mind. I'll take the thousand bucks."

"Fuck you. You had your chance," Peanuts told him. "You aren't getting a fucking penny. Your boss got it, now, and you better do what he tells you."

It was a bench trial, meaning there was no jury. Turning to Detective Hayes, the judge asked, "Is this the man who hit you?"

Glowering at Butch, Hayes responded, "Well, it looks like him."

"Looks like him is not good enough," the judge said. "Is Edward Panczko here the man who hit you or isn't he? Yes or no."

"Um, I can't be sure, your honor."

"Enter a ruling of not guilty," said the judge. "The defendant is discharged."

"What happened?" Butch asked as they walked out of court.

"How the fuck should I know?" Peanuts said. "I made the drop. Who got the money? The judge? The prosecutor? The police? I don't know. Don't worry about it."

While all this was going on, big brother Joey was not enjoying prison life one bit. He was confined to a small, windowless cell without plumbing in the "Old Prison" at Joliet. He and his cellmate took turns carrying out the "shit bucket" once a day. The rest of the time it reposed on the concrete floor between their bunks and the wall, in a space just wide enough for one man to stand up in at a time.

Joey was put to work in the mess hall, pouring coffee, and warding off advances from fellow inmates who winked at him and cooed, "Hello, baby," or called him "nice young stuff." For the first time in his life he was scared, but he put on a bold Panczko front and snarled, "How'd ya like a pot of boilin' hot coffee in yer lap?"

Joey's only recorded infraction at Joliet resulted in three days solitary confinement for "insolence" for staring at a guard. After that he learned to keep his eyes aimed at the ground when anyone of authority approached.

At the end of one year he was transferred to the new Stateville Penitentiary. "Dis is a palace!" he whooped excitedly, on being shoved into a bright, airy cell with running water, a flush toilet, and an earphone to listen to the radio.

He wasn't going to do anything that might get him sent back to the old prison, and his good behavior subsequently got him promoted to the honor farm, where he was put to work as a baker. A black inmate called "Cotton," who strawbossed the cooking staff, took an instant dislike to the North Side Polack and did his best to make life miserable for him.

Joey bided his time. On his day off from kitchen duty one afternoon he snuck in early and poured a bottle of cooking oil into the coffee urn. Before the end of the day an epidemic of galloping diarrhea had overcome the guards and prison population alike.

Joey and a handful of guffawing inmates who were in on the gag were among the few prisoners who did not spend the rest of the night on the commode. The next day he went about his business somewhat smugly as prison officials sternly chastised Cotton over the messy incident. "What the hell did you do to that fish you served?" they scolded.

When Joey came up for parole after three and a half years, Peter Fox & Sons sent a letter to Warden Joseph Ragen urging that parole be denied. "This man was stealing us blind," the letter explained. Neither the warden nor the parole board ever saw the letter. An inmate working as a clerk in Ragen's office intercepted the missive and ripped it to shreds.

Joey's parole hearing was still pending when he got word that his father, Peter, had died. In one of the few times in his life he ever begged a favor, he requested permission to attend his father's funeral. Permission denied.

A month later Joey was released. He had heard about the Peter Fox letter, and as soon as he got home he sent the inmate who had torn it up a gold pen and pencil set that Peanuts had stolen for him.

Then he got down to business, joining his two brothers in crime, making up for lost time.

On one of their first jobs together, Joey and Peanuts targeted a jewelry salesman, whom they decided to relieve of his sample cases. They followed him from a jewelry store on 43rd Street, on the South Side, all the way to the West Side, waiting for an opportune moment to strike.

Along the way Peanuts was amused by a couple of men he saw through a window, idling in a barber shop. One was tall and fat, the other thin and wiry. "Ha, ha. Laurel and Hardy," he laughed.

But wait a minute. As he and Joey sat in their car at Cicero Avenue and Madison Street, while the jeweler went into another store, there was the same Laurel and Hardy team, standing on the sidewalk.

"What the fuck? It's those same two guys from the barber shop," Peanuts said.

Joey gave the pair a squint. "Those are Pinkertons," he exclaimed. "I remember seeing da same two guys once when I was casin' a jewelry building downtown. "Lookit da little guy. Whaddya see? He's got a sawed-off shotgun against his leg."

"Jesus Christ, they're layin' for us, Joey," Peanuts said. "They're tryin' to catch us cold bang."

The brothers sat tight, nervously watching the Pinkerton detectives as the Pinkertons watched them. When a traffic policeman came up and engaged the Pinkertons in conversation, Peanuts and Joey pulled out of their parking space, U-turned and raced home.

"So? How'd you guys do today?" their sister asked when they ducked into the house. Her brothers' occupations were no deep, dark secret to Louise, who still lived under the Panczko roof with her husband, Frank.

"We're lucky to be alive," Peanuts said. "Honest to God! If it wasn't for Joey, we might be dead, fer crissake."

"What in the world happened?"

"Two Pinkertons had us made, but Joey recognized 'em. That's what saved us."

"Good lord! Don't say nothing to ma."

Not long afterward Joey was walking along Milwaukee Avenue when he ran into Patrolman John Glon. "Panczko, you are one lucky son-of-a-bitch," the officer said, shaking his head from side to side in a tut-tut-tut manner.

"Huh?"

"You know fucking well what I'm talking about. I warned you before to stay away from jewelry salesmen. If you and your dizzy brother had gone near that fucker's car, those Pinkerton dicks would have blasted you."

"Whatdya mean, Glon?"

"They were working together, with the salesman, you asshole."

"Ya mean dey were tailin' us?"

"Shit no! The Pinkerton's had the jewelry guy's schedule, and they were leap-frogging ahead while you clowns were following his car. They were just waiting for the salesman to get knocked off, and they were going to let you guys have it. Bang! The coroner'd be scraping you and your brother off the pavement."

Peanuts and Lover Boy Mendola, meanwhile, had already staked out a fur shop in west suburban Berwyn for one of their "Three Minute Gang" hits. Joey went along to help carry out the goods.

"Lookit. Ain't that beautiful?" Peanuts mused, as they drove by the front of the store, with a mannequin wearing a mink stole in the window. Circling the block, they drove down the alley to the rear of the building. Peanuts doused the headlights and pulled the car crossways in the alley, with the rear of the auto aimed at the back door.

"Okay, Joey. You take this here two-by-four and hold one end of it against the back bumper while I back up," Peanuts instructed, pulling a length of wood out of the trunk.

"What for? I don't get it."

"It's a battering ram, don'tcha see? We ram the son-of-a-bitch into the door and, Boom! it's open. Then, in we go and clean out the joint before the cops get here."

"Okay. Let 'er go!" Joey said, steadying the two-by-four. Mendola stood at the ready, poised to leap through the door the second it popped open.

Peanuts got into the car, rolled up the window to shut out the cool night air, shoved the gearshift in reverse, and gave it the gas. The battering ram hit the heavy door with a thud and snapped in two with a loud crack. Joey pitched backwards, and the car's rear bumper caught him smack across the belly.

"Owwwwwwwwwuuuuuu!" he screamed.

Peanuts, oblivious of his brother's condition, pulled ahead a few feet, put the car in reverse, and zoomed backward again. "Noooooooooo!" Joey yelled as the bumper flattened his gut for the second time, and sent him reeling backward into the door.

Joey was trying to struggle to his feet, broken battering ram in hand, when Peanuts pulled forward and backed up for a third shot. Joey got the square end of the two-by-four against the bumper just in time. The splintered end connected with the door in just the right spot, the doorjamb split, and the door crashed inward as the back bumper of Peanuts' car pinned Joey against the framework.

Joey rolled over in a cataclysm of pain, clutching his midsection, as Mendola, awaiting his cue, hopped over his injured partner and ran into the store. The three-minute plan was in split-second operation now, as the burglar alarm jangled its warning that all was not right with the world.

Peanuts dashed into the store and was helping Mendola toss furs into the back seat of the car when he spotted Joey, lying on the ground convulsed with pain.

"What the fuck you doin'? We got work to do."

"Ya runned over me, ya dumb shit!"

"Aw, Jeez. We gotta get outa here. Guy! Gimme a hand here, quick."

Peanuts and Lover Boy helped the groaning Joey to his feet, shoved him into the back seat with the furs, and sped off into the night as Berwyn police roared down the street from the opposite direction with sirens blaring.

Back in the safety of the old neighborhood, they woke up a doctor and took Joey inside. They laid him on his back on a table and the doctor undid his belt and pulled down his trousers and undershorts.

"Good lord! What in the world happened to you?"

"A car backed into me," Joey groaned, glaring at his brother through bloodshot eyes.

The doctor went to his medicine cabinet and came back with a long needle.

"Jeez! What ya gonna do to me, Doc?"

"Your abdomen is a mass of blood blisters. I'm going to drain them and relieve the pressure."

"I don't like needles, Doc."

"Hold him down while I work," the doctor nodded to Joey's companions.

After the "operation" Joey was driven home to recuperate from his near brush with death while Peanuts and Lover Boy took the furs to a fence.

Mendola's pals all called him Guy—his given name. Nobody called him Lover Boy to his face, any more than a person would walk up to Jacob Guzik and say, "Hi, Greasy Thumb," or greet Al Capone with, "How ya doin', Scarface?"

For years, tagging mobsters with unflattering nicknames had been a game played by the press. Most of the hoodlums of the day had their monikers laid on them by two newsmen in particular—Clem Lane, of the Chicago Daily News, and James Doherty, a Chicago Tribune crime reporter. It was their way of amusing themselves on slow news nights.

A major exception was Paul "Needle Nose" Labriola. He was so christened by Virginia Marmaduke, a street reporter for the Sun-Times, who looked at a photo of the small-time hoodlum and quipped, "His pointy nose looks like a needle." The name stuck, and so did the nickname other reporters pinned on Marmaduke, "The Duchess."

Peanuts Panczko was building a network of thieves on whom he could call as needed, depending on the job. He also varied his co-workers to confuse the cops. Needle Nose became a part of his ever-growing gang. On January 6, 1947, Panczko, Labriola and Steve Tomaras found themselves in deep trouble.

All three were arrested on a charge of disorderly conduct, which did not seem serious, until they discovered they were suspects in the murder of Otto Freund, a wealthy printing company executive, who had been stabbed and beaten to death by robbers in his Wilmette home.

For once Tomaras—who had been arrested fourteen times in the past two years, but never convicted—was grateful for his police record. It showed that he was in the jail on the night Freund was murdered. Panczko and Labriola, however, could not come up with an alibi without incriminating themselves in some other burglary.

Both were given lie detector tests and, to the surprise of the arresting officers, both passed the polygraph with flying colors. The lie box indicated neither had knowledge of the Freund homicide, and both were released. It would not be the last time, however, that Peanuts Panzcko was a murder suspect.

The next member of the Panczko clan to end up in the toil of the law was brother Butch—but it wasn't for thievery, it was mopery.

Butch, who the cops were just aching to nail, was booked on charges of disorderly conduct, assault and battery and using obscene language when Policeman Albert Bruns recognized him as he left the Criminal Courts building on August 1, after he'd gone there to appear on another matter.

Police had been looking for Butch for a week since the Togel sisters, Vera, 25, Wanda, 21, and Florence, 18, reported he had intercepted them with his automobile while they were riding their bicycles on Lawndale Avenue. They said he leered lasciviously at Vera, and made an obscene suggestion when she asked, "What are *you* looking at?"

They said he then tried to grab Florence, but was frightened away by an approaching car. The sisters jotted down his license plate as he drove off, and the cops checked it out to Butch.

Joey, meanwhile, was regaining his health by taking long, and productive, Sunday evening strolls through the Loop. The downtown area provided a grab bag of out-of-town cars to steal from. Most people from small towns never locked their cars, and they didn't think of doing so when they drove into Chicago.

While making his Sunday evening rounds Joey became fascinated with a jewelry store next to the Oriental Theatre on Randolph Street, between State and LaSalle Streets.

"It ain't got no burglar alarm," he told his disbelieving brothers. "It's right next to da movie theater, and dere's so many cops downtown dey probably figure dey don't need one. We wait 'til the movie lets out and da street's fulla people, and we go in. Nobody'll notice us."

There were several feet of snow on the ground on the night they picked for the invasion. They had to equip their car with full-length skid chains before they could even get out of the old neighborhood.

When the theater disgorged its crowd of late-night movie goers at midnight, Joey pulled the lock on the jewelry store door and he and Butch, each carrying a laundry bag, went in. Peanuts stayed in the car, monitoring the police radio.

His brothers were deep inside the store, working on the safe. "I can't get da son-of-a-bitch open," Joey sweated. "Then let's get the fuck outa here," Butch said, nervously.

"Just anudder minute," Joey said. "I think I found the spot wit' my chisel. Here, give it a whack." Butch hit the chisel with his mallet while Joey held it against the dial, and clink, the tumblers went down. Joey smiled as he swung the door open.

"Here, hold da bag," he told his brother. "No, no. Get one end in your teeth, like dis, and hold it open wit' yer two hands so I can trow the stuff in it. Yeah, dat's da way."

Joey cleaned out the safe in a matter of seconds, and he and Butch repaired to their getaway car—which was suddenly hemmed in by automobiles that had parked in front of and behind it. Other vehicles were stopped alongside it in the street, waiting to pick up theater goers and late night restaurant patrons.

"Hang on," yelled Peanuts, who was already proving to be one of the best wheelmen in the business. Cutting the steering wheel sharply to the right, he plowed through a snow bank with the skid-chains and took off down the sidewalk, leaning on the horn to warn pedestrians to get the fuck out of the way.

When they got home the three brothers divvied up the loot, about twenty expensive men's rings and $1,500 in cash.

"Ya know, dis ain't no good," Joey remarked, as they admired the results of evening's work.

"What d'ya mean? This is great," Peanuts said. "Right, Butch? We did okay."

"No, what I mean is, us tree brudders workin' together is no good," Joey continued. Ya know what I mean? 'Cause if we go into a place and dere's an ambush, or da cops start shootin', Ma's gonna have ta buy tree caskets, and she can't speak very good English."

"You maybe got something there, Joey," Peanuts agreed. "From now on we each do our own thing. It's better that way."

The Loop jewelry heist was the only job the three Panczko brothers ever did together. In addition to pocketing $500 apiece in cash, each of them eventually got about $6,000 for the rings. Butch and Peanuts unloaded theirs with a neighborhood fence, Lawrence Sylvester, 38, who was beginning to make quite a name for himself as a buyer of stolen merchandise.

Joey peddled his goodies with Sylvester, too, but in dibs and dabs. He brought in a ring bearing an $1,800 price tag and told him, "Ya kin have it fer a tousand bucks."

"Five hundred," Sylvester countered.

"Ya cheap bastard."

"Take it or leave it."

"Gimme da money."

Sylvester didn't see Joey again until the $500 was gone. Then he would bring in another ring.

"Jesus Christ, Joey, quit fuckin' me around this way," Sylvester protested. "Everybody knows you guys made that jewelry store. Why don't you bring me everything at once and get it over with?"

The midnight theft was never solved. The jeweler who did not believe in burglar alarms eventually went out of business. The store is now a peanut shop.

A few weeks after the brothers struck out on their own the year 1948 bowed in with a bang for Joey—literally.

He and 41-one-year-old Eddie Orloski, a fellow ex-convict, were busy transferring cases of liquor from the Concord Restaurant at 117 E. South Water Street to their car, parked downstairs on the lower level of Wacker Drive, when Detectives Al Curry and Frank Cusack pulled up in an unmarked police car. The detectives were suspicious because the New Year's Eve crowd had gone home, and the restaurant was closed for the night.

"Put your hands up and stand against the wall," Curry said. Panzcko and Orloski gingerly set the cases on the ground and did as they were told. Traffic Policeman Walter Dietz, who had arrived as a back-up, drew his service revolver and ordered the two to turn and face the wall while the detectives checked out their car.

It was not uncustomary for police to hold "street court" at the scene of a crime, and Joey mistakenly assumed court was in session. Digging into his pocket to "make bail," he withdrew $400 and said, "Why don't you give us a pass?"

Dietz thought he was going for a gun, however, and let him have it. The bullet slammed into Joey's left shoulder and exited from his back as he fell, bleeding profusely, to the pavement.

The detectives called for an ambulance and Orloski, who was still being covered by Dietz, carefully removed his cashmere coat and draped it over his fallen partner. "Dat copper, he din't mean ta shoot me. It was a accident," Joey moaned. "Tell da poor son-of-a-bitch not ta worry. I'll be okay."

Joey was taken to the Bridewell Hospital and Eddie went to jail. As soon as Joey was well enough to walk the two of them were brought before Judge Charles S. Dougherty in Criminal Court.

Dougherty was a Chicago original worthy of passing judgment on a member of the Panczko clan. A short, dignified jurist who wore granny glasses, he was the epitome of decorum as he sat in his black robe on the bench. He had a unique character flaw, however: He could not resist stealing Yellow Cabs.

Like all good Irishmen, Charlie took a nip now and again. He patronized only the finest bars, such as the Drake Hotel on Chicago's Gold Coast. When it came time to call it a night, the judge would not call a cab. He'd go out and get his own. He would stroll down Michigan Avenue until he spotted a Yellow Cab whose owner had ducked in for a cup of coffee and left the motor running. Cackling with glee, he would impishly jump behind the wheel and drive himself home.

Chicago police were aware of the judge's affinity for the color yellow, as long as it was painted on a taxi. Whenever a Yellow Cab was reported stolen late at night on the Gold Coast they routinely drove over to the judge's apartment, where they would invariably recover the vehicle and return it to the cabbie with a minimum of pomp.

When Panczko and Orloski were arraigned before Dougherty for the liquor theft, the judge listened to the evidence, slammed his gavel on the bench and declared, "Case dismissed!" He ruled that police failed to prove the two men had not found the whiskey in the alley behind the store, as they claimed.

Even though he'd beaten the rap, the arrest was a violation of Joey's parole, and he was returned to Stateville in chains.

When he was checked into the pen, he discovered that some rat had snitched on him over the celebrated diarrhea incident two years earlier. A notation on his registration card said, "Do not put Joseph Panczko near food."

CHAPTER 8

MAKING A NAME
FOR HIMSELF

When Joey got out of stir he slipped his parole officer a ten spot to help find him a job. The agent sent him to the Globe Beverage Company, a soda pop bottler at 2106 Superior Street, where he signed on as a $1-an-hour laborer. A month later, when one of the delivery truck drivers quit, Joey was given a shot at the job.

"You work on a commission basis, Joe. A good driver averages maybe ninety dollars a week in wintertime," Pete Salato, the foreman, told him. "But in the summer, when it's hot out and everyone's thirsty, you can make up to two hundred bucks if you hustle."

The first thing Joey did was drive through his own neighborhood, so everyone could see him behind the wheel of the big soda pop truck. "Here comes the pop man," he yelled out the window, beeping the horn. "Pop man!" Before long everybody on Iowa Street was referring to Joey as "the Pop Man."

Even his own brothers joshingly greeted him with, "Hi ya, Pop Man," or "Here comes Soda Pops." It did not take long before his friends shortened it to "Pops," and the moniker stuck like fingerprints on the dial of a safe. It was high time he had a nickname like Peanuts and Butch, and

Joey loved it. Pops Panczko. It had a peculiar ring to it. It was a name by which the public, police and the press would know Joseph Panczko for the rest of his life.

Pops quickly became one of the most industrious drivers Globe Beverage ever had on its payroll. Regular working hours meant nothing to him. He was on the go all the time, delivering pop throughout the city, and bringing back the empties. Even his parole officer marvelled at how well he had taken to honest toil.

What his legion of admirers did not know was that Pops was driving around town casing joints for burglaries. The innocuous soda pop truck was the ideal vehicle for such an undercover operation. The cops never suspected a thing.

Both Pops and Peanuts were specializing in jewelry stores during this period. Pops preferred the frontal assault, while Peanuts worked with a bit more finesse.

One evening, after enjoying just enough beers to put himself in a playful mood, Pops took off on a one-man crime spree down Devon Avenue.

Starting at California Avenue, he kicked in the back door of a jewelry store, setting off the ADT Security alarm. Knowing he had to move quickly because police would be there any minute, he was dismayed to discover that the jeweler had covered all the display cases with dust cloths, so he could not see what was inside of them. Taking pot-luck, Pops whipped off one of the covers and smashed the glass top with a tire iron. "Aw, nuts! Only four lousy watches."

Making the best of the situation, he scooped up the four watches as the alarm jangled, ducked out the back door, and headed east on foot.

He'd gone about four blocks before he came upon another jewelry store, and decided to duplicate the procedure, hoping this guy didn't use drop cloths. He was working on the back door when a woman who lived upstairs of the shop spotted him.

"Hey, you! What are you doing down there?" she yelled, loud enough to wake up the neighborhood.

"Nuttin'. Go to bed," Pops yelled as he took off down the alley. The woman picked up her phone and told the operator, "Give me the police."

By the time he had reached Western Avenue, Pops could see squad cars with their Mars lights flashing in front of the first break-in at California, while other squads, with sirens screaming, were pulling up at the second shop.

There was another jewelry store right on the corner where he stood. Pops circled the block until he found the back door, and pulled out the lock with a device he had perfected himself. To his chagrin, there was a set of bars on the inside, secured with a padlock he could not reach. "Nuts!" He went back around to the front, smashed the plate glass window, and grabbed six watches and five rings as the ADT alarm went off.

By now the district police had run out of squad cars, and had to answer the third burglar alarm in paddy wagons.

Pops picked up the newspaper the next day and read, to his amazement:

THIEVES GET $10,000
IN JEWELRY ON DEVON

"Dem dirty crooks," he fumed, shoving the newspaper in front of his brother, Butch. "Lookit! Dem fuckin' jewelers are da teeves. Dey padded da losses so dey could collect from dere insurance."

The jewelers weren't the only crooks in Pops Panczko's eyes. Early one morning, before reporting to his truck driving job, he pulled out the lock and pushed in the door at First Distributors, 2604 West North Avenue. While the alarm clanged loudly, he dashed inside.

Grabbing an armload of men's jackets with one hand, he smashed a glass show case with the other, and took $300 worth of watches. He got away just before a squad car screeched up in front with its red dome light flashing.

After stashing the loot in the trunk of his car at the end of the block, Pops sauntered casually back past the store to see what was going on. Cupping his hands to his face and peering through the front window, he could see several uniformed police officers standing over the broken jewelry case, stuffing their pockets with watches he'd left behind.

"Fuckin' teefs," he muttered under his breath as he headed back to his car.

Later that day, when he went to fence the goods, he discovered to his chagrin that Lawrence Sylvester had been sentenced to eighteen months in the federal pen for receiving stolen property from an interstate shipment. Federal agents had raided Sylvester's shop and found sixteen fur-trimmed coats he couldn't explain. Tough luck. Just when Pops found a dishonest man he could trust!

On the same night that Sylvester was packed off to prison, 29-year-old Edward "Butch" Panczko landed in the Fillmore Street police station on a charge of burglary. Detective Murray Royer found Butch, Guy Mendola, Mendola's 21-year-old wife, Donna, and 22-year-old Vincent Ficarrotta sitting in a car parked in front of a paint store at 3548 Roosevelt Road, where burglars had just taken $54 from a cash register.

By coincidence, when Royer questioned the quartet, he discovered that they had exactly $54 in their possession.

While Pops relied on a common tire iron to smash jewelry cases, Peanuts had hit on a far more sophisticated implement. It was a brick—gift wrapped.

Strolling innocently down the sidewalk, with what appeared to be a colorfully wrapped present under his arm, he would pause in front of a jewelry store window and study its contents. After making sure in the reflection that no one was watching, he would hurl the brick through the glass, scoop up all the rings, bracelets, necklaces and watches he could carry, and run to a waiting car.

The only injury Peanuts ever sustained in the line of duty came on one of his jewelry forays when he moved too fast for his own good. He and Steve Tomaras had targeted a store near Central and North Avenues. "You go park the car in the alley and wait for me," Peanuts instructed, as he tucked a gift-wrapped brick under his arm.

Walking up to the display window, Peanuts carefully made his selection and threw the brick. With the crash of broken glass still tinkling in his ears, he reached into the window and grabbed several trays of diamonds. Unfortunately, the glass wasn't done breaking yet, and a falling shard caught him right across the right wrist.

Yowling in pain, he left a crimson trail along the sidewalk as he hightailed it to the waiting car.

"You're bleeding like a stuck pig!" Tomaras exclaimed, as Peanuts jumped into the front seat beside him.

"Drive!" he yelled.

Tomaras drove to the office of a friendly physician at Lake Street and Ogden Avenue. He barely got his partner inside when Peanuts slumped into a chair and passed out from loss of blood. It was a subdued and heavily bandaged accomplice that Tomaras drove home afterward.

Peanuts had to lay low until the wound on his wrist healed, leaving a jagged scar that he bears to this day. As soon as he was well enough to work he picked up Walter Jednyak and they headed for a Holland Jewelry store on the South Side. Just in time for the holiday season. They were driving Peanuts' souped-up 1940 Ford getaway car, which was equipped with a spotlight and siren.

The gift-wrapped brick method had proved hazardous to one's health, so they tried a new tack. While Peanuts acted as lookout, Jednyak drew a sweeping circle on the display window with a glass cutter. Then he gave the glass several sharp taps in just the right places and the circle toppled inward, leaving a nice, large porthole. Each man grabbed a tray of diamonds and ran for the car, parked at the curb with the motor running. The entire operation took no more than ten seconds.

"Here we go!" yelled Peanuts as he jumped behind the wheel and rammed the gearshift into first. Off with tires squealing against the pavement, they headed north on Halsted

Street. But traffic was so heavy with Christmas shoppers they couldn't make any headway. Jednyak was listening to the police radio, and word of the jewelry break-in was already coming over the air.

"Hang on, Wally!" Peanuts said, as he flipped on the spotlight and hit the siren, weaving in and out of traffic.

As they came up on 63rd Street a traffic cop, alerted by the siren and fast approaching spotlight, mistook the bandits' auto for a police car. Blowing his whistle and raising his arms, he brought cross-traffic to a halt from both sides and waved the fleeing car through the intersection.

The next day Peanuts had a headline of his own to share with his brothers:

POLICE HELP JEWEL
THIEVES GET AWAY

By now the Ford get-away car was getting hotter than a pistol. It had been used on too many jobs, and the traffic cop had gotten a good look at it when he cleared a path for it in the wake of the Holland job. Peanuts decided to dump it in favor of a less conspicuous 1934 model. He took the old rattler over to the Bosworth-Devon Garage and had the owner, Henry Kleine, slip a 1947 Mercury engine under the hood.

The police got to test-drive it before Peanuts did, however.

Acting on a tip that the garage was a supply source of get-away cars for gangsters, Rogers Park District police, led by Lieutenant Eugene McNally, raided the place on the night of June 25, 1948.

They found all manner of hot-rod automobiles in various stages of rebuilding, and arrested the owner and four mechanics, all of whom had police records. Under questioning at the Rogers Park station, the mechanics admitted souping up cars for hoodlums so they could outrun pursuers, and even to patching bullet holes sustained during chases.

One of the cars found in the garage was Peanuts Panczko's 1934 Ford with the Mercury engine, dual carburetors, dual mufflers, double gas injectors, and special high-speed gears.

Detective Sergeants James Corbett and William Owens took it out for a little spin. To their amazement, the old Ford shot forward at 90 miles an hour seconds after they stepped on the gas, and quickly hit 140 on the straightaway.

"It's a goddam airplane without wings," Corbett gasped, clutching the wheel. "No wonder nobody can ever catch the son-of-a-bitch."

At about the time the cops were road-testing Peanuts' car on the North Side, Pops was about to get pulled over in the Loop. He and Jednyak had just popped the trunk of a salesman's car, and stolen four suitcases of men's underwear and socks. As they were leaving the scene in Panczko's 1940 Chevrolet, Detectives Max Rice and Donald O'Hara drove by from the opposite direction, and recognized them.

"It's Pops Panczko and some other guy," Rice said. "They're up to something, or they wouldn't be downtown at this time of night." The detectives made a U-turn and took off after them. They curbed the Chevy at Wacker Drive and Adams Street. Jednyak jumped out while the car was still moving and fled on foot, leaving Pops to face the music.

As the detectives examined the four suitcases Pops offered a suggestion. "Can't we work sometin' out here, officers? I mean, gimme a break and I'll take care of ya." He was on parole at the time and couldn't afford another bust.

"Yeah? How much?" Rice asked.

"Half a hunnert," Pops said, offering his friendliest smile. "Each."

"A grand," O'Hara said.

"A tousand bucks? I ain't got dat kinda dough on me," Pops protested.

"We'll go with you to get it," O'Hara said.

"Aw, Jeez, officers . . ."

"Would you rather to go back to the shithouse?"

"Naw. I . . ."

"Well, let's go get the money then."

Rice took a pair of belts out of one of the grips and strapped the rear doors shut on Pops' old Chevy. Then the three of them got into the police car and drove out to the Panczko home on Iowa Street.

Ma, Lou and Butch were all home when Pops arrived with the two detectives in tow. Since the cops were in plainclothes, everyone assumed they were co-workers whom they hadn't met. O'Hara and Rice stood by while Pops unlocked his old CCC footlocker, and dug out $700 he had salted away for an emergency.

"Lou," he said, turning to his sister. "Borrow me tree hunnert, will ya? I gotta have it right now. I'll tell ya later."

Lou went to a secret hiding place in her room and came back with $300.

The two detectives sat down at the kitchen table, and Ma gave them each a cup of coffee while they counted the money. "Okay, thanks a lot, Pops."

"Hey, ain't ya gonna take me back to my car?"

"Yeah, what the hell. Come on."

After dropping Pops off back downtown he thanked the detectives for the ride and told them, "Hey, do me a favor, will ya?"

"What?"

"Follow me. Ya got all my money, and I can't afford anudder stop."

"Where are you goin'?"

"Just follow me to Chicago and Western Avenues. Then don't follow me any more."

The two detectives obligingly tailed Pops's Chevrolet to the Near Northwest Side. When they reached Chicago and Western he waved them a thank you salute, and they turned off.

Making sure he was no longer being followed, Pops cut over to Superior Street and pulled into Louie Panozzo's garage. After Lawrence Sylvester got sent to prison Pops had discovered Louie.

Panozzo gave him $75 for the four suitcases of hot clothes. Pops was out $925 for his night's work.

When Pops got home his 80-year-old mother asked in Polish, "Who were those two men, Joey? They were so nice and polite."

"Dey were cops, Ma. Dey robbed me of all my money."

"Those crooks!" she said. "If I had known that, I would have killed them."

Another police officer who Pops supported on the side was Al Orkowski. Whenever Orkowski spotted his car he'd greet him with, "Open the trunk."

"What?"

"Open the trunk."

"Whatya want in my trunk? You're in my trunk more dan I am."

Pops would open the trunk. Orkowski would reach in, grab a handful of watches, and smirk away.

Late one night, after dropping a load of goods off at Louie Panozzo's, Pops went into a saloon at Superior and Western for a couple of cold beers. The place was packed. After a few drinks he went to the pay phone and telephoned Orkowski's home. Another police officer had given Pops the number for ten bucks.

"Al just went to sleep," the policeman's wife said.

"This is the lieutenant. It's an emergency," Pops explained.

Mrs. Orkowski awakened her husband and he came sleepily to the phone.

"Yes, lieutenant."

"Get up and piss, you son-of-a-bitch!"

Orkowski recognized the voice. He changed his phone number, but one of the cops sold Pops the new one. Several days later, when he knew Orkowski was on duty, Pops called the home again. Mrs. Orkowski answered.

"Listen, you tell that husband of yours to stay away from my wife," Pops snarled. "Or I'll kill 'em both!"

"Who is this?"

"Just give him the message. He's been sleeping with my wife. He'll know who it is."

The next time Pops was in the tavern near Panozzo's, Orkowski and his partner walked in. Orkowski grabbed Pops by the front of his shirt and slammed him against the wall. As he tried to clear his head, Orkowski's partner smacked him across the face with his night stick. They then drove him to the Racine Avenue station, where several officers, including O'Hara, worked him over. Pops spent the next two days in a hospital, where it cost $300 to have his face patched up.

Pops had another encounter with O'Hara after he was ticketed for parking in a snow removal zone at 5 o'clock one morning, while he was in a nearby bakery buying breakfast rolls for his family. He drove directly to the Albany Park District station, walked in and demanded, "What's dis all about?"

His presence in the police station drew a crowd of detectives and uniformed officers, who began questioning him about every unsolved burglary and neighborhood theft on the books.

"I don't know nuttin' about nuttin'," Pops insisted. "I just wanna know what dis here ticket is about."

"What's the matter, Pops?" It was Detective O'Hara.

Ignoring the fact that O'Hara had shaken him down for $1,000 the last time they met, Pops waved the ticket in his face and argued, "I been parkin' dere for ten years, and I never got a ticket before."

Possibly afraid that Pops might mention the shake-down, O'Hara reached out and said, "Give me the ticket. I'll straighten it out."

Pops thanked him and stormed out of the station. When he got back to his car the battery was dead. He'd left the emergency flashers on while he tarried too long in the station house. O'Hara got into a squad car, pulled up nose-to-nose with the Chevy, and gave Pops a jump to get him started.

Reaching into the front seat, Pops said, "Here!" and handed the detective the bag of rolls.

Pops was no sooner out of trouble with the law than Steve Tomaras was arrested for the twenty-second time in two years. He was accused of burglarizing a haberdashery on Archer Avenue, from which $4,200 worth of clothing was taken. A policeman recognized Tomaras as he ran from the store, dropped a bundle, and leaped onto the running board of a waiting car. As the get-away car lurched away from the curb, Tomaras fell off and was captured as he was trying to ditch the rubber gloves he'd been wearing.

When the case came up for trial, Tomaras was represented by George Bieber. Bieber, who started as a "slugger" for the Hearst newspapers during the circulation wars of the 1930s, had gone on to law school and become one of the city's better known criminal defense attorneys. In addition to his regular clients, he was on a $250,000-a-year retainer from the crime syndicate.

Tomaras was small potatoes to the mob, but whenever a burglar was arrested Bieber was notified to go to bat for him. Bieber's usual strategy, if he could not get a case thrown out of Felony Court, was to file a "motion to fix."

It was important to keep punks like Tomaras out of jail, lest they become unhappy and start telling who they fenced their merchandise with, or leak other syndicate secrets they might have picked up while plying their trade in exchange for a lighter sentence.

Tomaras went on trial before Judge Frank Bicek in Criminal Court.

After the arresting officers described in detail how they'd caught the burglar red-handed, Bieber put the defendant on the stand.

"Were you indeed in the neighborhood of 4163 Archer Avenue on the night in question?"

"Yes, sir, I was."

"And tell us, please, what were you doing there?"

"I had just brought my girlfriend home."

"You took your girlfriend home. And what is your girlfriend's name?"

"It's Eileen something. I can't remember her last name."

"Ah, all right. After you took, ah, Eileen home, what happened next?"

"Well, I saw this crowd by the hat store, and I stopped out of curiosity, to see what happened, you know."

"And?"

"And I was arrested."

It was an inspiring story, and the jury never got a chance to kick it around. After the prosecution and defense had presented their cases, Judge Bicek ordered a directed verdict of not guilty.

Virgil Peterson, operating director of the Chicago Crime Commission, was outraged. He protested to the press over what he termed "the phenomenal success of Steve Tomaras in getting himself acquitted in Criminal Court."

Tomaras and his buddies went out and got drunk.

Steve's "phenomenal success" did not escape Pops Panczko and his burglar brothers. While they had achieved much of their success in stealing from the Jews, they all knew a smart one when they saw one. They hired George Bieber as their lawyer.

CHAPTER 9

LETTING GEORGE DO IT

George R. Bieber was the best thing that ever happened to the Panczkos, and they were the best thing that ever happened to Bieber. One or the other of the brothers was in trouble so regularly that Bieber's name made the papers almost daily as their attorney of record, often on page one. It was the kind of advertising that money could not buy.

Tall, suave and fishy-faced, Georgie, as he was known among his colleagues, wore $500 suits and owned a "dese, dose and dem" vocabulary that made Pops comfortable. Had he not gone into law he might have become a song and dance man. Bouncy and ebullient, he was not above holding his briefcase out at arm's length and whipping off a short soft-shoe dance in the corridors of the Criminal Courts building whenever he got a defendant off the hook.

His partner was Mike Brodkin. Dour and foreboding, he wore a crewcut on his head and a perpetually angry look on his face. His booming voice earned him the nickname of "Loud Mike" whenever he appeared in court. No two men were ever more opposite than Bieber and Brodkin.

Georgie immediately set up ground rules for his new clients. Just as police officers walking a beat had to go to a corner call box and phone headquarters at regular intervals to let the desk sergeant know they were all right, the Panczkos had to "pull the box" with Bieber.

If his answering service did not hear from one of them on schedule, he or Brodkin would begin beating the bushes—checking precinct houses throughout the city to find where he was locked up.

One night Pops was arrested in connection with the burglary of a gun shop, which he and Walter Jednyak had disarmed of twenty to thirty shotguns. On the way downtown in the paddy wagon, Pops slipped $300 to an elderly patrol officer and said, "Here, make a phone call for me. Call Georgie Bieber."

Bieber never got the call. He found Pops the hard way, and posted bail. As they were leaving the station house the white haired policeman edged up to Panczko and said, "Here's your three hundred back. I couldn't make the call."

"How come? Didn't I pay ya enough?"

"No. The word is out—anybody that makes a call for Pops blows their job. I'm too close to retirement, Pops. I couldn't take the chance."

"Dat's okay. You tried," Pops said. "Keep da tree hunnert."

When the case came up in court Pops, with Bieber at his side, was found not guilty.

The parole officer, to whom Pops paid the $10 to get the job on the soft drink truck, came by the bottling plant once a week at 5 o'clock to make sure Panczko was working. Pops paid him $25 a week.

"Look, you do as you please," the parole agent said, slipping the money into his billfold. "Just don't get caught, understand?"

"I just drive dis here truck," Pops said.

"Yeah, I know," the parole officer said. "Ah, by the way, did I mention that my daughter's getting married?"

"Naw. I didn't know ya had a daughter."

"Yeah, well, she is. I was wondering, Pops. Do you think you could get me some whiskey for the wedding?"

"How much ya need?"

"Couple of cases, I figure."

Two weeks later Pops visited a liquor store, after it was closed for the day, and selected three cases of liquor, which he delivered to the parole officer's home. The state agent was so pleased he invited Pops to the wedding reception at the Lakeshore Athletic Club.

Pops showed up in a stolen suit, with his hair slicked down, and gave the bride and groom a $100 bill. The swank affair was so unlike the rough and rowdy Polish weddings he was accustomed to, however, that he did not feel comfortable. He hung around just long enough to be fashionable, then ducked.

On the way home two police officers in a squad car spotted Pops on Fullerton Avenue, executed a U-turn, and took off after him. Panczko's experiences with the law by this time were such that he fled every time he saw a cop, whether he had stolen goods in the car or not. When he saw the police car in his rear view mirror, he hit the gas.

By the time the cops caught up with him, they had a whole list of charges prepared, starting with speeding, reckless driving, driving on the wrong side of the road and going through half a dozen red lights. It soon became a harassing tactic for police to pursue Pops whenever they saw him, and shower him with traffic tickets.

Before long he had amassed so many tickets that the Illinois Secretary of State's office revoked his driver's license. Pops, of course, went right on driving. A man has to work, doesn't he? This was like telling police with their hands out, "There is a Santa Claus."

The first day after his revocation, Pops found a uniformed police officer standing in front of his house when he went out to get into his car.

"You're not going to drive that car, are you Pops?"

"What do you tink?"

"It'll cost you a hundred bucks."

The word was out. It seemed to Pops that every cop in the district knew that his license had been yanked. It was costing him $100 every time a policeman caught him behind the wheel.

"You're on borrowed time, Pops," one detective told him, as he pocketed the C-note.

Now that they were more or less working with Pops, police started placing orders with him.

"I need a new suit, Pops. Size 48."

"Pops, pick me up a couple of shirts, will you? Size 16–34."

"The tires on my car are going bald, Pops. Here, I wrote the size down for you on this slip of paper."

Cigars. Whiskey. Polish hams. Underwear. Socks. Whatever the police needed, they went to Pops. He was so busy providing for them that he barely had time to steal for himself.

In exchange for his cooperation, police kept Pops posted on areas to avoid. "Stay away from Halsted Street for the next couple of days, Pops. There's a stake-out going on." "Don't go near North Avenue tonight, Pops. The dicks are watching a couple of stores."

As if Pops wasn't having enough problems, Bieber needed a dog. "Pops," the lawyer said, calling him at home. "Can you get me a poodle?"

"I t'ougt you had a dog, Georgie. What's da matter? Did Troubles croak?"

"No, no, Troubles is fine. This is for a friend from Wisconsin. He wants a little poodle."

"Okay, I'll shop around."

Pops had never stolen a dog before. This took some planning. He reasoned that Bieber was Jewish, therefore the friend must also be Jewish, so he should steal him a Jewish dog. But where'd be the best place to pinch a Jewish dog? Jews don't keep yard dogs. They keep house pets. You just can't reach over the back fence and grab one. They even take their mutts along when they drive to the store. Of course! That's it!

Armed with a prybar and heavy leather work gloves, Pops drove over to the Ashkanez Deli on the North Side. He walked casually along the sidewalk, looking into parked cars.

His calculations proved correct. There was a new Cadillac parked at the curb with the cutest white poodle you ever saw in the front seat, standing on its hind legs, scratching at the window and wagging its tail.

Quickly looking around, Pops popped the vent window with the prybar, reached in, patted the pup on the head, and grabbed it by the scruff of the neck. It was a good thing he thought to wear the leather gloves, because the little shit nipped him on the thumb.

Pops delivered the poodle to his lawyer, who couldn't have been happier. "Pops, dis is perfect," Georgie gushed. "Dis is just what I ordered."

The next time he saw Bieber, Pops asked him, "How'd your friend from Wisconsin like the dog?"

"I didn't give it to him, Pops."

"Ya didn't?"

"You won't believe this, but another friend of mine, from Rogers Park, calls and says, 'Georgie, my poor little dog was stolen. Do you know where I can get another one? My wife's bawling her head off.' I told him to come on over, that I had a poodle he could have. The guy stops by my apartment, and do you know what, Pops?"

"Uh-uh."

"Honest to God! The pooch runs up to him, licking his hands. He's kissing the dog and crying, 'Schnappsie!' It was his own dog you stole, Pops."

"Fer cryin' out loud. What'd ya tell him?"

"What could I tell him? I said I got the mutt at the pet store. He said they must be crooks."

While Pops was pilfering poodles, Peanuts was after bigger game. There was a jewelers convention at the Hilton Hotel. Naturally the place had more security guards crawling the corridors than Fort Knox. He and Chester Gray, one of Pops' former partners, put the hotel under surveillance.

When one of the gem salesmen left, carrying two black leather jewelry cases along with his personal luggage, they shadowed his cab to the Chicago & North Western Station.

They were prepared to follow him all the way to California if necessary.

Inside the station, 34-year-old Milton Jaffe glanced at his watch. He was obviously in a hurry to catch a train. While Panczko and Gray watched from a discreet distance, the salesman hailed a Red Cap. "Please take my bags to Track 10 while I make reservations for a berth," he said. "I'm going to Los Angeles."

Everett Baker, the 35-year-old porter, put the luggage aboard a baggage cart and headed for the gate, with Peanuts on his tail, waving a $10 bill. "Red Cap!" he called officiously. "Will you pick up my brother-in-law's bags for me? Here's a ten for ya."

"Where are they?"

"The cab driver left 'em on the sidewalk. C'mon. I'll show ya. I've got a bum back."

Baker left the cart where it was, pocketed the ten spot, and followed Peanuts. Gray grabbed the two jewelry cases and ducked out the other door. "Can ya beat that? I don't see the damn bag," Peanuts said, looking up and down the sidewalk. "Well, never mind. Maybe my brother-in-law carried it in himself. Keep the ten for your trouble, pal."

Peanuts joined Gray and the two jewelry cases, containing $40,000 in gems, in their car as the bewildered Red Cap headed back to the gate. The grips weren't on the cart where he'd left them. The gentleman probably picked them up himself. Oh, well.

When the police weren't concentrating on Pops, they were working on Peanuts and his pals. Butch was keeping a low profile.

On August 13 Peanuts, Steve Tomaras, Martin "The Ox" Ochs, and three other men were arrested for disorderly conduct during a robbery investigation. Peanuts put in a call to Bieber. When the six were arraigned before Judge William V. Daly in South State Street Court, the judge declared, "The police have nothing on these men. They are dismissed."

Some cops don't know when to quit. Three days later they arrested Peanuts, Ochs, Tomaras, Needle Nose Labriola and two other men on the same charge.

Judge John J. Griffin in Racine Avenue Court wouldn't drop the charges, so Bieber asked for a jury trial and got a continuance. One of his tactics was to get so many continuances that witnesses eventually got tired coming to court, and on the one day a key witness failed to show up he would demand immediate trial.

While charges were pending against Peanuts in Racine Avenue Court he was arrested for breaking into a bakery on Irving Park Road and taking $225. Judge Charles S. Dougherty, who was getting tired of seeing him, set bond at $1,500 and bound him over to the grand jury.

Dougherty was also wrestling with an interesting case involving Lover Boy Mendola. Park Policemen Edward Robart and Frank Clay curbed his car after an 80-mile-an-hour chase on Lake Shore Drive. They charged him with possession of stolen property after finding two radios, taken during a burglary of a radio shop on 79th Street, in his car.

Dougherty threw the case out after Robart and Clay could give no valid reason for taking off after Mendola in the first place. The judge ordered a grand jury investigation of the entire incident after reviewing a City News Bureau report that the park policemen earlier said they arrested Mendola because he was driving without lights.

The grand jury probe was still pending when Mendola was arrested again, along with Steve Tomaras, for possession of burglary tools. They were sitting in a parked car loaded with burglar tools on Ashland Avenue. The vehicle checked out to Peanuts Panczko. He had just stepped out of the car, and was busy casing the place they were going to hit, when the over-eager cops moved in so fast they overlooked him.

Christmas was approaching, and Peanuts needed money —not for yuletide shopping, but to put on the account with Bieber, who seemed to be spending half his time getting or keeping the brothers out of jail.

The dapper attorney had boasted to reporters in the Criminal Courts Building, "The Panczkos are a charity case. I handle them for free, just to keep my mind sharp. Jeez, does it ever keep my mind sharp!"

"Free, my ass!" Peanuts scoffed, when he read Bieber's outrageous statement in the morning paper.

If the truth were known, Bieber's meter was running every time one of the brothers talked to him. He was getting wealthier off of Peanuts, Pops and Butch than the police officers who shook them down. He made a point of declaring that he was handling them out of the goodness of his heart, however, so he could avoid paying income taxes. He knew the Panczkos could not declare the proceeds of their thievery with the Internal Revenue Service, so he saw no useful purpose in declaring what he earned off them.

Peanuts needed cash to pay the lawyer, so he was looking around for instant money—not furs or something he would have to fence—when he and Lover Boy Mendola spotted an Illinois Bell Telephone Company panel truck in the Loop. The truck had a Christmas tree lashed to the roof.

Peanuts and Lover Boy tailed the driver as he went from one downtown building to the next, unlocked the pay phones, and dumped the contents of the cash boxes into a canvas money bag. "The guy's collecting from pay phones," Peanuts observed. "He's just about ready to knock off. He's already got his Christmas tree to take home."

In those days pay phones were a nickel. Every little metal box the service man dumped into the bag was full of nickels. It was 3 o'clock in the afternoon. After a full day on the route, his truck was a rolling piggy bank.

When the driver came out of his next stop and unlocked the truck, Panczko and Mendola shoved him inside and piled in after him. Mendola held a gun on the surprised driver while Peanuts took the wheel, circled the block, and pulled into the alley behind Marshall Field's.

"You can have the money, but please don't take my Christmas tree," the driver pleaded.

"Get out!" Peanuts ordered, opening the door and giving the driver the boot. As he and Mendola sped off in the phone company truck they could hear the man yelling, "My tree! My tree! You're taking my Christmas tree!"

They drove to where their car was parked, transferred the load, and abandoned the truck, leaving the Christmas tree tied on the roof. Then they drove the carload of nickels directly to Bieber's North Side apartment at 431 West Oakdale. The elevator creaked and groaned as it laboriously hoisted the weight of the two thieves, and all those bags of nickels, all the way to the tenth floor.

Peanuts had phoned ahead to make sure Bieber was home. Troubles, the lawyer's poodle, yapped excitedly as Panczko and Mendola dragged in the money bags and dumped the nickels all over the carpet. The three men got down on their hands and knees and counted them out. It was dark outside by the time they came up with a tally. There were more than 36,000 nickels, worth over $1,800.

"Just leave the bags and everything here. I'll take 'em to my bank in the morning," Bieber said. Then, putting his hand on Panczko's shoulder, he added confidentially, "Ah, don't tell Mike about dis."

"That kinky son-of-a-bitch," Peanuts fumed, as he and Mendola rode back down in the elevator. "He's holdin' out on his own fuckin' partner!"

"That's why he's a rich lawyer," Mendola explained. "And we're poor crooks."

CHAPTER 10

POPS STOPS
ANOTHER SLUG

January was never one of Joseph Panczko's better months. It was a cold and snowy January day when he first got caught stealing cheese from the Fulton Street Market, and got that year at St. Charles. And it was the first day of January, 1948, that the cop winged him on lower Wacker when he and Orloski got caught carrying liquor out of the closed restaurant.

By the time another January rolled around he still hadn't caught on. Thanks to Bieber's remarkable legal shenanigans he was getting cockier by the day. Convinced that the lawyer's success gave him a virtual license to steal, he unwittingly decided to engage in interstate commerce.

On the evening of January 26, Pops' immediate attention was focused on a Railway Express truck parked in the agency yard at 411 South Market Street, near the Eisenhower Expressway. He watched that truck for a long time. There appeared to be no one around.

Pops had knocked off several Railway Express trucks loaded with furs in recent weeks, and REA officials were beginning to show concern. They had decided to set a trap. Like the others, this truck was loaded with luxurious furs—but there was one difference. It also contained officer Carl Ohlin.

Ohlin, a former Chicago policeman, had been hired as a security officer by the REA to investigate the rash of thefts.

Bundled up against the cold, he sat huddled inside the locked truck with his service revolver in his lap.

Pops walked up to the truck and gave it the once-over. The rear doors were secured with a heavy case-hardened steel padlock. The kind that could not be cut, even with heavy-duty bolt cutters. Guaranteed to stop amateurs. He slipped a fingernail file into the slot, jiggled it a few times, and the theft-proof lock snapped open.

Pops swung open the hinged doors, climbed into the back of the truck, and selected a cardboard box containing a fur coat. "Hold it right there!" Ohlin ordered. Pops instinctively dropped the box and started to turn to run. Ohlin squeezed off two fast shots. One of the bullets struck Panczko in the groin, and sent him sprawling to the ground, bleeding profusely and writhing in pain.

He was taken by ambulance to the now-familiar Bridewell Hospital. Since the REA did business across state lines, a federal grand jury subsequently indicted him for theft from an interstate shipment.

Pops was still in the Bridewell recovering from his latest gunshot experience six weeks later when brother Butch was nabbed after a police chase in which five shots were fired at his fleeing car. The bullet-riddled auto, loaded with ten suspicious looking cases of whiskey, was found abandoned at Erie and Aberdeen Streets. Thirty-three year old Butch was discovered strolling in the area a short time later.

"I ain't doin' nothing," he protested, when the police asked him what he was up to. "Just walking home. Somebody stole my car."

The cops wouldn't swallow it. Butch was booked on suspicion of burglary after James Pseris, owner of the Amelia Restaurant on Grand Avenue, identified the liquor as having been taken from the restaurant earlier in the evening.

Over on Huron Street and Ashland Avenue, meanwhile, other squads of police were busy arresting Peanuts, Steve Tomaras, Walter Jednyak, and six other men in connection with a series of North Side break-ins.

Police Captain Thomas Harrison, who supervised the

roundup, surmised, "It appears that Peanuts and his pals were attempting to raise a defense fund for Butch and Pops."

It was the first time all three brothers, working independently, found themselves under lock and key at the same time. There was no rest for Bieber. "I'm being persecuted," Peanuts complained, as he waited for the lawyer to come down and pull some strings.

Butch uttered the same complaint several weeks later when Captain Harrison and Sergeant Richard Stahlman arrested him for disorderly conduct when they found him loitering at 12:30 a.m. in Washington Square, a Near North rendezvous for soap box orators, more commonly referred to as "Bughouse Square."

Assuming, and quite correctly so, that no Panczko in his right mind would be prowling such a neighborhood after midnight unless he was looking for something to steal, Harrison asked, "What the hell would you be doing here at this hour of the morning?"

"Nothin'. I, ah, I just had to take a leak, and I stopped to use the wash room."

"Oh, is that a fact now?"

"Yeah."

"Well, my friend, the wash rooms closed eight hours ago, and they're still locked tight." Harrison explained. "We'll let you use the can over at the station house. See if the cuffs still fit him, sergeant."

No one had ever made the Chicago papers for having to go to the toilet before, but the Panczko brothers were becoming good copy. The press gave Butch's bladder problem four generous inches under the headline:

POLICE CAPTAIN TOURS
BUGHOUSE SQUARE AND
HOODLUM GOES TO CELL

Back in the old neighborhood, Butch's cronies found it hard to keep a straight face when he walked into the corner tavern the following afternoon and said, "Give me a beer."

CHAPTER 11

THE PARKER
PEN CAPER

Things were beginning to heat up for the Panczko brothers in Chicago. Pops was hurting in the Bridewell from a bullet in the groin, Peanuts had been jailed sixteen times in the past twelve months, and Butch couldn't even take a midnight pee without the police pouncing on him.

For all of his sixteen arrests, Peanuts had dished out only $25 in fines—$15 for parking and $10 for disorderly conduct. The rest of his money went to Bieber.

"Maybe we ought to hit the road for awhile, give the coppers a chance to forget what we look like," he suggested to Walter Marko one evening as they sipped beer in a neighborhood saloon frequented by burglars.

"Somebody told me there's a good score in Janesville, Wisconsin," Marko suggested.

"Yeah? Well, see what ya can find out."

On Sunday, March 23, 1949, they picked up a friend, gassed up the car, grabbed a free road map and headed for the Southern Wisconsin town, 109 miles northwest of Chicago. They were using their work car, the souped-up 1940 Chevrolet owned jointly by Panczko and Marko. Peanuts was behind the wheel.

Once they reached Janesville they followed directions Marko's friend had scrawled on a slip of paper until they came to a large warehouse along a railroad siding at the edge of town. It was the world-wide shipping depot for the Parker Pen Company. Easing the car between the tracks and the rear of the building, so as not to be visible from the road, the trio battered down the back door.

Peanuts was the first inside. Standing in the doorway he gasped in amazement, "Jeeeeezus Christ! Lookit all the fuckin' pens! There's t'ousands of 'em!"

"Maybe millions," Marko said. "Where the hell should we start?"

"Go for the gold ones," Peanuts said. "C'mon. Let's get moving."

This was one job the celebrated "Three Minute Gang" would not accomplish in the allotted time. Carefully selecting only the gold-filled pen and pencil sets, they carried nearly forty large boxes out to the car and dumped their contents into the back seat. When the back seat started to run over they poured the rest into the trunk.

"We shoulda brought a lousy truck!" Peanuts complained. "Jeez. This is all we can take. Let's get outa here."

Back in Chicago the trio stored the pens in a friend's garage at Central and Lawrence Avenues, covered with blankets, while they went out to look for a fence.

Peanuts didn't know until he picked up the newspaper the next day that he had scored the biggest haul of his career. Parker Pen Company officials listed the loss at 40,300 pens and pencils, having a market value of $363,000. That would be the equivalent of between three and four million dollars in today's currency.

The boys went to Meyer Gordon's Loop jewelry store, where the fence said he would take the shipment off their hands for $100,000. When it came time to deliver the goods, however, he reneged on the deal.

"I'm scared to touch it," he said. "This thing's in all the papers. And now the FBI has gone in to help the police from Wisconsin and Illinois. It's too hot. Look. Here's five grand for your trouble, and I don't know nothin' from nothin'."

Peanuts pocketed the $5,000, and went out looking for a fence who wasn't quite so skittish. Nobody in Chicago would touch the hot pens, however, and he ended up dumping them in New York with a fence who sent the entire lot overseas. This explains the sudden popularity of Parker Pens in Europe as the 1940s drew to a close.

Despite the combined efforts of the Federal Bureau of Investigation and police from two states, the Parker Pen heist was never solved. And the statute of limitations has long run out.

Peanuts was not the only brother to go interstate about that time. Pops took the same route—but his venture wasn't intentional.

Pops and Lover Boy Mendola figured they were on a routine stake-out when they shifted their operations to west suburban Aurora, to avoid some of the heat in Chicago. The immediate focus of their attention was the first jewelry store they could find.

"Dere goes a guy wit' a black suitcase, into da store. It's gotta be a jewelry salesman," Pops noted, getting out of the car.

"Where ya goin'?"

"I'll be right back. I'm gonna pretend I'm lookin' at da window display."

Peering through the plate glass, while pretending to look down at the watches in the window, Pops watched as the store manager and the other man went into the back room, suitcase and all.

"It looks like a jewelry salesman, all right," he told Mendola. "I'm gonna see if I can find where he parked his car."

Setting out on foot, Pops discovered a late model Buick with New York license plates parked around the corner. Inside the locked car was another black leather suitcase. "We got 'em!" he told Mendola, triumphantly. "Let's find a pay phone."

Pops dropped a nickel into the slot, dialed "0" and told the operator, "Gimme New York Information." When Information came on the line he asked for the number of the New York Motor Vehicle Department.

"Dis is Sergeant Brown, Chicago P.D.," he said, when he got through to the Motor Vehicle Department. "I need a fast license plate check. We're workin' on a hit-run accident." The New York authorities told him the plates checked out to a Marvin Cohen, a resident of Brooklyn.

More nickels into the slot. The next call was to the auto dealer in Brooklyn, whose insignia was on the trunk of Cohen's Buick. Pops was now the Ace Lock Company, trying to help a customer of theirs who had locked himself out of his car. "Look on the invoice, would you? Give me the serial number of his door key so I can make him a new one. Thanks a lot."

Using the key maker, which he carried whenever he was out on a job, he popped out a key for Cohen's Buick.

"Make sure he ain't comin'," he told Mendola. "I'm gonna check that big suitcase in his car." Pops returned minutes later and told Lover Boy, "It's a giant magnifyin' glass. He's a diamond guy!"

"Are we gonna make him here?"

"Naw, too many people. When he comes out, we follow him."

The jeweler came out of the store and put the grip on the front seat beside him, started up the Buick and pulled away from the curb. He drove out to U.S. Highway 30 and headed for Joliet. Pops and Lover Boy were right behind him.

Pops had "hot" plates on his car. He had stolen them off a policeman's auto, just in case any witness took down their license number while he and Lover Boy were robbing the salesman. After making good their escape he would put his own plates back on the car before heading back to Chicago.

"Dere's a red light up ahead. He's gotta stop," Pops said, as they approached Joliet. Handing Lover Boy a large hunting knife he carried under the front seat, he instructed, "Here. Jump out and give 'em a flat tire."

When the salesman pulled up at the traffic signal, Mendola slid out of the car, hunched down beside the right rear wheel of the Buick and gave the tire two good jabs with the knife. A short distance down the road the tire went flat. The salesman pulled off over to the side, near a manufacturing plant, and got out of his car.

"Okay, when he takes a hike to find a gas station to get his tire fixed, we grab the jewelry case outa his car and take off," Pops said. "Den we . . ."

"Hold it," Mendola interrupted. "What the hell's he doing? He's taking off his coat. Aw, shit, he's opening the trunk. Now he's getting the jack out."

"Jeez. He's fixin' his own fuckin' tire!" Pops said, banging the steering wheel with his fist. "Let's just grab da suitcase and beat it. It's sittin' on da front seat wit' da door open. He can't follow us wit' the wheel off."

They waited while the salesman jacked up the car, removed the right rear wheel and got the spare out of the trunk. "Okay," Pops said. "Let's move!"

"Wait a minute," Mendola cautioned, putting his hand on Panczko's arm. "Where's all them fuckin' people coming from? There's thousands of 'em."

"What da hell?" Pops exclaimed. "Da factory's lettin' out. We can't do nuttin' wit' all dese people on da street. We gotta wait 'til everybody goes home."

By the time the crowd had cleared, however, the salesman had replaced the flat tire. He put the tools back into the trunk, wiped off his hands, got back into his car, and took off down the road.

"Man, it's gettin' dark," Pops observed. "Let's stick wit' dis guy. He ain't drivin' all da way back t' New York tonight. He's gotta get a motel and go to sleep some time. Most salesmen hide dere stuff in da bath tub or under da bed, den dey go out an' get somethin' ta eat."

"Yeah," Mendola salivated. "When he goes to eat we'll knock the door down and grab the stuff."

There was only one flaw in the plan. The jewelry salesman did not stop for the night. He continued on through Joliet on U.S. 30, following the road around the bottom of Lake Michigan through Indiana, and up into Michigan. He was going to cross the state to Port Huron, and then take the shortcut through Ontario to New York.

By midnight the jewelry salesman and the jewel thieves were the only cars on the road. The salesman had kicked the Buick up to seventy miles an hour. Pops was forced to lag a mile or so behind, so as not to make the pursuit obvious.

"As long as we can see his taillights, we're okay," he told Mendola. "Help me keep an eye on dem lights."

"What the hell is that?" Mendola asked, as a red light coming up from behind bathed the inside of their car. "I hear a siren."

"Aw, nertz. Nuttin's goin' right," Pops groaned, as he pulled off to the side of the road.

"Going a little fast, weren't you boys? Let's see your driver's license." It was a Michigan state trooper. Pops handed him his suspended license. The trooper shined his flashlight into the car. He spotted the extra set of license plates and the hunting knife.

"We just passed the police station in Saint Joe," the trooper said. "Turn your car around and head back there. I'll be right behind you."

Pops made a U-turn and headed back down the darkened highway toward St. Joseph. "Jeez, I'm already on parole. I can't afford anudder bust," he said, squinting at the rear-view mirror.

"What are we gonna do?"

"Da copper's laggin' back. Let's make a run for it." Pops floored the gas pedal. The Michigan trooper picked up the chase and unlimbered his service revolver.

"Jesus Christ! He's shooting at us," Mendola yelled, seeing flashes coming from the pursuing police car. Climbing over the seat, he pulled up the back seat and held it against the rear window as a shield. "Drive, Pops," he yelled.

"Watch for lights," Pops told him as he hunched over the steering wheel. "Dis is a two-lane road. We ain't got nowhere to go. It's black as midnight out dere. I can't see anywhere to turn off. We gotta find a town and give him the slip."

The speedometer on the old Chevy said 100 miles an hour as Pops careened down the Michigan highway, the trooper in pursuit. Ahead he saw the lights of a town. "Here we go," he told Lover Boy. "We'll lose him now."

It was not to be. As he approached the St. Joseph city limits, Pops could see that a barricade had been erected across the road. The trooper had radioed ahead, and police were waiting for him. Pops slammed into the wooden sawhorses and splintered the barricade as he roared into town.

Hitting the brakes, he swerved into a side street. As he slowed to make the next corner, Mendola threw open the door and jumped out. Pops drove another block, turned another corner, skidded to a stop and jumped out himself. He took off on foot through the nearest yard, and ran smack into a chicken wire fence.

Police, who were right on his tail, grabbed him before he could get his bearings. A local reporter, who snapped his picture for the Herald-Press, asked, "Is that car stolen?"

"Naw, it's mine," Pops said as the cops slapped the cuffs on him.

"Then, why were you running from the police?"

"'Cause I'm on parole, and I ain't supposed to leave the state."

It was cold and starting to rain. Mendola broke into a summer cottage on Lake Michigan and stole a blanket. Police picked him up a half hour later, wrapped in the blanket and hitch-hiking.

"We never did get that salesman," Lover Boy lamented as he and Pops sat in the bullpen in the St. Joseph jail.

"Hey, don't say nothin'. This room is bugged," another inmate cautioned.

"I'm callin' Bieber," Pops said. "Hey, Guard! I wanna make a phone call."

The next day the small town paper bannered:

POLICE NAB HOODLUMS
IN 100 MPH CHASE

Panczko and Mendola were marched into court first thing in the morning, to be arraigned before Justice of the Peace Joseph R. Collins. "Where's da judge?" Pops asked a woman, who appeared to be the court stenographer.

"He's already here," she said, nodding toward a man in bib overalls, who was mopping the floor.

"Dat's da judge?"

"Yeah, that's him," she giggled.

Bieber arrived with an associate, whom he introduced as Spitzer. They talked briefly to the man in the bib overalls, then motioned to Panczko and Mendola. "C'mon, Pops, Lover Boy. We just made bail. We're gettin' outa here."

"When's da trial?" Pops asked, as soon as they were outside.

"There ain't gonna be none," Bieber explained. "The judge set bail at three hundred for each of ya. The agreement is that you forfeit the bonds and he sticks the six hundred bucks in his pocket."

"Where's my car?" was Panczko's next question.

"Forget the car," Bieber said. "The cops are waiting at the state line to pinch Mendola. They want him for burglary in Indiana. We're headin' for the airport. You guys are gonna fly right over their heads."

"Wait a minute! I ain't never been in a plane before."

"There's a first time for everything, Pops. Unless ya want to try to run another roadblock."

Leaving Spitzer behind, Bieber drove the two men in his black Chrysler New Yorker to the Benton Harbor-St. Joseph airport. There they boarded a small plane, and Bieber gave the pilot fifty dollars to fly the two thieves back to Meigs Field on Northerly Island.

The pilot hugged the shoreline as he headed for Chicago, rather than risk flying over water. "Hey, driver. What's dat place wit' all dose buildings down dere?" Pops asked, shortly after take-off.

"We're over Michigan City," the pilot said. "That's the Indiana State Pen."

Pops gave Lover Boy a weak smile.

After landing at Meigs Field, he and Mendola took a taxi home. The next day Pops telephoned Bieber and asked, "Say, Georgie. Where da hell's my car?"

"The cops kept it," Bieber said.

"Dey can't do dat. It's illegal."

"Is it worth three hunnert dollars to ya?" Bieber asked. "I'll have to make the drop."

"Yeah. It's da only car I got."

That afternoon Pops stopped by Bieber's apartment on Oakdale, paid the lawyer $300 and picked up his car. Pops later learned that Spitzer had driven the Chevrolet home, and Bieber had pocketed the $300.

Bieber also got a piece of the $600 he claimed to have paid the justice of the peace in Michigan. The defendants did not forfeit bail at all, as he had indicated. Instead, Bieber hired a St. Joseph attorney, Maurice Weber, to plead them both guilty when their cases were called.

Justice Collins fined the absent Panczko $100 and $7.25 in costs for reckless driving, and fined Mendola $25 and $8.55 in costs for vagrancy. Weber paid the fines. In addition to his legal fee, Bieber made $460 on the deal, less what he paid Weber to make a five-minute court appearance.

For Pops things quickly went from bad to worse.

He no sooner got back to Chicago than he went on trial before Judge Michael L. Igoe in federal court for theft from interstate shipments, in connection with the REA truck break-in, in which he'd been shot.

Pops was sentenced to two years in prison, to be followed by three years probation. He was sent to the federal prison at

Terre Haute, Indiana, and then transferred to Leavenworth. Upon his release in November of 1950 he was taken directly to the Illinois State Penitentiary as a parole violator. He would not see the streets of the city again until 1953.

Butch and Peanuts were having their days in court, too. Bieber was barely getting a moment's rest.

First it was Butch's turn for the midnight pee incident in Bughouse Square. That was his thirty-fourth arrest. He demanded a jury trial before Judge Mason S. Sullivan in Chicago Avenue Court. Georgie proved that the police had no cause to arrest him.

Then Butch went before Judge Alan E. Ashcraft in Criminal Court for the liquor theft from the Amelia Restaurant. Veteran detective Emil Smicklas was on the witness stand, relating events that led up to Panczko's arrest following the bullet-punctuated police chase.

"I recognized Edward Panczko right away," he testified. "I knew him because I had arrested him many times."

"Objection!" shouted Bieber, leaping to his feet and raising his hand. "Move for a mistrial! Your honor, the officer's testimony violates every rule of evidence."

Judge Ashcraft agreed. He dismissed the jury and told Butch he could go home.

Peanuts, meanwhile, had added eleven more arrests to his record. The most serious bust was for the theft of the salesman's suitcases, containing $40,000 worth of jewels, from the North Western railway depot. Police figured the theft had all the earmarks of a Panczko caper, and brought Peanuts in for questioning.

He was charged with grand larceny after Everett Baker, the porter, picked him out of a seven-man lineup at the Desplaines Street Police Station as the man who had lured him away from the jewelry bags; and LeRoy Moss, another porter, identified Peanuts as the man he had seen loitering near the luggage before it disappeared.

When the case came up for trial Judge William V. Daly, a frequent freer of the Panczkos, threw the matter out of court.

"The prosecution has not produced any witnesses who actually saw Mr. Panczko pick up the bag," he ruled.

The decade ended in violence for several associates of the Panczko brothers.

Elmer "Whitey" Madsen, the friendly fence who worked for Fish Johnson, was shot to death by two gunmen as he emerged from Johnson's candy store on Armitage Avenue on the night of October 10. Homicide investigators found seventy men's suits on racks in the back room of the confectionery. The original price tags had been removed, and the suits bore exaggerated labels scaled down to make them look like bargains.

Johnson dropped out of sight after the shooting. Three days later he walked into the Shakespeare Station and told police, "My barber says you gentlemen were looking for me."

Authorities were still investigating the Madsen murder when two burglars were shot and critically wounded by police during a break-in at a Michigan Avenue women's apparel shop. The wounded men were identified as Charles Scislo and John Di Franzo, both members of Peanuts Panczko's fabled Three Minute Gang.

Peanuts was among those being sought for questioning.

CHAPTER 12

THE NASHVILLE DIAMOND HEIST

While Whitey Madsen's murder remained unsolved, the inside story of the gangland execution quickly spread through the underworld as a pointed message to others: Don't mess with the Mob.

"Hey, the word's out," Peanuts told Walter Jednyak and Lover Boy Mendola. "Here's why Whitey got popped. Some punk kid robbed some jewels off some woman and, guess what? She's De Biase's old lady!"

"Johnny Bananas' wife? Are you kidding?"

John De Biase, known as Johnny Bananas, was the fixer for the Outfit, as the crime syndicate was known. If there was a problem, he fixed it. Somebody stole his wife's jewels. That was a problem that needed fixing.

"That's right," Peanuts continued. "So Johnny's people go to Fish Johnson and say, 'Do you know where the jewels are? Johnny would like to get 'em back.' Fish says, 'Go ask Whitey.' But Whitey says he don't know nothin' about no jewels."

"So, what happened?"

"So the punk who swiped 'em gets pinched. He cops a plea, and says he sold the stuff to Whitey. The word gets back to Johnny Bananas. His guys go back to Whitey and tell him,

'We want to buy back the jewels.' Whitey says, 'I don't know what you're talkin' about.' Those were his last words—'I don't know what you're talkin' about.' That's when he got popped."

"It's getting dangerous around here," Mendola lamented.

"Maybe we oughta take a little vacation," Peanuts suggested. "You guys ever been to the Mardi Gras down in New Orleans?"

"Naw, what's that?" Jednyak asked.

"The town's full of people, millions of 'em maybe, and the stores'll be raking in the money. We go down there, knock off a jewelry store while everyone's watchin' the Mardi Gras parade, and we're gone before the cops find their way through the crowd."

It sounded like a good idea. Peanuts drove home and threw some clothes in a suitcase, kissed his wife and infant daughter good-bye, and picked up his traveling companions. Peanuts was living with his in-laws at the time, so he figured Lauretta and the baby would be all right while he was away.

The first overnight stop on the way down was Nashville, where the boys checked into the Hermitage. Much to their surprise, they discovered that there was a jewelry convention in town.

"Hey, why not make expenses?" Peanuts suggested, with a broad grin. "What the hell!"

It didn't take long to determine that the Andrew Jackson Hotel, right around the corner, was the center of activity. All they had to do was wait for a salesman with a jewelry satchel to show himself, and he belonged to them.

They did not have long to wait. Jacob Davis, 51, of Pittsburgh, emerged from the hotel carrying a black satchel, and hailed a taxi. Peanuts and his partners were in their own car, right on its back bumper. They curbed the cab at the first opportunity, alongside the imposing statue of Andrew Jackson.

Mendola leaped out of the bandit car, waving his revolver. The taxi driver, Lawrence Herd, abandoned ship and took off on the run. The bewildered salesman swung open the back door and tried to get out, but Lover Boy was on top of him before he knew what happened. The two men struggled briefly over the satchel, containing $100,000 worth of unset diamonds. Mendola finally fired a shot through the roof of the cab for effect, and Davis let go of the prize.

Lover Boy grabbed it, sprinted back to the waiting car, and Peanuts took off.

"I lost my fuckin' hat wrestling with that guy," Mendola puffed, as Peanuts wheeled the get-away car through traffic.

"Well, we ain't goin' back for it now," Peanuts said.

Jednyak laughed, "You can buy a new hat with what we got here."

"Hey, I think we better forget about Mardi Gras," Peanuts suggested as he headed out of town. "Let's get the hell back to Chicago before these hicks start lookin' for us."

"What if they stop us and find this stuff in the car?" Jednyak worried. "These hill-billies will kill us. I heard they don't set no bond or nothing down here."

"Especially with Illinois license plates on the car," Mendola agreed.

"We're stickin' out like a sore thumb. We gotta get rid of the stuff," Peanuts said. "Then, if there's a road block or somethin', we ain't got nuttin in the car."

As they raced north in U.S. Hwy. 41, a giant billboard loomed alongside the roadway about 15 miles out of town. Peanuts hit the brakes and screeched to a stop in the shadow of the sign. Not a word was said. Everybody knew exactly what had to be done. Digging a shallow hole behind the billboard, they dropped the satchel in and covered it over with dirt. Then they returned to the car and continued on to Chicago.

Three days later they returned, accompanied by their wives, to claim the booty. They figured that if the police were looking for three robbers, they would pay little attention to three couples. They drove all the way in to Nashville so they could retrace the route exactly, to make sure they found the right billboard.

While in town, Peanuts bought a newspaper. "Holy Christ!" he exploded.

"What?"

"Lookit! Holy Christ!"

He shoved the newspaper at his companions. "Holy Christ!"

What they were looking at was their own pictures, plastered all over page one, under the headline:

POLICE SEEK JEWEL THIEVES

"That headline's bigger than World War Two!" Peanuts exclaimed. "They even got our names."

Each of the photographs, taken from police mug shots, was correctly labeled—Paul "Peanuts" Panczko, Guy "Lover Boy" Mendola and Walter "The German" Jednyak. Warrants had been issued charging the three with highway robbery.

"Holy Christ," was all Peanuts could think to say. "We gotta get the fuck outa here!" Handing the keys to Lauretta he said, "Here, you drive."

With Panczko, Jednyak and Mendola crouched down in the back seat, and the three women in front, the car headed out of town. When they came to the place where the jewelry pouch was hidden, Peanuts jumped out. "I'll go dig 'em up," he said. "Drive on down the road and come back for me in fifteen minutes."

When the car returned, he had the jeweler's satchel under his arm. He jumped into the back seat with his buddies and the group drove nervously back to Chicago, making sure not to go even one mile over the speed limit. When they got back to town the peddled the jewels to Meyer Gordon.

How the "hill-billy" police in Nashville got such a fast line on the trio eventually became clear. It was all thanks to Lover Boy's hat, which he lost in the scuffle with the jeweler. The hat bore the label: Jack's Men's Shop, Cicero, Ill. He might as well have given out his name and address.

Nashville authorities sent a query to Chicago, and Chicago police sent down a folder containing mug shots of all known Chicago jewel thieves. Nashville detectives made the rounds of downtown hotels, and a desk clerk and bell hops at the Hermitage picked out the photos of Panczko, Mendola and Jednyak as the three men who had stayed there the night before the heist.

The cab driver and Jacob Davis, the Pittsburgh jewelry salesman, also picked out Mendola's and Panczko's photos.

By the time the group got back to Chicago with the jewels, the story was in the local papers, and police were seeking them on the Tennessee warrants, issued by District Attorney General J. Carlton Loser.

With no place to hide, Jednyak threw in the towel and surrendered. He was returned to Nashville, where he was booked on a charge of highway robbery. Peanuts, on the other hand, had worked out a dandy place to hide. He knocked a large hole in the wall behind the bed in the attic apartment at his mother-in-law's home.

Whenever police came by with the warrant, Peanuts crawled through the hole into the attic and pulled the bed up against the wall to conceal the opening. His mother-in-law dutifully conducted one team of detectives after another up to Peanuts' room and said, "Well, here it is. As you can see, he isn't here."

By now even the mother-in-law had deduced that Peanuts was hardly a paragon of virtue.

Peanuts hid in the attic for seven weeks, until he tired of playing hide and seek with the law, and telephoned Bieber. "Georgie, how am I gonna get outa this?" he asked.

"That warrant ain't gonna go away," Bieber told him. "I think you oughta go down and give yourself up, unless you want to sit in the attic until your hair turns gray."

On his lawyer's advice, Peanuts reluctantly took a plane to Nashville, surrendered, posted $10,000 bond, and flew back to Chicago where it was now safe to walk the streets—he thought. He no sooner got back in town than Patrolmen Raymond O'Malley and John McCormick, wondering what he was doing wandering on the West Side at 6 o'clock in the morning, pinched him for disorderly conduct.

Peanuts' luck continued to run bad a week later when he and Steve Tomaras were arrested after their car collided with another and overturned during a police chase. Panczko and Tomaras suffered only bruises in the crash. But Policeman Paul Katilus, who had stood in the street with drawn revolver in a futile attempt to halt the bandits, ended up with a sprained right wrist and a sprained ankle when he jumped out of the way in the nick of time.

Police threw every traffic charge they could think of at Peanuts. It was his 47th arrest in five years, but he had yet to be convicted. And he wasn't this time, either. When the matter came up in court Peanuts failed to appear; however, Judge George B. Weiss dismissed the charges after the other motorist said she did not want to prosecute.

Brother Butch's conviction record also remained unblemished when he was arrested after a ten-block police chase in North Avenue. Bieber won his release on a writ of habeas corpus because police were unable to identify him as the man they had originally taken out after.

Peanuts Panczko, Walter Jednyak and Lover Boy Mendola went on trial before Judge Charles Gilbert in Nashville on October 9, 1950, for the great jewel heist. The Nashville Jewelers' Association exerted every pressure it could to make an example of the Chicago hoodlums.

Bieber and Brodkin could not practice law in Tennessee, so the trio had to rely on a local attorney, Jack Norman, while Brodkin sat in as an advisor. Prosecutor Loser threw everything he had at the trio, prompting Peanuts to whisper to Mendola, "Jeez, I think they're more upset because it happened by the Andrew Jackson statue than they are over what we stole."

At the end of a two-week trial, all three were found guilty. Judge Gilbert gave them the maximum sentence, five to fifteen years at hard labor in the Tennessee State Penitentiary.

CHAPTER 13

![black bar]

BULLETS BUSTING OUT ALL OVER

Wednesday, the first of the month, was the hottest November day in Chicago's history. The record was set at 1:45 p.m. when the temperature soared to 80.9 degrees, according to I.W. Brunk of the U.S. Weather Bureau. It broke the previous record, set six years earlier in 1944.

Vincent Ficarrotta, 25, had just been freed on bond in connection with the burglary of a Gary, Indiana, tavern, and was pacing the hot sidewalk in front of his home in the 1300 block of West Roosevelt Road. A working member of Peanuts Panczko's gang, Ficarrotta walked with a slight limp, the result of having been shot in the leg by a retired police sergeant a year earlier while burglarizing a West Side grocery.

He had just received a phone call from Lover Boy Mendola, who told him, "Vince, I got something for you. Wait for me out in front. I'll be by in two minutes."

Mendola, like Panczko and Walter Jednyak, was free on appeal bond in connection with the Nashville caper. Ficarrotta turned to meet his fellow gang member as Lover Boy drove up, got out of the car, and started blasting away with his .45. One of the slugs struck the astonished Ficarrotta in the right arm and he fell to the ground. Mendola stuffed the smoking gun into his waist band, hopped back into his shiny new 1950 model auto and sped off.

Police Officers James Turner and Nyland Woods happened to be passing just as the shots were fired, and gave chase. Mendola threw his .45 caliber automatic pistol out the window of his car as he barrelled down the street with the law in pursuit. He abandoned the car at Adams and Paulina Streets when another squad car screamed in from the opposite direction, and fled on foot.

Officers Emil Smicklas, John Alcock and Ray Duffy scoured the area, but the gunman had given them the slip. His abandoned car was equipped with a police radio and a baseball bat.

The identity of the gunman was not a mystery for long. Police, who interviewed the wounded Ficarrotta at his bedside in the Bridewell asked, "Who shot you, Vince?" They did not expect an answer. The underworld's Code of Silence requires the victim to mumble something like, "I didn't see nothin'."

Ficarrotta did not honor the code, however. "That son of a bitch Mendola shot me," he declared.

Lover Boy, who was picked up the following day on a charge of assault to kill, was equally voluble as police slapped on the cuffs: "Yeah, I shot the son of a bitch. He stole my wife, Donna, from me."

By the time his wound had healed and his assailant was arraigned in Felony Court, however, Ficarrotta had reassessed the situation. "I don't want to press charges," he told the impetuous Judge Charlie Dougherty. "I don't have anything to say."

"Your honor," interjected Lieutenant James Dakey of the State's Attorney's Police. "We have Mr. Ficarrotta's earlier statement naming Guy Mendola as the shooter, and we have the defendant's admission that he shot this man."

"I've heard enough," Dougherty snapped. "The defendant is bound over to the Grand Jury. Bond is set at $1,500. Next case."

"Edward Panczko!" the bailiff called out.

Dougherty might as well have been holding court in a Milwaukee Avenue saloon. It seemed as though half the Panczko gang was in court.

While Ficarrotta was licking his wound, Butch had been arrested for the holdup of a baking company in Gary, Indiana. Several witnesses identified him as one of five gunmen who held employees at bay while they carried out two safes containing $4,000. Butch was now busy resisting attempts to send him back to Indiana for trial.

"Case dismissed for lack of evidence!" Dougherty declared, with a bang of his gavel.

Next Butch found himself in Superior Court, where he was being sued for $25,000 by Guglielmo Bertonicini, a 50-year-old maker of religious icons. The statue maker claimed he was seriously injured when Butch ran a red light and struck him with his car at North Avenue and Clark Street.

Butch shrugged his shoulders and walked out of court after the matter was put over indefinitely. There was a seven or eight year backlog of lawsuits in civil courts of Cook County at that time.

The year 1950 ended on a strange note. Chicago Avenue District police announced in the press on New Year's Eve that they had solved the December 26 burglary of Mosel's Clothing Store on North Michigan Avenue, in which a band of thieves, with football team coordination, had carried off 750 men's suits worth $75,000 in a matter of minutes.

It was Peanuts Panczko and his "Three Minute Gang," police asserted. They identified other members of the theft crew as Guy Mendola, Steve Tomaras, Bruno Scordo, and Edward "Butch" Panczko.

Curiously, no arrests were made. Police just declared that the case had been solved, and those were the guys who had done it. If the cops didn't have enough proof to make an arrest, they at least wanted to give the gang some bad press. Happy New Year, boys.

* * *

Two weeks later Tomaras, suffering from a bullet wound in the left thigh, was dumped off at the entrance to Walther Memorial Hospital. He was transferred to the Bridewell hospital where Lieutenant Thomas Mackey asked the usual question: "Who shot you, Steve?"

"Gee, I don't know," Tomaras insisted. "A couple of guys tried to rob me at North and Francisco, and shot me when I resisted. Honest, lieutenant. I never saw 'em before."

"You're full of shit, Steve," Mackey said, shaking his head.

Police then brought Butch Panczko in for questioning, since he had been seen with Tomaras a short time earlier. Butch didn't know anything, either.

Since neither man would talk, police charged both Tomaras and Panczko with disorderly conduct. When they were arraigned before Judge Edward P. Luczak in Municipal Court, both demanded jury trials, and the case was continued.

* * *

Butch was up bright and early on February 24, hoping to pick up some ready cash to pay his legal fees, when everything that could possibly go wrong, did.

Police Officers Fred Triner and Harry Goelz were cruising on the Southwest Side in their patrol car in the pre-dawn hours when they heard a radio alert that a burglar alarm had gone off in the National Currency Exchange at 6457 S. Cicero Avenue.

"That's right around the corner," Triner said. "Let's roll."

They wheeled the squad car around the corner and screeched to a halt just in time to see a group of men struggling to hoist a three-foot-square safe into their car.

Goelz and Triner stepped out of the car and announced, "Police!"

The burglars dropped the safe and started to scatter. Goelz and Triner opened fire, and Butch Panczko took two bullets in the gut. As Panczko fell to the ground, clutching his abdomen, one of his companions, James Murray, 30, raised his arms and surrendered. The rest of the thieves disappeared into the darkness.

Police called an ambulance, and Butch was rushed to Holy Cross Hospital, where his condition was listed as "serious."

In checking out the gang's souped-up automobile, Goelz and Triner found another safe, which the burglars had removed from the currency exchange before police arrived. Also found in the car were a shotgun and a pistol, crowbars, pinchbars, wirecutters, and other assorted burglar tools.

Police announced the next day that they were searching for two of the wounded man's brothers, Paul "Peanuts" and Joseph "Pops" Panczko, believed to have been among the thieves who fled into the night.

This was wishful thinking on the part of police, since Pops was still in the state pen, serving time as a parole violator.

The get-away car was towed to the auto pound, where police discovered a bullet hole in the trunk. Jefferson Park police reported that they had fired on a similar auto a week earlier when its occupants refused to stop for questioning.

As police continued to go over the car for clues, George Bieber filed a writ of habeas corpus, seeking Butch Panczko's release. Butch was carried into court on a stretcher for a hearing on the motion, before Chief Justice Thomas E. Kluczynski of Criminal Court. Murray, in handcuffs, hobbled along at his side.

"Was this defendant shot too?" Kluczynski asked.

"No, your honor," his lawyer, Max Lurie, responded. "Mr. Murray fell while trying to get away, and aggravated an old leg wound he received on Luzon during World War II."

"So, he's a veteran, is he? And who is this little lady here?" Kluczynski inquired, nodding toward a slender, be-spectacled woman who stood before the bench with a large paper bag clutched tightly in her arms.

"I'm Butchie's sister, Louise," she explained. "I got money in the bag here to put up his bail. She posted $9,200 cash bond for her brother, so he could be transferred from the Bridewell to Ravenswood Hospital, closer to home.

Butch was still in the hospital when the case came up before Judge Dougherty the next day for arraignment. Dougherty ordered the $9,200 forfeited, and increased Murray's bond to $23,500.

"If Mr. Panczko should decide, at some future date, to honor us with his presence, we might consider returning the bail money," the judge said. "Next case."

It took Butch a full month to recover from his wounds to the extent that he was able to get back to work. When he did he teamed up with his brother, Peanuts—something Pops had advised against years earlier. The wisdom of Pops' warning soon became apparent.

While free on appeal bond from the Tennessee conviction, Peanuts had been focusing his attention upon a currency exchange at Wabansia and Central Avenues, operated by 51-year-old Frank Palzen.

"This guy goes to the bank at Division and Ashland every Friday morning," he explained to his brother. "Him and another guy, they got their own like bulletproof van. He picks up his own money and delivers it to his own currency exchanges. Actually he owns three of 'em. Remember them old coal bags like Pa used to carry stuff in? Well, this guy and his partner take the coal bags to the bank to get 'em filled with money to cash people's paychecks every Friday at the currency exchanges."

"So we grab 'em?"

"It ain't that easy," Peanuts cautioned. "Him and his partner, they come out of the bank with their guns out and go into their little bullshit van, like an armored truck. He leaves there and goes down Ashland to Elston."

"Couldn't we get 'em when they stop at the currency exchange and carry in the dough?"

"We thought of that," Peanuts said. "I had a guy dressed up in an Army uniform. He got a carbine under his coat. I got another guy pushin' a street cleaner cart. He's got a shotgun. But we never got a chance to do it because there's always a copper by this school crossing by his first currency exchange."

"So, how ya figure on working it?"

"We ask ourself, where is this bulletproof truck comin' out of? He's gotta keep it in a garage someplace, right? So we followed 'em and found the garage, right by the guy's house on Karlov Avenue. Now, here's what we're gonna do . . ."

Before dawn on a chilly Friday morning, March 30, 1951, Peanuts smashed a window and broke into Palzen's two-car garage. The armored vehicle was in there all right, along with a Jeep station wagon. Peanuts unscrewed the armored truck's gas cap and carefully poured several quarts of water into the fuel tank. When Palzen got into the money wagon several hours later he was unable to start it. He and his partner, 46-year-old Edward Meyer, were forced to take the unprotected Jeep to the bank.

When they left the Manufacturers' National Bank on Ashland Avenue with their loaded money bags, Butch Panczko and Nick Civella, with a submachine gun on his lap, were right behind them in a late model Ford stolen the night before. Peanuts and another gang member, armed with a shotgun, were waiting down the road as Palzen made a left turn into Elston Avenue.

As Palzen turned right off Elston into Logan Boulevard, to cut over to Diversey, where one of his exchanges was located, Peanuts pulled in front of the Jeep and stopped. The traffic signal was green, and Palzen blew his horn impatiently. As he did so, Butch pulled up behind him in the stolen Ford and rammed the Jeep, pinning it tightly between the two cars.

A fifth gang member, Skeets Szymanski, who had been standing on the corner, stepped off the curb, unlimbered a carbine, and ordered Palzen and Meyer out of the Jeep. Meyer dutifully obeyed, but Palzen came out shooting.

He jumped out from the driver's side of the Jeep and took refuge behind the Ford, blasting away at the robbers with his .38 caliber revolver. Peanuts' companion let go with several blasts from the shotgun, striking Palzen in the right shoulder.

Civella cut loose with the submachine gun and the wounded Palzen returned the fire, hitting him in the left leg.

Civella collapsed to the pavement, dropping the machine gun as he fell. As two of the other bandits pinned Palzen down with gunfire, Peanuts grabbed the wounded man by the armpits and dragged him into his car as Butch made a run for the Jeep and grabbed one of the money bags, containing $53,500.

The bandits fled in Panczko's souped up car, leaving Palzen in the street behind the stolen Ford. Francis Black, a 42-year-old Chicago Tribune driver who witnessed the gun battle, gave chase in his circulation truck. He slowed at Diversey and Damen Avenues to pick up Park Policeman Walter Schultz, who was directing traffic. They followed the bandit car south in Damen Avenue to Fullerton, where they lost it in traffic.

Peanuts drove out to Melrose Park, where a friendly doctor treated Civella for his wound, which did not require hospitalization. They then returned to the safety of their neighborhood, where they divvied up the loot. It came to $10,700 apiece.

Like the Parker Pen caper, the currency exchange holdup was never solved. Police checked area hospitals, but could find no record of anyone having been brought in for treatment for gunshot. Civella's wound healed nicely, and he ultimately went on to become head of the Kansas City mob.

Pops, still stewing in Stateville penitentiary at Joliet, was working every angle he could figure to get out and get in on the fun. In one of his more unique pleas for freedom, he filed a writ of habeas corpus, arguing that he should not be serving time in a state prison because he was on probation for a federal offense.

He was returned to Chicago in shackles and leg irons for a hearing before Federal Judge Walter J. La Buy on May 25. Judge La Buy denied the writ, and Pops was whisked back to Joliet.

Peanuts and his boys continued "making safes" with clocklike regularity—one every Sunday night—for an average of $20,000 to $30,000 a pop. He was building up a nest egg to take care of his family while he was away.

The popular Barney's Market Club at Randolph and Halsted Streets was one of their victims. Neilsen's Restaurant in Elmwood Park was another. So was Amlings Florists on North Avenue.

The safes were hauled away in a stolen 1948 Chevy, from which the seats had been removed. The driver sat on a milk carton. There was no center post on the right side of the car, and the doors were rigged so they could slide open, like a modern-day van. The car was also equipped with special overload springs

The safes were taken to a North Side garage where one of the boys, Bruno Scordo, known as Polack Bruno, burned them open.

Early in June Peanuts and his pals visited the drive-in movie theater near Harlem Avenue and Irving Park Road, after the crowd had gone home. The yard lights were on, and a lone employee was busy spearing napkins and ice cream wrappers with a stick with a nail in one end. Peanuts and the boys tied him to a chair and told him to keep his mouth shut while they carted off the office safe.

The next day they heard on the radio that the employee, still tied to the chair, had wheeled himself all the way down the street to a State Police post to report the theft.

While Peanuts was busy doing drive-ins, Butch and James Murray went off on their own and broke into another currency exchange on South Cicero Avenue, by chipping through the wall of an adjoining building during a heavy fog. Police, answering an alarm, arrested the two as they fled from the building.

A Criminal Court jury set them free, however, after Bieber argued that police could not have actually seen the two men come out of the exchange because of the heavy fog.

The heat was now on, and Peanuts figured it was about time for another out-of-town expedition. He, Polack Bruno, and Irish Jimmy Murray took a quick trip to Lima, Ohio, where they picked up the trail of a jewelry salesman. They tailed his Cadillac all the way home to the Cleveland suburb of Shaker Heights.

Peanuts pulled his Oldsmobile 88 right into the salesman's driveway behind him, so he couldn't back out. The man's wife, who had apparently been awaiting her husband's return, was looking out the window as Peanuts and his pals got out of their car.

The frightened salesman, sensing what was about to happen, pushed the door buttons down and locked himself inside the Cadillac. Bruno pulled out his pistol, smashed the car's side window, and fished out the sample case. It contained nearly $400,000 worth of rings and loose diamonds. As Peanuts and his pals drove off in the darkness they could hear the salesman's wife screaming.

Peanuts used his share of the loot to pay off gambling debts, and to enrich Bieber and Brodkin.

The appeal of the Tennessee prison sentence, meanwhile, was denied. Peanuts was resigned to the fact that he would have to do time in stir, and had begun getting his affairs in order.

He also moved out of his mother-in-law's attic, and bought a home at Melvina Avenue and School Street. As much as possible, he was trying to give his wife and four-year-old daughter, Paulette, a normal life.

On the last Saturday morning in June an envelope bearing his name turned up in the mailbox at his new address. This was unusual, since a man in Panczko's position rarely received mail. Ripping open the envelope, Peanuts stared dumbfounded at its contents. It was a note, written in longhand. He read and reread the note like it was a bad dream:

"If you like your child and wife, you had better have $5,000 for us Wednesday or else. Put a chair in the middle of your back yard by Tuesday. You'll hear from us Tuesday. Don't tell anyone. That is all. Your house is being watched."

The note was signed, "Pal."

CHAPTER 14

A SHAKEDOWN BACKFIRES

Peanuts showed the note to Lauretta.

"There's sometin' I shoulda told ya," he said.

"What's this all about?"

"I dunno. But the other night when I pulled up in front of the house, I looked up and down the street like I always do, and a car pulled up behind me. I pulled away and they chased me about eight, ten blocks."

"Well, who was it?"

"Who knows? I never got caught. That's why I'm always the wheelman. I'm considered one of the best drivers there ever was. You know that. Hell, I can back up faster than most people can go frontwards. So, I got rid of them guys. Now I get a note in my mailbox."

"What are you going to do? Paul, I'm scared to death."

"Look, you take the kid and go stay at your ma's house. I'm gonna go see Bieber and Brodkin."

Peanuts drove his wife and daughter to her mother's home on Waveland Avenue. Then he continued on downtown, parked his Cadillac in a bus stop, and went up to the lawyers' offices at 188 W. Randolph Street. Handing the note to Bieber he said, "They're messing wit' my family, now, Georgie. Should I take care of this myself, or what? What am

I supposed to do?"

Bieber studied the note. "Call the FBI," he said.

"The FBI? What'll they do wit' me? I'm a thief. I'm goin' to jail in Tennessee."

"You ought to do what Georgie says," Brodkin advised. "You handle this yourself, you could get your fuckin' head blown off. Somebody's threatening your family. This is nothing to fool around with. It don't matter who you are."

Leaving the Caddy where it was, Peanuts hiked over to FBI headquarters at Adams and Clark Streets. It was an entirely new experience, looking for the guys who usually looked for him. After explaining the nature of his call, he was ushered in to the office of George R. McSwain, head of the Chicago office. He showed McSwain the note.

"Okay, we don't know who we're dealing with here. Do exactly what they say," McSwain told him. "Put a chair in your back yard, and see if they take the bait. Do you have the $5,000?"

"Are you kidding? I'm fuckin' broke and I'm goin' to jail. That's why I was crashin' and robbin' everything."

"All right. Just put a chair in your back yard like they say. Then it's their move."

Peanuts felt like an idiot, but he carried a kitchen chair out the back door and set it in the middle of the yard. It sat there through the weekend, all day Monday and Monday night. On Tuesday he found another letter in his mail box:

"Peanuts: Now, here's what you should do with the $5,000. It should be in 100s, 50s, and 20s. About 1:30 a.m. Thursday morning, drive north on Meade from Belmont and toss the bundle at Newport on west side of street at lamp post. I hope for your wife and kids so you don't try to pull anything smart because we will have to take care of them while you are away. (Signed) Pal. P.S. Have money wrapped in a paper bag."

Accompanying the note was a newspaper clipping with a photo of a distraught father bending over his child, who had been killed by an automobile. Written on the clipping were the words, "Enclosed photo shows man in grief over a dead child. His kid found dead. Don't let this happen to you if anything happens."

Peanuts turned the second note and the clipping over to the FBI. McSwain said, "Okay, make the drop, just like they say. We'll be there. I'll have my men all over the place, but you won't see them."

Panczko might have been a crook, but he was also a father. The FBI chief assigned twenty-five agents to the case. Shortly after midnight on June 28, McSwain gave Peanuts a brown paper bag filled with blank paper, cut in the shape of currency. The paper had been treated with a chemical substance that would turn the hands of anyone who handled it a bright green.

At exactly 1:30 a.m. Panczko's Cadillac made a left turn off Belmont and headed north in Meade Avenue opposite Wright Junior College. Peanuts, more jittery than he'd ever been on any heist, was behind the wheel. An FBI agent, armed with a rifle and a walkie-talkie radio, crouched on the floor in the back seat.

As the car approached Newport Avenue Peanuts slowed down, dropped the bag out the window onto the pavement, and continued on. He drove about six blocks, pulled over to the curb near his home, and doused the lights.

He and the FBI man sat in the darkened auto, listening as the drama unfolded over the two-way radio. "Here comes a car around the corner . . . it's slowing up where the bag is . . . Nobody getting out . . . Now it's leaving . . . They're going around the block . . . Here it comes again . . . Now they're stopping . . . No plates on the car . . . One man is getting out of the car . . . He's walking toward the college parking lot . . . He's picking up the bag . . . He's checking it out . . . Now he's taking it back to the car . . . Close in! Close in!"

Two agents leaped out of a panel delivery truck parked in the college lot, brandishing their weapons. Other agents, all heavily armed, swarmed in from all directions. The would-be extortionists were frisked, handcuffed and photographed before they knew what was happening to them.

The suspect who had retrieved the paper bag carried a loaded revolver under his coat. The one who had remained in the car had a shotgun across his lap.

"Wait a minute! Wait a minute! You guys are making a mistake," they protested. "We're cops! We're cops!"

"You are police officers?"

"Christ, yes. Check our IDs."

The suspects were indeed Chicago police officers. Both were beatmen, assigned to the Cragin District. One was identified as 30-year-old Thomas J. Moloney. The other was Peter M. Foley, 29, the same age as Peanuts.

"If you two are police officers, what in the hell are you doing here at this hour of the morning?"

"We've been investigating Panczko for a series of burglaries in our district, and we lured him so we could pinch him," Foley explained.

"Then why in the hell did you let him drive away?" McSwain asked. "And what's that green stuff all over your hands?"

"Huh?" Foley sputtered, glancing at the palms of his hands. He tried frantically to rub the coloring off, but it wouldn't go away.

The two were taken downtown to FBI headquarters for questioning. Foley eventually admitted writing and mailing the two extortion notes.

"Yeah, we were going to shake Panczko down for five thou. We knew he was going away, and figured he'd pay off so nothing would happen to his family," he said. "I'm in debt up to my ass, and I'm all fouled up at home, because my wife caught me with some other women. I needed the money."

Moloney claimed he knew nothing about the extortion plot, but gave conflicting explanations as to why he was with Foley at 1:30 in the morning, toting a shotgun.

Both were booked on charges of violating the Federal Extortion Act. McSwain told Peanuts afterward, "It's a good thing you didn't try to take care of this in your own way, Panczko. You might have walked up to those guys and said,

'Whattya doin'?' and—BOOM!—they'd have blown you away. Two coppers? They could have said you were resisting arrest, and they'd have gotten away with it."

"Jeezus Christ," Peanuts said. "Me, saved by the FBI. That makes me laugh."

Police Commissioner Timothy J. O'Connor suspended Foley and Moloney as soon as he was informed of their arrests.

The two were indicted by a federal grand jury, and went on trial before Judge John P. Barnes in U.S. District Court. It was a bizarre situation of the kind that could only happen in Chicago. There was Peanuts Panczko, the convicted robber, testifying on behalf of the United States government against two Chicago police officers.

A jury of six men and six women found both officers guilty. Judge Barnes sentenced Foley to ten years in prison, and sentenced Moloney to five years. The United States Court of Appeals subsequently reversed Moloney's conviction, after Foley swore that his partner wasn't in on the plot.

Meanwhile, Peanuts got the phone call he wasn't waiting for. It was Mike Brodkin. "We lost our appeal," the lawyer told him. "You gotta report to the state pen in Nashville first thing Monday morning. We've got a seat for you on a plane flying out of here at 10 o'clock Sunday night."

Peanuts spent the weekend saying good bye to his friends. His brother, John, who had gone into the tavern business after helping to build the subway, organized a farewell party for him at his Joy Club at Maplewood and North Avenues.

"Well, I have to go," Peanuts told Lauretta. He didn't tell her about the party. She was moping around the house, long-faced, and daubing away tears with her handkerchief. "At least I can go to the airport with you," she said.

"Naw, naw, naw. You stay home with Paulette," he argued. "I don't want any emotional thing at the airport. What the hell."

"I'll write to you, Paul," Lauretta sobbed. "Please take care of yourself. The baby and I'll be here when you get back."

Peanuts gave her one last hug. "My plane leaves at 8 o'clock. I gotta get outa here."

He took a cab to the Joy Club, where John had gotten together a bunch of his cronies. Steve Tomaras was there, along with Walter Marko, Marty Gariti and Snuffy Ryan. Even Polack Bruno. Brother Butch was there, too, and Frank, the "legit" member of the family. Everybody but Pops. He was still in stir.

Peanuts enjoyed one last evening, hoisting a few at the bar with his pals. At 9:30 his big brother, John, gave him the high sign. It was time to go. John drove him to the airport. They got there just in time. The flight to Nashville seemed like it was over before it had hardly begun. Peanuts took a cab downtown from the airport, and checked into the Hermitage, the same hotel he had stayed at during the ill fated jewel robbery.

The next morning he turned himself in at the Tennessee State Prison.

The next thing he heard from Lauretta, she had filed suit for divorce, and asked the court's permission to sell the house.

CHAPTER 15

███

TENNESSEE
STATE PRISON

Peanuts entered the Tennessee State Penitentiary on July 27, 1951. The prison had an inmate population of 2,500, and a staff of 500. For the next eight years and seven months he would be known as inmate No. 44555. The moment he was ushered through the front door he knew that he would not be enjoying "soft time."

"Yankee! Yankee! Lookit the fuckin' blue-bellied Yankee!" other inmates taunted as Panczko was marched to the laundry room for his clothing issue. He hadn't opened his mouth yet, but they knew. They could tell by his complexion, by his determined gait, and by the way he carried himself that he was not one of them.

It didn't take him long to realize, either, that from here on out his crime would not be that Nashville jewel robbery, but the fact that fate had caused him to be born on the upper side of the Mason-Dixon Line.

"Them are stone hillbillies there. And they don't like you one fuckin' bit, Yankee," smirked the guard who was marching him down the hall. The guard, wearing soiled bib overalls and chewing tobacco, was obviously one himself. He made no secret of the fact that he relished his job of lording it over the northern prisoner almost as much as eating watermelon.

Peanuts hadn't been there a week before he was forced to defend himself in a vicious fist fight. When Deputy Warden W.S. Neil quizzed him afterward, in an effort to find out what it was about, he rubbed his bruises and said, "I don't know nothin'."

"Just remember, you're out of your element here, Pan-ZeeKo," Neil told him. "Try not to be smarter than everybody else, even if you think you are, 'cause there's a lot o' fellers down here a lot meaner than you. Do I make myself clear?"

"I can't believe I'm here," Peanuts told him. "Up north we always beat the rap. I don't understand you people."

"Well, long as you're here with us, just watch your ass."

There were more battles, and after every one Peanuts told his guards, "I'm not a beefer. I can take care of my own problems." Begrudgingly, the Rebel prisoners were finally forced to admit that the Yankee might be their kind of guy after all.

Once he'd been accepted, Peanuts began to do what he knew best, next to stealing. He set up a prison gambling operation, which made him even more popular with his fellow inmates.

He used his winnings to buy candy bars to augment his forced diet. Prison food consisted mainly of grits and gravy, seven days a week. The only exceptions were Easter, Thanksgiving and Christmas, when the cons were served meat.

On learning that Peanuts had once worked in Chicago as a lathe operator, Neil assigned him to machine shop. Attentiveness to duty and a sunny disposition eventually earned him a promotion to the paint shop, where the work was less physical. There were also greater opportunities for hanky-pank.

A golden opportunity came rolling along in the form of a 55-gallon drum of wood alcohol. Peanuts immediately saw possibilities. With the help of an inmate chemist, he would distill the alky to cook out the harmful ingredients, and peddle the resulting "white lightning" to fellow prisoners.

As soon as the paint room supervisor went to lunch, Peanuts emptied the contents of the drum into eleven five-gallon containers, which were then stored in an out-of-the way corner. He and his cohorts took a hose and refilled the 55-gallon drum with tap water, and locked it in the warden's office.

The trouble was, word of the would-be alky spread like wildfire through the prison grapevine, and several of the smaller containers mysteriously disappeared before Panczko's chemist had a chance to complete the refining process.

The next morning three prisoners were found dead in their bunks. Several others had gone blind, and half the surviving inmates in Panczko's cell block were deathly ill or raving mad and foaming at the mouth. A full-scale medical emergency was called. Doctors and ambulances from Nashville converged on the penitentiary, and Governor Frank G. Clement, a former FBI agent, arrived to confer with the warden.

"Jeez, what the hell's going on around here?" Peanuts asked as he and a handful of workers in the paint shop watched jailers carry out the dead bodies of three of the victims, while medical teams rushed in to tend prisoners too sick to be moved.

"It's that fuckin' alky. Them dumb bastards drank it before it was ready."

"Christ, we gotta get rid of it, fast," Peanuts said.

"What are we gonna do with it?"

"Pour it down the fuckin' shower," he said. "Come on. Let's go."

Panczko and his cohorts took one can into the shower area at a time and began pouring the lethal liquid down the drain. They were almost home free when a tobacco chewing guard spotted Peanuts carrying the last five-gallon can toward the shower.

"Hey, boy! Whatcha got in that there can?"

"Who, me?"

"I don't see no one else around. What's in the can, I ast ya?"

"Oh, nothin'. Just some paint remover."

"Oh, yeah? Well, I'll just take me a little look if you don't mind."

The guard unscrewed the cap and took a whiff. "Whew! Paint remover, my ass!" he snorted. "That there's booze!"

"I can't believe it," Peanuts shrugged, feigning utter amazement.

"Buuulllll-sheeet! Lock this boy up," the guard ordered, beckoning to several of his deputies.

As the hacks marched Peanuts down the corridor they passed the governor and a group of prison officials. "Here comes one of 'em now," the warden said, nodding toward the prisoner.

Governor Clement motioned for the group to hold up for a moment. "Tell me, boy. Where's you get the alky?" he asked. Peanuts stood silent.

"This here's Paul PanZeeKo. Cocky bastard won't tell you nothin'," the warden said. "We're charging him with murder. Take the son-of-a-bitch away."

Peanuts was ushered directly to the "hole," an iron cage with no light, no toilet facilities, and only bread and water for sustenance. The governor headed into the hospital ward, to pay a call on the stricken inmates.

"Say, who's that boy over there?" he asked the deputy warden. "He looks familiar to me."

"Who, him? That's Johnny Bragg," Neil told him.

"The entertainer?"

"Yeah, that's him. He drank some of that poisoned hooch."

Bragg, 27, who was doing six 99-year terms for rape, turned out to be the lead tenor in a singing group of five black convicts who called themselves The Prisonaires. As soon as he recovered from his ordeal the governor had him and the rest of The Prisonaires over to the executive mansion to put on a show.

Peanuts, meanwhile, languished in the "hole," all but forgotten. "Let the son-of-a-bitch rot," the warden told Neil. Meals consisted of corn bread every morning, and cooked carrots every third day. By the time he was brought out at the end of 30 interminable days, his weight had dropped from 260 pounds to 160, and his clothes no longer fit.

Nothing further came of the murder charges the warden had threatened, but Peanuts was judged a troublemaker, and was transferred to Brushy Mountain Prison near the small town of Petros, about 30 miles west of Knoxville.

The main industry at Brushy Mountain was coal. Prisoners worked in the mines, where each was paid the grand sum of eighty cents a month. For that eighty cents he was expected to fill four tram cars of coal a day. For Peanuts it was the end of the world.

He had never been underground before. He could hear loud cracks as the veins of coal shifted, and showered coal dust down from the roof of the mine. One of the three mines had been closed because of a fatal cave-in. Each prisoner was assigned a number and given a piece of chalk. He wrote his number on the side of each car he filled, so the guards could ascertain whether the cons were making their quotas.

The narrow-gauge rail cars were pulled by mules, who could drag as many as fifteen cars behind them. How the mules counted, no one knew, but if a sixteenth car was added to the train, they refused to pull it.

Along with the mules were mice, skittering throughout the mine, looking for crumbs from the prisoners' sandwiches. The first thing a prisoner learned was not to harm the mice. If he killed one, the guards beat him half to death. The mice were sensitive to mine gas, and as long as they were running around on the floor, that meant the air was clean enough to breath. If the mice started to keel over, or to abandon the mine, that was the signal to get out.

The trouble with sharing the mine with the mice, was that they also thought they were entitled to share the prisoners' food. The trick, Peanuts learned, was hiding his luncheon sandwiches up in the rafters where the mice couldn't find them.

There were frequent cave-ins, and convict laborers were killed or maimed. There were no doctors at the mine, and injured inmates had to be taken by ambulance to Knoxville.

"How do ya get outa this filthy joint?" Peanuts asked a fellow con as they sweated over their shovels, scooping up coal that had been dynamited out of the walls.

"You try to make a break and they'll shoot ya."

"Naw, I don't mean that. I mean, like, how d'ya get a different job, like in the kitchen or the shop?"

"You play baseball?"

"Whaddya talkin' about? I bet on baseball, I don't play it."

"Well, everybody goes to the mines unless they're a good ballplayer. Then you go to the kitchen or the laundry. The baseball team plays other prison teams, and Warden Boone wants to keep 'em happy. The wardens, they bet big money against each other's teams. Know what I mean?"

The only bat Peanuts ever swung was at a window, so he dug coal. Heaven help any prisoner who balked. The son of a Tennessee preacher was brought in one day, and promptly told Warden Dan Boone, "I cannot dig that coal."

"Why can't you, now? asked Boone, a short, skinny man who had run the prison for the last twenty years.

"Moses put that coal there, and he didn't put it there to be taken away."

"I don't give a rat's ass who put the coal in them hills," Boone sneered. "YOU, are going to take it OUT."

"Warden Boone, I told you, sir, I cannot dig that coal."

"Bring him down the hill," Boone commanded.

The preacher's son was taken to a guard station, where the hacks laid a thick leather strap to him. After several good whaps across his back he turned to Boone and cried, "Warden, lemme get back up there. I don't give a dam if Moses put that coal in there. Just let me get it out!"

Warden Boone had a way with men. The guards, as well as the cons, were terrified of the man. Peanuts dug coal for an entire year, until Boone got tired of him booking bets on baseball games, and shipped him back to Nashville as a bad influence on prison life.

He wasn't back long before he was in trouble again, this time for helping three fellow inmates escape. One of them was his cellmate, Ralph Cosellino, a known jailbreaker who once bribed his guards in an Alabama prison to let him crawl over the wall.

At Nashville, Cosellino and two other cons slipped a trusty $1,500 to let them hide inside of garbage cans, scheduled to be hauled out of the yard by a scavenger truck. As soon as each man was in place, he was covered with garbage, and the can was loaded aboard the truck.

At 4 p.m., before going off their twelve-hour shift, the guards, slouching in overalls and spitting tobacco juice, held the daily "countdown" of prisoners.

"Hey, PanZeeKo, where the hell's Cosellino?" one hack queried, standing outside the cell.

"Jeez, how the hell should I know?" Peanuts responded.

There was another investigation, and the truck driver ultimately put the finger on Peanuts. In what was becoming a familiar routine, he was returned to the hole. After he'd done the usual 30 days he was shipped out to Fort Pillow, a prison farm on the outskirts of Memphis. There he discovered something that he had never known before—that cotton grew on bushes. If nothing else, prison was giving him a well-rounded education.

"Hey, Peanuts!" he was greeted as he alit from the prison van at his new quarters. "How the hell are ya?" It was like old home week. By now he had been in and out of so many prisons he had friends all over the state of Tennessee.

"I'm terrific," Peanuts beamed. "Hey, what kind of a place is this?"

"It's a bad-ass joint, with miles and miles and miles of cotton fields."

"So what?"

"So you pick cotton, you asshole."

"You pick it?"

"Hell, yes. Where did you think cotton comes from?"

"I never thought about it."

Peanuts soon learned that each convict was given a sack and told, "Go to it." Every man was expected to pick 100 pounds of cotton a day, or he was given the strap. Guards on horseback, with pistols in their holsters and rifles or shotguns across their saddles, rode up and down the rows warning, "Don't miss no boll weevils!" Any con who let a weevil slip by in the cotton balls was held down on a mattress by four black inmates and whipped, until he learned to pay better attention to his work.

It was at Fort Pillow that Peanuts witnessed two graphic examples of prison life that would be marked indelibly on his mind.

The first involved blisters. Every morning at dawn the cons were lined up like soldiers and marched five miles to the Mississippi bottomland, where the cotton was grown. All had been issued new shoes that needed breaking in. When darkness fell, after a day of picking cotton, the exhausted cons were marched back to the penal colony.

By nightfall one man's feet were so badly blistered that he could not make the five-mile trek. Part way home he collapsed to the ground. A guard named Thumb dismounted, walked over to the fallen inmate, and kicked him in the side. "Get up, boy," he ordered.

"Warden, I can't. My feet are bleedin' somethin' awful," he said.

"Well, ain't that too bad," Thumb commented, as he unbuttoned his trousers. As the other prisoners looked on, Thumb stood over the con and urinated on his face.

Other convicts then helped the man to his feet and half dragged him back to the base.

The second incident was an axe murder. It was autumn, and the inmates were working in a wooded area, felling trees and burning the branches to clear the land for more cotton fields. Three of the men in the group had been partners in a robbery. After their arrests, one had turned state's evidence and testified against the others. For cooperating with the prosecution, he was sentenced to six years in prison, while his partners got twenty years each.

Incredibly, all three were sent to Fort Pillow, where they were assigned to the same work crew.

During the lunch break one day, one of the robbers walked up behind the informant, swung the razor-sharp axe in a high arc, and brought it down with a sickening squish, splitting his ex-partner's head right down the middle.

The con was dead before he hit the ground, blood spurting from the gaping wound above his shoulders. The killer dropped the bloody axe and picked up the clean one the slain man had been using, walked over to a nearby tree, and sat down to enjoy his lunch.

Peanuts and the rest of the inmates continued eating their lunches as if nothing had happened. One of the first rules you learn in prison is, "you don't see nothing." If a con sticks another con in the ribs with a knife in the chow line, you keep on walking, right over the dead man, as if he isn't there. It's the only way to survive in the human jungle.

Thumb rode up on his horse and looked at the bloody mess. "What happened here?" he asked. The cons kept right on eating.

Turning to Peanuts, Thumb said, "Hey, boy! I ast what happened here?"

Panczko shrugged his wide shoulders.

The men were marched back to Fort Pillow where Peanuts, and several others suspected of witnessing the incident, were thrown into the hole. One evening about a week later Peanuts was taken in handcuffs to Warden Joseph Barfield's office for questioning. Thumb and several other guards were present.

"All we want to know, Panzcko, is who killed the guy with the axe," Barfield explained. "I didn't see what happened," Peanuts said. The warden nodded, and several of the guards went to work on the prisoner with a walking cane and blackjacks.

At the end of the beating Barfield talked to him again. "I know you saw who killed that fucker. Who was it?" Peanuts shook his head. Two guards then held the manacled prisoner while the warden slipped on a pair of brass knuckles and punched him in the face, breaking his nose and his right ear drum.

Still refusing to talk, Peanuts was delivered back to the hole to lick his wounds. Shortly thereafter he received a visit from Lena Fiore, a friend from Chicago. Visibly upset on seeing his battered face, she told Peanuts' sister, Louise, what had happened when she got back to Chicago. Lou leaked word to the press and filed a complaint with the FBI that her brother was being mistreated in the southern prison.

FBI agents were dispatched to interview Warden Barfield. He admitted punching Peanuts, but claimed it was in self defense. When confronted by the prisoner, in the presence of FBI agents, Barfield asserted, "Why, Peanuts, you tried to attack me and I had to defend myself."

Butch then got on the phone and complained directly to the city desks of all four major Chicago newspapers that his kid brother was being mistreated in the southern prison. "Just because Peanuts is a Yankee, they sent him to the coal mines and the cotton fields," he asserted. "They even beat up on him because they heard us talking Polish when I went to visit him."

It was a novel situation. Here was one of Chicago's best known law breakers, telephoning the press—which he abhored—urging an investigation of penal conditions in another state.

The papers made their own inquiries, but reporters were assured by Warden Barfield, "Ol' Peanuts hasn't sent in any complaints to me. Hell, he's leadin' a good, healthy outdoor life. It's doing him a world of good, too."

The reporters took the warden at his word. For the most part, authorities in Chicago had learned over the years to level with the press, and it did not occur to the newsmen that the southern warden was any different. The matter got nowhere, and Peanuts was forced to tough it out.

When he came up for parole after serving 38 months he was turned down by the parole board. Every time he came up for parole after that his request was denied. The Memphis jewelers association was exerting heavy pressure on the parole board—which included a prominent jeweler from Clarksville—to keep him behind bars as long as was legally possible.

A subsequent investigation of conditions in the Tennessee penal system revealed that prison officials had been confiscating meat intended for inmate meals, and giving it free to FBI agents, who were also permitted free use of the prison pistol range for target practice.

CHAPTER 16

BUTCH TAKES OVER

With both Pops and Peanuts on ice, it fell upon Butch to uphold the family honor. This was hardly fair, since it seemed as though every cop in town was suddenly relying upon Butch as a source of amusement and/or income on the side.

But even one Panczko on the loose was enough to keep Bieber and Brodkin busy.

Butch celebrated February 29—Leap Year Day—by leading police on a 70-mile-an-hour chase through the Northwest Side. Sergeant Robert Hunt and Patrolman Frank Kalusa were on routine patrol when they spotted him and two other men in an approaching car at high noon. Nothing might have happened, except that Butch hit the gas when he spied the squad car, so the cops took off after him.

The chase ended in an alley near Damen and Armitage Avenues, where Butch and 21-year-old Thaddeus Holod were taken into custody. The third man got away, and called George Bieber.

Less than ten minutes after Butch and his pal were brought into the Shakespeare Avenue station, the arresting officers got a call from the state's attorney's office informing them that Bieber's office had filed habeas corpus petitions in behalf of the prisoners.

At a 3 p.m. hearing before Criminal Court Judge William Lindsay, Panczko and Holod were ordered freed immediately. It was a possible record for brevity in custody, at least for a Panczko. Butch was arrested at 12:10 p.m., and back on the streets at 3:30.

Two weeks later, when he was arrested for disorderly conduct while riding in a car that ran a red light, he didn't bother going to court. His $25 bond was forfeited. He jumped a $10 bond shortly after that when he and 450-pound Joe Valente were arrested for disorderly conduct after robbery detail detectives found them loitering at Armitage and Milwaukee Avenues.

Shortly thereafter, when he and Rocco Agerone were booked for "investigation" after police found them hanging around a building at Erie Street and Western Avenue, Judge Joseph Geary threw the matter out of court because police admitted they had no evidence that any crime had been committed.

And so it went, arrest after arrest after arrest—more than sixty, and still counting—as police resorted to every device they could devise to put the remaining Panczko behind bars. Nothing worked.

Then, in October of 1952, Pops was freed on parole to join his brother in crime. He had served five years, three months and one day of the one year to life sentence for burglary.

Joseph D. Lohman, chairman of the Illinois Parole Board, declared, "Releasing this man from prison will be in the best interests of the inmate and the community. We examined his record on its merits, and we felt the time was ready to see if Joseph Panczko had made a successful adjustment. He gave evidence of being inspired by his continued incarceration."

Police Commissioner Timothy J. O'Connor all but doubled up with laughter when he read Lohman's bizarre statement in the press. "Inspired by his incarceration? Ha! I know Pops well," he chuckled. "Unless he toes the mark he'll find himself right back where he came from."

The fact that the police commissioner would go on record as knowing Pops at all was a ringing testimonial to Panczko's growing notoriety as a chronic lawbreaker in a city of more than three million inhabitants.

The intellectual Lohman, a University of Chicago sociologist, harbored a burning desire to become governor of Illinois, and the Panczko case gave him an opportunity to get his own name before the public. He was subsequently elected sheriff of Cook County, and proved to be one of the most inept lawmen ever to hold that position. That was the end of his political career.

Now, with two Panczkos working the streets, it became a toss-up over who was kept busier, the police or Bieber and Brodkin.

Pops, who had been freed "in the best interests of the community," set right to work relieving the community of anything that wasn't properly fastened down.

The first thing he spotted, on making his old rounds on a cold and rainy Saturday, was a clothing salesman's shiny new Oldsmobile, parked unattended outside the Merchandise Mart. Pops made the customary phone calls, popped out a key for the Olds, hopped in and drove off.

Hey, what the hell's this? As Pops headed down Orleans Street a golden haired cocker spaniel jumped over from the back seat and took its place beside him, thoroughly enjoying the ride. Only slightly rattled, Pops, an inveterate animal lover, drove over to Barney's Market Club, a popular steak house on Randolph Street, and parked around the corner on Halsted where the Olds would blend in with those of Barney's well-heeled customers.

From Barney's he hailed a cab and went back to the Mart to pick up his own car. Then he drove back to Barney's and double-parked alongside the Olds.

"Stay dere," he instructed the animal, as he transferred three large garment bags of women's dresses to his own car. "Okay, doggie. C'mon wit' Pops," he called when he had finished his chore. "I can't leave ya dere. Ya might freeze yer little hind end."

Pops drove back to his neighborhood, where he fenced the dresses for several hundred dollars. Then he made the rounds of his usual haunts, trying to get rid of the dog. "Who wants a pooch?" he pleaded. "A really nice dog. Make a good pet. Jeez. Don't nobody want dis nice little puppy?"

Louise wouldn't let Pops bring the dog home, and he didn't want to turn it loose, for fear it might get hit by a car. So he got back into his own car and drove around with the animal, trying to dope out his next move while listening to the radio. When the regular newscast came on, the theft of the car full of dresses and the cocker spaniel was the lead story.

At the end of the report the dog's owner, Daniel E. Byrnes, made an impassioned plea. "Whoever stole my new Oldsmobile, you can keep the car. And you can keep the dresses. But please bring Rusty back to us. He's part of our family."

The newscast was repeated every hour—"Please bring Rusty back to us." Pops looked at the dog and, for one of the few times in his life, experienced a guilty conscience. He knew what he had to do. Fortunately, Byrnes was listed in the telephone directory, so Pops could tell right where he lived. But he couldn't just walk up to the house, ring the doorbell, and say, "Here's yer dog I stole."

This called for a dose of Panczko ingenuity. Pops drove over to California and Foster Avenues, three blocks from the Byrnes home, and tied the dog to a tree in front of a synagog. "Nice doggie. Stay dere," he instructed. Then he went to a pay phone and called the owner.

"Mr. Byrnes? I got yer dog."

"Is Rusty okay?" the salesman asked. "Look, we don't care about the car. You can have it. You can have everything that was in it. But, please don't hurt Rusty."

"Naw, naw. The mutt's okay," Pops assured him. "He's tied up here waitin' for ya, a couple of blocks away."

"It's raining. He'll catch cold," Byrnes protested.

"Naw, I told ya, everyting's okay," Pops said. "Ya got anudder car?"

"My wife has an old car, but . . ."

"Okay. Get in yer wife's car and drive over by the Jewish church at California and Foster, wit da restaurant in the back. Yer dog's waitin' for ya under a tree. An' ya can pick up yer Olds at Barney's steak house at Randolph and Halsted."

There was a click on the other end of the line. Pops knew that the dog's owner was on the way.

He drove down the block and parked, so he could keep the dog in view to make sure everything went off as scheduled. A minute later a car pulled up and a man got out. The dog went wild, jumping up and down, wagging its tail and pawing the air. The man cuddled the dog, untied the knot on its collar, and took the animal back to the car.

As Pops watched Byrnes head home with Rusty he felt warm all over, despite the chilly rain spattering against his windshield. "Dat's one guy who won't prosecute me if I get caught," he told himself. "Pops just made him a happy man."

The closest Pops came to getting caught with the goods, since the time he posed as a department store dummy, came not long afterwards when he made an after-hours visit to the haberdashery in the Stevens (now the Chicago Hilton & Towers) Hotel. Pops arrived with four garment bags, pulled the lock out of the door, and went on a one-man shopping spree.

Some people might select suits, or shirts, or sweaters or socks. But Joseph Panczko was looking for something any man could wear, regardless of size. He filled all four bags to the bursting point with neckties. Looking like just another hotel guest as he carried the garment bags out past the security men, Pops headed straight for his car, parked out front in a taxi zone, with the trunk lid open and the emergency lights brazenly flashing. He carefully placed two of the bags in the trunk and laid the other two across the back seat. Then he headed for Louie Panozzo's. Louie was his current fence.

Pops approached Panozzo's place on Superior Street via the alley and pulled into Louie's garage. While he was getting the garment bags out of his trunk to display his wares Panozzo burst in, shaking like a leaf. "Jesus Christ, Pops, get the hell out of here! The cops are all over the place!" he stammered.

"Oh, man, I just unloaded. They'll see me drivin' away wit da stuff if I put it back in da car."

"Whaddya got in them bags?"

"Ties to da mammy."

"Neckties?"

"Tousands of 'em, Looie. Gimme a fast deal. You got maybe fifteen hunnert bucks worth here."

"Here's three hundred. Get the hell outa here."

Pops pocketed the $300 without counting it, and Louie stashed the garment bags out of sight without checking their contents. When he left, Pops couldn't resist driving around the block, now that there was nothing incriminating in his car. Sure enough, several squad cars were parked in front of Panozzo's, and uniformed police officers were carrying furs and other contraband items out of the house.

Pops pulled his head in like a turtle and drove on by, as inconspicuously as possible. Sure enough, he had just delivered a load of stolen merchandise in the midst of a full blown police raid.

The close call did nothing to dampen his enthusiasm, however. Pops was developing a fascination for the swank Michigan Avenue hotel strip. But by the summer of 1953 it was getting more and more difficult for him to pull off the "guest act." In police circles, at least, he had become every bit as well known as Mayor Martin Kennelly.

And so it was no wonder that Detectives George Kush and Patrick Daly were somewhat abashed when he showed up at 7:30 a.m. one Sunday at the Conrad Hilton Hotel, where the National Jewelry Fair was in progress.

Few conventioneers were around at that early hour, and Pops was drawn like a magnet to a room where dozens and dozens of jewelry sample and display cases were lined up in a cordoned off area. Kush and Daly, who had been assigned to guard the fortune in gems, did a double take when they looked up and saw who was admiring the display.

"All right, Pops. What the hell are you doing here?"

"Who, me? Nutin'. I just come down to take a walk in Grant Park."

"Oh, yeah? Well, how about taking a walk with us?"

The two detectives escorted Pops out of the hotel, where they found the borrowed car he had arrived in. The trunk was unlocked, the keys were in the ignition, and the front wheels were positioned for a fast U-turn. This was known in the trade as the "get-away position."

Pops was taken to police headquarters at 11th and State Streets, where he was charged with possession of burglary tools, since a screw driver was found in his car.

When he was arraigned the next morning in Felony Court, Bieber moved to suppress the evidence on grounds that the arrest was illegal. He argued that police had no reason to suspect Pops in the first place. Judge Harold P. O'Connell agreed and threw the case out. As Pops was leaving the building with his brother, Butch, he was cornered by Lt. Ralph Petacque of the police Confidence Detail.

"You son-of-a-bitch!" Petacque raged, shaking an angry finger at Pops. "You got me out of bed for nothing. I ought to get paid for this!"

"How much ya want?" Pops asked, instinctively reaching for his wallet.

"Get your Polack ass out of here!" Petacque snarled, pointing to the door.

Several weeks later Pops was back behind bars, charged with attempted bribery by police Sergeants William Jannick and John Magner of the Summerdale District. They said he offered them $100 "for a pass" when they stopped to question him in the 5900 block of North Campbell Avenue, where there had been a rash of recent burglaries.

As soon as he made bond Pops hit the streets again, to raise money to pay Bieber to get him off. For this particular venture he selected a South Side furniture store, miles from his home neighborhood, at approximately 1 o'clock Sunday morning.

By all appearances the coast was clear as Pops broke in through the front door. Had he looked a little more closely at a car parked in the nearby shadows, however, he would have noticed a young couple enjoying a sexual experience in the back seat.

The noise of the break-in caused the young man to look up momentarily and, despite his moment of ecstasy, he was able to memorize the license number on Panczko's get-away car.

Pops was long gone by the time Lawndale District police responded to the burglar alarm, but the unruffled swain remained on the scene to give them the license plate number. The number checked out to Joseph Panczko, who was promptly picked up at his sister's North Side home and taken to the Lawndale Avenue station for interrogation.

The questioning consisted of a detective penning a "confession," handing it to Panczko, and ordering him, "Sign it." When Pops refused, he was strung up by a rope, looped over the top bars in the station lockup, and beaten unconscious. When he came to he was handed the confession and told to sign it. When he refused he was beaten again until he blacked out.

After being thoroughly worked over, Pops was dragged to a cell. A detective placed the confession and a pencil on the cot and told him, "We'll be back." As Pops sat in the cell rubbing his bruises he overhead the watch captain admonish the detectives, "Take it easy or you'll kill the son-of-a-bitch. We can't let that happen."

When he heard that, Pops tore up the "confession" and flushed it down the toilet.

Pops was held incommunicado, and it took Bieber several days to locate him when he failed to make his customary telephone check. Bieber bailed him out, and he limped home to let his latest wounds heal. When the case came up before the judge Pops was turned loose after the young lover, who

The five Panczko brothers, in the late 1940s, are shown at the wedding of brother John Panczko, standing right, next to Frank Panczko. In foreground, from left, are Edward "Butch" Panczko, Joseph "Pops" Panczko and Paul "Peanuts" Panczko.

Choir boy he was not, but Joseph Panczko did make his First Holy Communion looking like a little angel.

Eva and Peter Panczko on their wedding day. The union would produce five sons and a daughter, and send the crime index rate sky high.

Louise Panczko married Frank Grygiel in 1938 but always had time for her brothers. Especially when they needed to be bonded out of jail.

Edward "Butch" Panczko, ruggedly handsome, was quick as a cat for his size.

Edward "Butch" Panczko said he was home drunk when police arrested him as a suspect in a 1956 burglary of a clothing store warehouse in which one burglar was slain by police. Butch beat the rap.

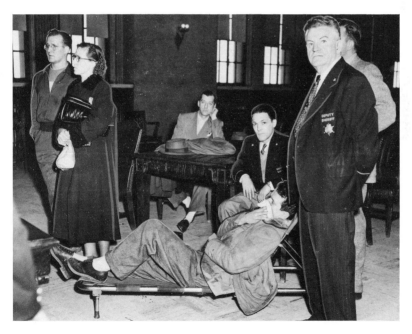

Carried to court on a stretcher, Edward "Butch" Panczko was shot by police responding to the alarm of a currency exchange holup in February of 1951. At left are Panczko's sister, Louise, and a brother, John.

Walking wounded. Joseph "Pops" Panczko is led to an ambulance after being shot in the groin while trying to steal furs from a truck on Jan. 26, 1949.

Joseph "Pops" Panczko isn't fighting a cold as he is led to lockup by Officer Jack Muller, nemesis of Chicago criminals for many years.

Joseph "Pops" Panczko was shot and his Buick riddled with shotgun slugs when, according to police, he attempted to burgle a jewelry store in Wilmette, Illinois, in 1957. He survived and was acquitted of all charges.

Joseph "Pops" Panczko finds something to grimace about while in the custody of Chicago police detectives for another jewelry theft, this one in 1960.

Hamming it up for the camera, Joseph "Pops" Panczko displays a comic sense of humor that often angered no-nonsense partners in crime.

Paul "Peanuts" Panczko (sunglasses) listens to attorney George Bieber explain to him and fellow thieves Joseph D'Argento and Anthony D'Antonio (hand on chin) what they should say to police. Questioning centered on 1964 murder of Guy Mendola, another theft ring member.

Attired in his Sunday best, Joseph "Pops" Panczko awaits another legal ruling in Chicago's Criminal Courts Building (circa 1964).

Famed Chicago defense attorney George Bieber gives advice to Joseph "Pops" Panczko outside court. Bieber frequently represented Panczko brothers "Pops," "Butch" and "Peanuts," often successfully. "They are my lucky charm," the lawyer said of his thieving clients.

Paul "Peanuts" Panczko tried to outdistance police but slammed on the brakes when detectives fired on his car. Here Sgt. James Walsh of Cook county sheriff's police points to bullet hole. Slug narrowly missed Peanuts' auto companion, Joseph D'Argento. (1964 photo.)

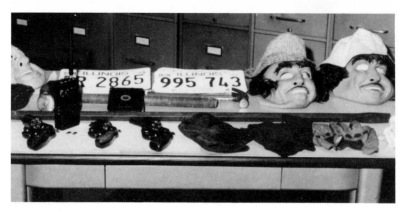

Rubber face masks, a five-foot crowbar and other tools of crime were recovered by Chicago police detectives from Paul "Peanuts" Panczko and four other prominent thieves near a suburban Chicago bank in 1979. Peanuts was later convicted of possessing three pistols displayed on table. Police radio scanner, also displayed, was found in his Cadillac.

U.S. Secret Service agents who arrested Paul "Peanuts" Panczko on charges of passing counterfeit $10 bills said they found these guns and masks in his home. Here a Chicago police detective models one of the masks. Peanuts claims he was the first bigtime jewel thief to don rubber Halloween masks when making a "score."

Paul "Peanuts" Panczko blew the whistle on his brother Joseph "Pops" Panczko and helped the FBI send others to prison to win leniency for himself.

had given police his license plate number, was unable to point him out in court.

Pops was equally lucky when the police bribery case came up before the now familiar Judge O'Connell in Felony Court. Sergeant Magner testified that Pops had offered him and his partner $100 "to give him a pass" after they stopped him for questioning about the series of burglaries in the Campbell Avenue neighborhood.

He admitted, however, that police had no cause to stop Panczko in the first place, and allowed that nothing incriminating was found on him or in his car.

After hearing the evidence, Judge O'Connell rendered a remarkable decision: "Since the police had no reason for suspecting the defendant, there is no way he could be guilty of offering a bribe to escape being held for something of which he was innocent. Case dismissed."

While Pops was making legal history, Butch was busy dodging bullets. Police took out after him when he was seen hurriedly leaving the scene of a hardware break-in on West Chicago Avenue. Sergeant Patrick Flynn of the Park Police emptied his gun at Butch's fleeing car in a chase that ended at Chicago Avenue and Wood Street when one of the slugs struck Panczko in the right arm.

After his wound was bandaged up, Butch was brought in for questioning, but refused to tell police the time of day. He was booked for reckless driving and resisting arrest, and released on $225 bond. When the case came up in court, Bieber worked his usual magic and he went home a free man.

Police hopes of finally seeing the end of Butch were buoyed when a late model sports car was found, apparently abandoned, in the 3500 block of Wabansia Avenue just five days before Christmas in 1954. Shakespeare Avenue police ran a license plate check and discovered that the auto, which had been there for two days, was registered to none other than Edward Panczko.

"That's Butch!" Policeman Peter Storm told his partner, Arthur Raguse.

"Do you think somebody took the son-of-a-bitch for a ride?" Raguse suggested. "Do you think he could be in the trunk?"

"Don't touch anything. We got to call homicide," Storm said. "Just in case."

Raguse and Storm kept the car under surveillance until Homicide Sergeant William Clark arrived and took command of the investigation. "If Butch is in the trunk we'll know in a minute," he smiled.

As the two patrol officers stood by hopefully, Clark took a crowbar and popped open the trunk. There was a spare tire and a jack, but no dead body. "Nuts," he said. "There goes Christmas."

With Butch's car seemingly abandoned, and him nowhere to be seen, police ordered a city-wide search. "Since he ain't in his own trunk, he might have been taken for a ride and dumped somewhere," Clark speculated. "We'll have to establish whether he's dead or alive, one way or the other."

Efforts to locate Butch were unsuccessful, but detectives did learn from associates that he'd been playing hide and seek with a finance company. He was delinquent in his payments, and was moving the car every few days to stymie efforts to repossess the vehicle. When police went back to Wabansia Avenue to have the car towed to the auto pound, it was no longer there.

"Well, I guess that proves Butch is very much alive," Clark said wistfully. "He moved the frickin' car again while we weren't looking."

CHAPTER 17

THE ROAD TO MANDEL-LEAR

Early in January of 1956 an event transpired that would have a profound effect on the life of Butch Panczko, who had become known in police circles as "Burglary, Inc." The new year had barely taken its icy grip on Chicago when authorities picked up a rumble that the giant Mandel-Lear warehouse, just east of Michigan Avenue on the north bank of the Chicago River, was going to be hit by burglars.

Police, under the direction of Lieutenant James Lynch, set a lethal trap.

After warehouse employees went home for the day, shotgun-toting lawmen slipped into the building on Friday night and positioned themselves around the most likely targets on the first floor.

Lieutenant Lynch, Sergeant James O'Neill, and Detectives Harold Olson and William Cooper hunkered down in the darkness alongside a walk-in vault containing $235,000 worth of furs destined for the Mandel Brothers Department Store. Detectives Russell Sweeney, Vincent Martin and James Kelleher were posted near the warehouse safe.

Throughout the night and into the early hours of Saturday they huddled in the drafty, red brick building, talking in hushed tones, waiting for something to happen.

On the next night, it did. At 4 a.m. Sunday, January 8th, a car pulled up to the north side of the building, on North Water Street. "Everybody pipe down. This could be it," Lynch cautioned.

As the police investigators held their breaths, three men got out of the car. Two of them scanned the neighborhood to make sure the coast was clear. The third took a crowbar and ripped the lock off the door. Several of the lawmen waiting inside clutched their shotguns. A stakeout can be a scary thing, especially when you don't know who you're waiting for, and what he might do if cornered.

Swiftly and efficiently, the three intruders slipped into the darkened building and headed for the fur storage vault. They obviously knew exactly what they were after.

"Hold it right there!" Cooper shouted. "We're police officers."

One of the trio drew a revolver from his belt, as his companions turned to flee.

"Watch it, he's got a gun!" Cooper warned.

As he yelled, Cooper squeezed off three shots from his pistol while both Olson and O'Neill cut loose with their shotguns. When the smoke cleared, one of the burglars lay dead on the floor with twenty-one shotgun pellets in his body. His two accomplices fled into the night. Somebody yelled, "Turn on the lights."

"Did anybody get a look at the other two guys?" O'Neill asked.

"Damn right," Cooper answered. "One of 'em was Butch Panczko. I think the other was Albert Tomasello. I'm also pretty sure I hit one or the other."

"I made Panczko, too," O'Neill agreed. "No question about it. And everybody knows Tomasello works with the son-of-a-bitch. Who's this guy?"

Olson bent over the dead man and went through his trouser pockets. Cards in his wallet identified him as Robert Behnke, age 27. "Yeah, I know this guy," Olson remarked. "He works as a tile setter, but he's got a rap sheet for burglary."

"Well, let's call the coroner's office and put out the word for Panczko," Lynch said. The body was removed to the Cook County Morgue, while police set out to round up Edward "Butch" Panczko. Patrolmen John Cooney and Don Byrne picked him up a short time later when they spotted him at California Avenue and Division Street. Taken to the detective bureau for questioning, he denied any knowledge of the fatal breakin.

"You got the wrong guy," Butch told Lieutenant Lynch. "I was out drinkin' all night on Division Street, and at 4 o'clock in the morning I was home sleeping it off."

"What bars were you in?" Lynch asked. "We can check them out easily enough, and if you got any witnesses who saw you there, you can go home."

"I don't remember," Butch claimed. "I think I musta been in just about all of 'em. I been drinkin' all night."

At a showup in detective headquarters, O'Neill, Olson and Cooper all identified Butch as one of the intruders. He was charged with burglary, and released on $10,000 bail provided by a professional bondsman, with orders to appear at an inquest later in the day.

All three police officers again identified Butch at the inquest as one of the bandits who got away. Butch refused to testify under oath, but commented to Deputy Coroner Louis J. Nadherny, "Your honor, I was blind drunk in bed at 4 a.m."

Meanwhile the search for Tomasello continued. In addition to his usual haunts, police checked hospitals and doctors' offices, on the possibility that he had been wounded in the shootout and would have to seek medical attention. He was nowhere to be found, which convinced police all the more that he was the third man they were after.

Suddenly he turned up right under their noses. On January 12 a federal grand jury indicted him for possession of heroin, in an unrelated matter. Tomasello showed up at the Federal Building a few hours later and surrendered to the United States marshal. Chicago police were alerted that he was there, and surrounded the building. Tomasello routinely posted bond, and as he walked out of the building, police took him into custody.

At a showup in detective headquarters, however, the police case against Tomasello fell apart before it was ever put together. After O'Neill, Cooper and Olson got a good look at the suspect, they told Lynch, "That's not the guy who was with Butch Panczko at Mandel-Lear, lieutenant."

Before releasing Tomasello, Lynch questioned him out of curiosity. "If you weren't involved in the Mandel-Lear thing, Al, how come you took a duck so nobody could find you?"

"I was out cabareting with my wife that night, lieutenant," he explained. "Then, when I heard what Bob Behnke got, I figured I'd better blow town because everybody knew me and him were friends."

That left only Butch facing charges that Bieber could normally handle blindfolded and with his hands tied behind his back. Then State's Attorney John Gutknecht announced he intended to make Illinois legal history by seeking an indictment charging Panczko with murder.

"Butch didn't kill anybody. The cops did," a reporter reminded the prosecutor.

"I'm looking at a case in Pennsylvania, where it's been held that where two or more persons are involved in a common crime and police kill one in intercepting them, the other or others may be tried and convicted of murder," Gutknecht explained. "The ground on which such action rests is that the killing by police is a natural and foreseeable result of the initial criminal act. Now, while there's never been such a prosecution in Illinois, I certainly believe it is legal."

Suddenly, in a case without precedent in Illinois, Butch found himself charged with Behnke's murder. He was arraigned in Criminal Court before Judge Elmer Holmgren, who released him on $7,500 bond.

Prosecutors decided to try Butch separately on the burglary and murder charges. This would double the odds in favor of conviction, by exposing him to two different juries. If they couldn't nail him on one rap, they figured, they might get him on the other. Of course, what they did not make allowances for was the Panczko factor.

Butch's first burglary trial ended in a mistrial after *The Chicago Tribune* wrote him up as "a reputed member of a notorious burglary gang, whose police record includes 62 arrests in 12 years." Judge Holmgren agreed with Panczko's lawyers, Bieber and Richard Devine, that such a statement, true though it might be, could not help but prejudice any juror who saw it in the paper.

Four months later he went on trial again, and this time—despite eye witness identification by three Chicago police officers—a Criminal Court jury found him innocent of the aborted Mandel-Lear burglary.

"I knowed Georgie would get ya off," Pops congratulated his brother, as the two of them left the Criminal Courts building together. "It's da Bieber magic."

"Magic my ass," Butch scoffed. "Bieber had to spread around fifteen big ones to the right people."

"Fifteen tousand bucks?"

"Fuckin' right. And my partner—it wasn't Tomasello like they said in the papers, it was Steve Tomaras—it cost him ten grand after the coppers found out he was the guy."

"So, anyhow, yer home free, Butch."

"Justice ain't free in Cook County, Pops."

The state's attorney's office now found itself in the awkward position of having to prosecute him for a murder that occurred when one of his gang members was shot to death by police in a burglary that a jury said Butch had nothing to do with.

Judge Holmgren quickly grasped the folly of the situation, and threw out the murder indictment in order to save the state the expense and embarrassment of a futile trial.

Having been charged with murder, and the possibility that he might have ended up in Cook County's electric chair, had a sobering effect on Butch. From that day on—for the most part—he would keep a very low profile.

Suburban police, meanwhile, were having no better luck in trying to put Butch's brother, Pops, back behind bars.

In north suburban Evanston, he was arrested in connection with the $30,000 robbery of Marguerite Ortman, a wealthy North Shore widow and clubwoman. But Judge Cornelius J. Harrington turned him loose after Mrs. Ortman failed to pick Pops out of a lineup in the Evanston police station.

Next he was picked up by police in the near west suburb of Forest Park, after $26,000 in jewels and watches was taken in a lunch hour burglary of jewelry store. Again, Pops was released after Police Magistrate Edward G. Schultz ruled that there was insufficient evidence against him.

Then Pops was arrested by Chicago police who spotted him loitering late at night in the lobby of the Pittsfield Building, the Loop headquarters for a number of prestigious jewelry firms.

"I could spot you a mile away, Pops," Sergeant George Kush told him. "You're not fooling anybody. You're waiting for some jewelry salesman to come out so you can follow him and clean out his car."

"Naw, ya got it all wrong, honest," Pops protested. "I'm just waitin' for my sweetie. Please don't take me in. I'm on parole, but I'm workin', drivin' a truck. Besides, my ma's awful sick, and . . ."

"Stick out your hands, Pops. You're under arrest," Kush told him.

As he slapped the handcuffs on Panczko he noticed that Pops was wearing a $1,000 diamond ring."

"Where'd you get the sparkler, huh?" Kush asked him.

"I bought it," Pops insisted.

"Yeah? Who from?"

"I don't remember."

Police couldn't prove otherwise, and a fast phone call to Bieber got Pops sprung as usual.

The ongoing saga of Pops, Butch and Peanuts prompted the *Chicago American* to observe: "Probably no single family has given Chicago police as much trouble as the three Panczko brothers."

The newspaper went on to suggest that their adventures would make a marvelous soap opera, entitled "In and Out of Court With the Panczko Brothers: or, Adrift on the Docket."

CHAPTER 18

POPS GETS BUCKSHOT OF THE BRAIN

"So the doctor took my brains out, set 'em on the table, and took six shotgun pellets out. Today he goes to medical meetings and shows pictures of me, before and after he took my brains out. Dr. Joseph Tarkington. If Kennedy had him, he would be alive today."

It was a snowy February morning in 1957 when Pops and his latest sidekick, Ralph Campagna, decided to knock over the T.J. Cullen Jewelers at Edens Plaza in the exclusive North Shore suburb of Wilmette.

Pops and his 34-year-old companion had been watching the shop for some time. They knew that the owner, Thomas J. Cullen, showed up at 8 a.m. to open the store, unlock the safe, and place jewelry displays in the show windows. The vault remained open throughout the day, until he removed the displays from the showcases and replaced them in the safe at night.

They also knew that Cullen locked up and went to lunch around 11:30 a.m., leaving the store unattended. What they didn't know was that the FBI had been watching them while they spied on Cullen.

The feds promptly advised Wilmette Police Chief Edwin Whiteside that it looked like Pops was planning a jewelry job. On Friday morning, February 8, Policeman Harold Graf was hiding in the back of the jewelry store with a shotgun in his lap, waiting to see if the rumor was true.

Panczko and Campagna were sitting in Pops' Oldsmobile, watching the store, when Cullen emerged at 11:30 and locked the door. "Dere he goes now. He's goin' to lunch," Pops said. "Here we go."

Each man carried a large cardboard box to put the loot into as they circled around to the rear of the store. Pops also toted a heavy crowbar, to open the door.

"You clean out da window display and da showcases in front and I'll take da safe," Pops told Campagna, as he deftly pried the lock off the back door. Campagna slipped into the shop while Pops wiped his fingerprints off the crowbar and tossed it into a trash bin. Then he picked up his box and went in after Campagna.

Pops entered the store just in time to hear Graf yell, "Don't move, kid, or I'll kill you!" Campagna, who was unarmed, hurled the cardboard box at the lawman and bolted for the back door as Pops was coming in. Pops found himself looking straight down the barrel of Graf's shotgun.

"Put your arms up!" ordered Graf, a World War II combat veteran who was still wearing his khakis.

Pops, who never carried a gun, instinctively heaved his cardboard box in the direction of the lawman as he heard a loud "BOOM!" and felt a blast of hot air and lead rip into his face. The force of the blast spun him around, and he lurched out the door after Campagna, as fast as his legs would move.

Graf was in pursuit as the fleeing burglars sprinted past the Carson Pirie Scott store and made for the parking lot. He was shouting at them to stop, but dared not shoot because of the noontime crowd of shoppers. Campagna, the shorter of the two men, zig-zagged between parked cars and hurdled a fence at the far end of the lot, while Pops, with blood streaming from his face, headed for the get-away car.

He jumped into the Oldsmobile and started the engine, just as Graf reined up on the opposite side of the car. As Pops hit the gas, Graf fired two more shotgun blasts, blowing out the right front window. Unable to see through the blood pouring from his forehead, Panczko smashed into a parked car.

He wasn't ready to concede defeat yet, however. He rolled out of the car and raced toward a National Tea store, still under construction. Graf fired several shots from his service revolver as Pops ducked into the store and loped past astonished workmen.

Not realizing he was a police officer, because of his Army khakis, the store workers ran for cover when Graf barged in, waving a shotgun with one hand and a revolver with the other. Graf followed the trail of blood to the men's room, where Pops was hunched over a washbowl, trying to wipe the blood off his face with a wet handkerchief.

As Graf burst into the room, Pops backed into a stall and sat down on the commode, still wiping blood from his face. A store worker, who flung open the door to see what was going on, shouted, "Let the guy alone. Can't you see he's hurt?"

"I'm a police officer. Call the patrol wagon," Graf responded.

When the worker left the room to make the call, Pops looked up through the bloody handkerchief to see the 30-year-old police officer pointing his service revolver directly at his head. Figuring Graf was going to finish him off and claim he had tried to escape, Panczko moaned as loud as he could, "Get me a doctor! I'm dyin'! I'm hurt bad!"

An ambulance arrived minutes later and took the wounded burglar to Evanston Hospital. Other police officers tried to pick up his partner's trail. Footprints in the snow indicated he had run southwest through a wooded area, and into the adjoining suburb of Glenview, where his tracks were lost on the pavement near Juniper Street and Beverly Lane.

Back at Wilmette police headquarters, Graf viewed mug shots of known burglars, and picked out a photo of Campagna as the man they were after. Police squads from five North Shore suburbs combed the area, but Campagna had made good his escape.

Back at Evanston Hospital, Panczko was stretched out on a table in the emergency room, wearing a $1,000 wrist watch, a $1,000 diamond ring, and with $1,200 cash in his pockets for bribing cops in case he got caught. As attendants began stripping him down so he could be X-rayed he protested weakly, "Hey, hey—dat's my watch."

He vaguely remembered someone saying, "You'll get it back," as he lapsed into unconsciousness. A Roman Catholic priest administered the last rites, and he was wheeled into the operating room.

Dr. Joseph A. Tarkington, a skilled surgeon, removed six shotgun pellets from Panzcko's head and five from his face, and excised a wad of brain tissue that was so badly damaged it would be of no further use to anyone, even Pops.

Listed in critical condition, the patient hovered at death's door for two weeks while Bieber managed to get him "released on bond." In this case, with Panczko still in a coma, it meant that police could unlock the shackles and remove the around-the-clock-guard at his bedside.

Pops spent forty days in the hospital before he was released. After giving $100 to the priest who had administered the extreme unction, he went home with his head swathed in bandages like an Egyptian mummy.

Bieber, meanwhile, won fifteen continuances from six different judges before finally maneuvering his battle-scarred client into what he hoped would be a friendly courtroom. Bieber's fee was $30,000—up front. Part of it would go to attorney Richard Devine, whom he brought in to assist with the defense. Bieber was wise enough to recognize his own limitations. He was a fixer, not a trial lawyer.

Pops did not go to trial until the following December. Campagna, who had avoided arrest until September 24, appeared as a co-defendant before Judge Julius H. Miner.

Campagna did not testify but contended, through his lawyer, Harry J. Busch, that he had never been to Wilmette on the day in question.

Pops could make no such claim. The prosecution produced seventeen witnesses who positively placed him at the scene of the crime, including FBI agents, police officers, ambulance crew members and medical personnel. Dr. Tarkington testified that he removed six pellets "as big as your fingernails" from inside Panczko's head.

Throughout the testimony Pops sat at the defense table with his face painfully contorted, as if to emphasize to the jury that he'd been so horribly disfigured that he could never again lead a normal life.

When it came time for the defense to present its case, Bieber put Pops on the stand to offer his own version of the near-fatal shooting.

"What is your occupation, Mr. Panczko?" the lawyer asked loudly.

"I'm a teef," he mumbled, through twisted lips.

"You mean you are a thief?"

"Yeah. I steal tings," he agonized.

The jury of eight men and four women, clearly impressed by such unabashed honesty, leaned forward to catch the poor man's every tormented word.

"Now Pops, er, Mr. Panczko, please tell the judge and the jury, in your own words, exactly what happened on February 8, 1957."

Putting on his best Quasimodo face, Pops leaned toward the jury box as he slowly related, "Dat day I was out lookin' for a nice house to buy for my mother. I got hungry. I seen dat shoppin' center and stopped, tinkin' to get a sandwich and a cup of coffee. I was gettin' outa da car and somebody shot me in da head an' just about killed me."

The jurors were spellbound. While they were out deliberating after the defense rested, Pops turned to Bieber and asked, "Whadya tink, Georgie?" Did I do okay?"

"You know what they say, Pops. Never bet on a jury or a precinct captain. But I got a good feeling about this one. I think we're okay."

Bieber was prophetic. The jury came back at midnight, and the foreman announced, "We find the defendants, Joseph Panczko and Ralph Campagna, not guilty."

"Tank you! Tank you!" Pops shouted, rising to his feet and bowing humbly. Campagna clasped his hands over his head like a boxer who had just kayoed his opponent.

Reporters ran to the phones and flashed their offices: "Pops did it again!"

As jurors, lawyers and spectators filed out into the corridor after court was dismissed, prosecutors Joseph Tobin and Irving Lang scornfully asked one of the male panel members, "How the hell could you people come up with such a verdict?"

"Well," the juror explained. "We all felt the dumb bastard was guilty, but he paid the penalty when he got his head half shot off. The poor guy's suffered enough."

"Pops," Bieber beamed, on overhearing the remark. "Ya won your own case?"

"Den how about givin' me back my thirty grand?"

"Ha, ha. Pops, you're a real comedian."

As luck would have it, Pops found himself riding down in the elevator with Judge Miner after the cheering was over. "Yer honor. Is it okay if I say somethin'?" he asked.

"You can say anything you want, but not if it's concerning your case," Judge Miner answered tartly.

"Naw. I just wanna say dat I've been around dis here buildin' for years, and you're da best judge I ever faced. You gave me and Ralph a fair and impartial trial."

Miner frowned and said something to the elevator operator, then disembarked briskly as the car reached the ground floor.

"What did he say?" Pops asked.

"The judge said you're the biggest con man he's ever seen," the operator laughed.

After digesting his press clippings the following day, Pops urged Bieber to sue Edens Plaza shopping center and the Wilmette Police Department, since it was now a matter of court record that an innocent man had been shot down while getting out of his car to fetch a cup of coffee.

"You got it, Pops," Bieber promised. "I'll take care of everything."

No suit was ever filed. Pops knew that it was in Bieber's best interest to remain on friendly terms with as many police departments as possible. If a police officer owed Bieber a favor he might be inclined to give weak testimony against one of the lawyer's clients. As for the shopping center, Pops heard via the grapevine that Bieber got paid under the table to let the matter drop.

Once again it appeared that the resourceful attorney had been able to collect a generous fee from both sides.

With all eyes on Pops and his dramatic brush with death, Butch had been all but forgotten since the Mandel-Lear job. By all accounts he was the most religious member of the Panczko family. Although not a regular churchgoer, he adhered to the Roman Catholic faith, and abstained from eating meat on Fridays long after it was no longer required.

Finding himself charged with a murder he did not commit had caused him to rethink his lifestyle. Besides, after seeing what happened to young Behnke at Mandel-Lear, and Pops at Edens Plaza, he began to realize that he was not exactly in what might be called a low-risk profession.

Butch decided to call it quits. No more jewels. No more furs. No more men's suits. As far as anyone could tell, he walked a Boy Scout path for more than a year. Then, just as police were almost forgetting what he looked like, he was arrested for stealing—of all things—a cement mixer.

The ponderous machine, valued at $800, had been parked in a vacant lot at 2300 Belmont Avenue, on the Northwest Side. When Hans Martin, a building contractor with offices nearby, went to haul the mixer to a new construction site he discovered it was missing.

Now a cement mixer is not an easy thing to hide, and Martin quickly located it in a junkyard on Elston Avenue, where Butch had sold it for scrap for $36. Butch and 26-year-old James Panos, who had helped him haul it away, were promptly arrested for grand larceny.

A call was put in to Bieber, and he lined up Devine to help him out, since the defendants demanded a jury trial. The press had a field day, speculating as to whether police had enough "concrete evidence" to put Panczko away this time.

A jury of five men and seven women was selected to hear the case before Judge Henry Dieringer in Criminal Court. Butch admitted straight on that he had, indeed, taken the cement mixer.

"We spotted it in this vacant lot, and I walked up to the man who was standing there and said, 'Is it all right if I take the mixer?' He said, 'I don't care.' So I took it."

The prosecutors called Hans Martin, the building contractor. He denied having given Butch permission to haul away the mixer. Butch took a close look at him and agreed, "That's not the gentleman who told me I could take it."

It now appeared that Butch had asked a casual passer-by, who couldn't have cared less. When Panczko asked if he could take the machine, the bystander had truthfully told him, "I don't care." Butch interpreted this as permission granted.

Judge Dieringer did not wait for the jurors to render their decision. He sustained a motion for a directed verdict of acquittal, on the grounds that the prosecution had failed to show "felonious intent" on Butch's part.

The cops were mad now. Shakespeare Avenue Detective Lieutenant John Neurauter put a bounty on the brothers' heads, promising a $300 bonus to any of his officers who shot either Butch or Pops dead. "Take a good look at them," he said. "Kill them on sight."

Detective Donald Kelly, on the department only four years, felt that such extreme measures were unnecessary, even by Chicago police standards. Kelly, a highly decorated Marine

Corps hero from World War II, decided he would show more seasoned police veterans how to deal with the Panczkos legally. He set out to get the brothers, but got more than he bargained for instead.

There had been a series of burglaries, in which a suspect seen leaving the scenes closely resembled Pops. Learning that Pops frequented Ricky's restaurant on Division Street, Kelly drove by and spotted the suspect loitering on the sidewalk. He parked his unmarked car and walked over to him.

"I'm a police officer," he said. "I'd like to talk to you."

"Go fuck yerself," responded Pops, as he put both hands against the detective's chest and shoved him out of the way.

The astonished Kelly grabbed Pops roughly by the upper arm and escorted him into the restaurant, so he could phone for the wagon. Butch, who was having a cup of coffee inside, grabbed the detective and demanded, "Hey! What the fuck are you doing with my brother?"

Before Kelly knew it he was engaged in a shoving match with Butch, while still holding tightly to Pops, so he couldn't get away. Restaurant patrons began to cheer and boo as the struggle continued. The cheering got Kelly's adrenaline flowing until he realized, to his dismay, that the spectators were jeering at him and rooting for the bad guys.

The restaurant manager called for police reinforcements, but the melee only grew in intensity before they arrived. The next thing Kelly knew he had 190 pounds of Lu Florio on his back, gripping him in a headlock. Miss Florio was the waitress. Kelly lurched to the floor with Lu wrapped around his neck. When the patrol wagon got there the detective was still sprawled out on the deck, where the waitress had locked a stranglehold on him.

"I barely restrained myself from taking out my pistol and clouting her with it," Kelly sheepishly explained, as fellow officers picked him up off the floor.

Pops and Butch were herded into the wagon and taken to the Shakespeare Avenue station, where they were charged with simple assault, aggravated assault, assault and battery and resisting an officer—which was every charge Kelly could come up with on such short notice.

They had barely been booked when a new player arrived on the scene, Herbert Barsey. A highly successful prosecutor, he had been lured away from the state's attorney's office by Bieber and Brodkin, and was now a part of the Panczko defense team. Barsey, a bespectacled scrawny lawyer whose trousers were baggy because he couldn't fill out the seat of his pants, was known among the Criminal Courts press corps as "Charles Assless."

It was a bedraggled pair of brothers who appeared with Assless before Judge Harold P. O'Connell the following day. Their hair hung down over their foreheads and their clothing was dripping wet.

"My, my my. What have we here?" the amused jurist smiled as he looked down at the woebegone defendants.

The Panczkos explained that they had been kept up all night by police, who refused to feed them and repeatedly doused them with cold water. Judge O'Connell ordered them released on bonds of $450 each, so they could go home and towel off.

When the matter came up for trial, Pops and Butch produced five witnesses who testified that Pops was peacefully sipping a cup of coffee outside the restaurant when Kelly vigorously placed him under arrest. Butch's only role, they said, was to ask Kelly, "What are you arresting my brother for?"

Judge William V. Daly declared the defendants not guilty, and told them they could go.

"Wait a minute, your honor. I believe there is another matter pending against Joseph Panczko," said Police Officer John Curtin, approaching the bench. Curtin explained that he had charged Pops with attempted bribery after Pops offered to buy him dinner in exchange for letting him go when Curtin arrested him for prowling.

Curtin's partner was called to verify the bribe offer. "Um, I remember Pops offering to buy John and me some supper, but I don't recall anything about a bribe," he stated.

"Case dismissed," said Daly, raising his eyebrows at Curtin.

Pops' final encounter with police that year was a most unusual one. Detective Kevin Ryan looked up from his desk in the North Avenue police station on Christmas Eve to find Panczko towering over him.

"Merry Christmas. Who brought you in this time?" Ryan asked. "And who took the handcuffs off?"

"I come in by myself," Pops explained.

"You mean you're actually surrendering?"

"Naw, some son-of-a-bitchen teef stole da radio outa my new '58 Olds and I wanna file a complaint."

"Somebody stole something off of *you*?"

"Yeah. Dis neighborhood is gettin' so bad a guy can't park his car witout somebody breakin' into it."

"Are you sure you didn't break into your own car by mistake?" Ryan asked seriously.

"Hell no," Pops insisted. "I know my car when I see it."

"Well, maybe your brother broke into it. Maybe we'd better pick Butch up to see if he knows anything about this crime."

"Fuck youse guys," Pops said in disgust. "You don't tink we got our reputation by breakin into cars, do ya? Dere's a teef loose in da neighborhood."

"Yeah, and I tink I'm lookin' at 'em," the detective said, mockingly.

Realizing he was going to get no help from the law, Pops left the station and went to look for another Oldsmobile, so he could replace his own radio. He wanted to listen to Christmas music.

CHAPTER 19

SOMETHING FISHY AT 26TH AND CAL

The Cook County Criminal Courts building at Twenty-sixth Street and South California Avenue, known by all who walked or worked within its gray stone walls as "Twenty-Sixth and Cal," was a warren of humanity worthy of Damon Runyon.

The venerable structure, of Greco-Roman style architecture with an Egyptian interior, was a scandal from the day it was built back in the '20s, in a remote part of town on land owned by Mayor Anton Cermak. Criminal lawyers who had to represent clients there hated it, because of the valuable time lost traveling between the courts and their downtown offices. And when they were out at Twenty-Sixth and Cal their offices couldn't reach them, forcing them to make frequent phone checks.

Among the heavy hitters who practiced law five days a week in the building were Bieber, Brodkin, Barsey, Harry J. Busch and Charlie Bellows, a suave orator who turned ham acting into a successful career before the bench. Collectively they were known as the B-Boys.

Most of the other regular defense lawyers were sleaze bags or characters. Among the latter was the dapper George Crane, a brother of Charlie Cohn, the roly-poly bail bondsman. Crane, who changed his name for professional purposes, liked to sip from a tall glass of clear liquid as he sat at the defense table.

"This ain't what you might think it is, folks—just water," he once quipped to a jury, holding the glass aloft for all to see. As he set the glass down and stepped away from the table to cross-examine a witness, he tripped over a heavy brass spittoon, lurched forward and landed on his face.

Another defense lawyer had perfected the art of snapping his toes inside his shoes. As the opposing counsel was trying to make a point before a jury he would sit innocently at the defense table, snapping his toes, while the judge, bailiff and prosecutors tried in vain to figure out where the distracting sound was coming from.

Felony Court, where defendants were first arraigned before being bound over for trial, was a cesspool. The crime syndicate usually owned the prosecutor, whose job it was to muff the preliminary hearing, so the judge could throw the case out of court.

The courtroom was always jammed, and busy lawyers walked forward, one after another, to drop twenty-dollar bills into the court clerk's desk drawer. By mid morning the drawer contained hundreds and hundreds of dollars. Attorneys who made the drop got their cases called early, so they could get back to other business. Those who didn't pay waited all day.

Taking pictures while court was in session was prohibited, yet the Chicago papers regularly ran front page photos of accused criminals standing before the bench.

This was accomplished quite simply. When a news photographer showed up to get a picture of someone on trial, a reporter from the same paper would walk up to the bench while court was in session and wink, "Excuse me, judge, but you have a phone call."

"Oh," said the judge. "Five minute recess." The judge then retired to his chambers to look out the window or grab a quick nip from a bottle, while the photographer took the judge's seat on the bench and snapped the startled defendant's picture with his flash camera.

Among the fledging prosecutors just out of law school in the late 1950s were Lou Garippo, an intense young Italian, and Jim Thompson, a tall, blond Scandinavian. Garippo went on to become a highly respected judge, and Thompson would ultimately become governor of Illinois.

Reporters who covered the building quickly deduced that Garippo was arrow-straight when he invited them to lunch, and insisted that each person pay his own share of the bill.

Garippo's honesty got in the way of his conscience when a distant cousin was arrested on a felony charge. Garippo was fearful that whichever judge heard the case would recognize the defendant's last name and give him a pass, as a favor to the prosecutor, thus making it look like Lou had put in the fix. At the same, Garippo's family didn't want the cousin to go to jail.

Garippo took his problem to George Wright. The snowy-haired *Chicago Tribune* reporter who had been covering the building since the Leopold-Loeb case was the undisputed dean of the Criminal Courts press corps. He knew more law than most of the legitimate attorneys who worked the building, and was often consulted on knotty cases.

"Just keep your ass out of it completely, Lou. I'll take care of it," Wright told the Garippo. Wright was always willing to do favors for lawyers, which meant that they owed him, and frequently tipped him off on stories before other reporters got wind of them.

Wright sought out Bieber, and told him, "Georgie, this kid is in trouble, and we gotta get him off. If there's anybody who can get this thing laughed out of court, it's you."

"George, whaddya askin' me for?" he said. "Jeez, you know I'll be glad to do it. You don't have to ask. What's the kid's name? I'll handle the case."

The case had been assigned to seventy-three-year-old Judge William J. Lindsay, a tough jurist, who was also known to take a drink on occasion. Bieber boned up on the case like he never had before, because he did not want to blow something in which the *Tribune* reporter was interested.

Wright, meanwhile, played double-safe by talking to the judge on the side, a practice that was not uncommon in those days.

On the day the case came to trial, the judge was quite obviously in his cups. Bieber broke out into a sweat when he noticed the venerable Wright, in a sincere brown suit, standing next to the judge on the bench.

Judge Lindsay remained impassive, and even dozed a bit, while the prosecution presented its case. When it came time for the defense, Bieber was ready. As he rose to call his first witness, Wright nudged the judge in the ribs and whispered, "This is the one I was telling you about."

"Oh?" said the judge, sitting bolt upright in the plush leather chair. "Defendant not guilty!" with a bang of the gavel.

Bieber gawked in astonishment, first at the boozy-eyed judge, then at Wright, who flashed him a wink. Turning to his young client, Bieber said, "Let's get the hell outa here. You're home."

A grateful Garippo, on hearing that Bieber had won the case, tried to pay the high priced defense lawyer, but Bieber refused. "Lou, you can't pay me because you didn't hire me," Bieber said. "I won it for Georgie."

Judge Lindsay subsequently eloped with a thirty-seven-year-old woman.

Bieber's climb to success had it's genesis with the arrest of a West-Side triggerman named Sam "Mooney" Giancana, for the theft of a bathtub. Giancana and a companion had stolen a milkman's delivery truck, with sliding side doors, and were using it to cart off the gleaming white tub from an apartment building under construction when they were caught in the act. They were astonished when the arresting officer turned down the standard $500 bribe offer. Furthermore, the cop added charges of attempted bribery of a police officer.

It was a hot case, because young Giancana was considered a "comer" in the local crime syndicate. The Mob's lawyer, Anthony Champagne, a fixer but no legal scholar, feared the wrath of the higher-ups if he bungled the defense.

He went to Bieber. "Georgie, would you handle this one in court for me?" Bieber accepted the challenge.

After studying the arrest sheet he went to the case prosecutor, Assistant State's Attorney Edward Egan. "Look, Eddie, the state ain't got a case here and you know it," he said. "First, you gotta prove the bathtub was stolen, right? Now, bathtubs don't have no serial numbers, and nobody has reported this one missing, and if they did, how would they prove it was theirs? There must be three hundred bathtubs in this building they swiped this one outa, and if they come up one short, how are they gonna know when it was taken, or if it was lost in shipment, or what? Right?"

Egan pondered the logic for a moment. "Well, Georgie, you're right. It is hard to identify a stolen bathtub—they all look alike. But, those two dagos did try to bribe a copper. We've got 'em by the short hairs on that, and they aren't getting off."

"Okay, Ed. We'll cop a plea to bribery, but I don't want no jail time. Just a fine. Okay?"

"I don't care what they get, as long as they're guilty," Egan said.

Bieber then made the customary approach to the judge, in chambers, explaining that his clients had agreed to plead guilty in exchange for a $1,000 fine. The judge agreed, "That sounds reasonable."

By the time the case was called, the judge was so drunk he had to be helped onto the dais, and he had his robe on backward. He listened bleary-eyed as the theft charges were dropped. Then the prosecutor stepped aside while Bieber pleaded his clients guilty of attempting to bribe an officer of the law.

"Wait a minute," the judge interrupted unexpectedly. "I want to hear the evidence before sentencing."

The astonished Bieber, sensing a double-cross, stepped back in dismay, holding his arms out in a "what did I do?" gesture as Giancana gave him the evil eye. The judge then called the arresting officer, who gave his account of the arrest.

"And this man offered you a $500 bribe?" the judge asked incredulously.

"Yes, your honor, he did," responded the policeman.

"And you refused a $500 bribe?"

"Yes, your honor."

"That's a goddam lie!" shouted the judge, pointing an angry finger at the police officer. "Not guilty! Case dismissed!"

"What the hell is this? Ain't we supposed to pay a fine?" asked the confused Giancana.

"Don't ask no questions, Mooney. Just get the hell outa here," instructed Bieber, making a quick exit himself.

Giancana later tried to pay Bieber, who turned down the money, saying, "You didn't hire me." Bieber collected a fat fee from Champagne, who billed Giancana an even larger amount.

Giancana subsequently rose to take over as god-father of the all-powerful crime syndicate in Chicago, and put Bieber on a flat retainer of $250,000 a year to represent any mob figure who was hailed into court.

While most defense attorneys found working out of Twenty-sixth and Cal a terrible inconvenience, Bieber and his fellow B-Boys, along with Crane and a select handful of the more interesting criminal lawyers, used the fourth floor press room as an office away from home.

Covering the building for the *Tribune*, in addition to George Wright, were George Woltman and Clay Gowran. Eddie Bush was the reporter for the *Chicago American*, Jesse L. Cook handled the beat for the *Sun-Times*, Ed Baumann worked the courts for the old *Chicago Daily News*, Jim Foree was assigned by the *Daily Defender*, and Bill E. Garrett and Dan Friedlander represented the City News Bureau.

There were no TV reporters, shouting inane questions and pushing microphones into people's faces, in that glory era.

The reporters worked out of a large room on the southwest corner of the building. The entire east wall was taken up by a long, bench-like desk, with a small section partitioned off for each reporter, who sat facing the wall, with a direct phone line to his city desk.

There was also a refrigerator, a coffee urn, a table and chairs for card playing, a leather couch for snoozing, and a large lavatory and shower. The north wall was occupied by an expensive array of aquariums, well stocked with colorful tropical fish.

In exchange for the privilege of hanging their coats in the press room, and receiving phone messages, the defense lawyers paid for the fish and financed their upkeep. There was no television in those days, and idle hours between trials were often spent seated in front of the tanks, hypnotically watching the fish.

Only one other person was permitted free run of the press room: Joseph Panczko. Pops, who frequently had cases pending before as many as three different judges, manned the phones and took messages while the reporters were busy making their rounds.

On a typical day Pops arrived at the building shortly after seven o'clock, carrying several bags of sweet rolls. One morning, as he clambered aboard the elevator, a seductive looking black woman with blonde hair, foggy eyes, and the tightest fitting dress he had ever seen got on with him.

Lenny, the elevator operator, knew without asking that Pops was getting off at the fourth floor. He looked at the woman. "Take me to Dreamland, baby," she said.

"Fifth floor, Narcotics Court," Lenny sang out.

Pops' first stop was Judge Daniel Ryan's courtroom, where he walked directly into the judge's chambers and laid a clean napkin and sweet roll on his desk. When the judge showed up he would note the roll and remark to his bailiff, "I see we have Pops in court again today."

From Ryan's court Pops headed for the press room, where he distributed the rolls to reporters and defense attorneys and brewed their morning coffee. On busy days, when several important trials were in session, and reporters could not be everywhere at once, Pops would dutifully report back to them on his own court appearances.

The Criminal Courts building was not air-conditioned, and one insufferably hot summer afternoon when the temperature climbed past 100, seventeen of the press room's precious fish turned belly-up and died. Pops came into the room during a recess in one of his trials while Bush was dipping out the dead fish and Cook was dropping ice cubes into the water to try to make the survivors more comfortable.

"What the hell happened?" asked the concerned burglar.

"The water's so warm the fish are keeling over," Bush told him.

Pops shook his head sadly. "Tell me what you guys need. I'll make a pet store on my way home tonight."

"Pops, you son-of-a-bitch. Mind your own business. You will NOT steal any fish," Wright reprimanded as he walked out the door to check a case.

When Wright returned he found that Pops had taken all seventeen dead fish out of the waste basket, and had lined them up on the table on a newspaper. With a pencil and note pad, he was painstakingly writing down a description of each of the corpses, along with their approximate measurements.

"What the hell are you up to now?" asked Wright in exasperation.

"Don't worry, George," Pops assured him. "Just tell me what da names of dese fishes are."

"Why?"

"Because I wanna stop at a pet store on my way down here tomorrow and BUY you gents a new fish for every one that died."

"Don't shit me, Pops."

"Honest to God. I won't steal nuttin. I'll pay for every one of 'em."

"Jesus Christ," said Wright in mock amazement. "I had you all wrong, Pops. You have my deepest apology."

"Then," continued Panczko, "I'm gonna take all dese dead fish back to da store tomorrow night and tell da guy dat all da fish he sold me died, an I want my money back."

"I give up," moaned Wright. "I'm going down to see what the grand jury's doing."

The grand jurors met in secret, but reporters discovered that by going into an unoccupied room, next to the grand jury quarters, and putting their ear to a drinking glass held against the wall, they could pick up bits of conversation. It was also customary to go into the room after the jurors had gone home for the day and empty out the waste baskets, which frequently contained notes of their deliberations.

Prosecutors were often accused of leaking grand jury proceedings to the press, but they were as baffled as anyone as to how reporters were getting the inside information.

Like the defense lawyers, Pops was always anxious to ingratiate himself to the reporters for letting him hang out in the press room.

When he overheard Cook lamenting the fact that it was hard getting by on a reporter's salary of $137 a week, Pops told him, "Ya wanna make some extra money?"

"Doing what?"

"We need somebody to sit in da car at night an' listen for police calls."

"Thanks, Pops, but I'd rather cover the trials, not end up as one of the players," Cook laughed.

Bush, an early admirer of Frank Sinatra, was addicted to bow ties. One morning Pops handed him a package saying, "Dis is for you. I know ya kin use 'em." The package contained a dozen snap-on bow ties, for which the *American* reporter was indeed grateful. He was not the least bit surprised to read in his own newspaper that evening that a clothing salesman's car had been broken into.

On seeing the Daily News reporter poring over a boat catalog, Pops inquired about his interest in watercraft, how big a boat he dreamed of owning, the type of engine—inboard or outboard—cabin cruiser or open. The reporter answered every question, flattered at Panczko's interest, until it dawned on him that Pops was taking an order, and intended to break into Rodi's Boatyard.

"I really don't want a boat, Pops. I just like to look at the pictures," he lied.

"It won't cost ya nuttin."

"No, thanks, Pops."

"Well, I gotta be in Morrissey's court at tree o'clock. Lemme know if ya change yer mind."

This was Twenty-Sixth and Cal, where Pops spent most of his non-working hours.

CHAPTER 20

ONE SCREWDRIVE, HOLD THE ONIONS

Probably no case in Pops Panczko's vast repertoire of court performances attracted more attention than the celebrated "screwdrive" trial of 1959.

Edward Koniecki, forty-three, and his nineteen-year-old son, Dennis, made a citizens' arrest at gunpoint after their homemade burglar alarm went off in the middle of the night, and they surprised Pops in the garage behind their house at 1715 North Wood Street with a large screwdriver in his hand.

Koniecki was a hosiery salesman. Pops had spotted his car some days earlier, made a license plate check, and got his home address. After letting himself into the garage Pops discovered that Koniecki had such a large inventory, that he raised the overhead door to make it easier to move the stuff out.

That's when he encountered Koniecki, standing in the driveway with a revolver in his hand. Pops turned to duck out the side door, but found his way blocked by Koniecki's six-foot, 250-pound son, brandishing a hunting knife.

"Lay down on the floor," the burly teen-ager commanded.

"Hey, I got tree hunnert in my pocket," Pops replied. "Take da money. I got a record and dis won't look so good for me."

"Throw the money on the floor."

Pops threw the three hundred on the floor, just as several squad cars pulled up. Koniecki's wife had phoned police when the burglar alarm went off in the couple's bedroom. Panczko stooped over and scooped up the money as police entered the garage with guns drawn.

"Hey, Pops. What's going on?" one of them asked.

Pops shrugged his shoulders. He couldn't figure it out himself. A wagon was called, and he was taken to the Racine Avenue station and charged with burglary.

Police Captain Thomas Murphy had a hunch on this one. On the following night he assigned Patrolmen Henry Glazik and Cornelius Casey to visit the Koniecki home and stay awhile. At 7 o'clock the telephone rang, and Casey picked it up.

"This is a friend of Panczko," the caller explained. "He's a nice guy, and maybe if you lay off, it might be worth your while."

"Well, ah, okay," Casey said. "But if you want to make it worth my while you'd better come over right now, because I got to go out with my wife."

A few minutes later the doorbell rang. Casey opened it and smiled, "Hi, Butch. You're under arrest." Butch and his companion, William Heneghan, were charged with intimidating a home owner.

"We weren't doing nothin'," Butch complained. "We were just out, and thought we'd drop in and say hello."

The charges against Butch and his pal were thrown out of court by Judge William V. Daly when Koniecki failed to identify either man as those who had tried to intimidate him. In their zealousness to arrest the pair, police had whisked the two culprits off to jail before Koniecki ever got a look at them.

But the burglary charge against Pops stuck. He had been caught in the act. George Bieber was at his imaginative best as he skilfully guided the case through the court system. Then Pops missed an appearance before Chief Justice Abraham Lincoln Marovitz. "Your honor," Bieber prevaricated. "Mr.

Panczko simply made a mistake. He went to church with his little grandchildren this morning when he should have been here in your honor's court."

Marovitz was touched. The judge placed a high value on the family structure, and often lectured defendants in his court about the responsibilities of parenthood. Unaware that the forty-year-old thief had neither children nor grandchildren, he routinely ordered Panczko's $5,000 bond forfeited, but quietly assured Bieber he would return the money as soon as Pops showed up.

The real reason Pops hadn't appeared in court was that police had arrested him on a warrant from Wisconsin in connection with the $25,000 robbery of a jewelry store in Madison. Pops refused to waive extradition. A hearing was held, and Wisconsin Governor Vernon Thompson dismissed the arrest warrant after Dane County District Atty. Joseph Bloodgood admitted under oath that he lacked sufficient evidence to make the charges stick.

Next Pops had the misfortune of running afoul of Sergeant George Kush, the same cop who had once arrested him in a downtown hotel while a jewelers convention was in progress. Kush, along with Detectives Thomas Gaughn and Patrick Daley decided to see what Panczko was up to when they spotted him at California and Division Streets, where he had been busted so many times before.

Pops opted not to tell them, and a twenty-minute donnybrook ensued before the three police officers were able to put the wiry suspect into handcuffs. "I don't know nothin' about nothin'," Panczko insisted after he was taken to the lockup.

"We'll see about that," Kush said.

A search of Panczko's car turned up a ring of keys, none of which fit Pops' Oldsmobile. Then Kush put on his thinking cap, and recalled that a jewelry salesman from Warrenville, Ohio, had complained to Chicago police a month earlier that somebody had been following him. Kush went through a batch of month-old reports and came up with the salesman's name, Linn Bates.

On a hunch Kush drove all the way to Warrenville with Panczko's ring of keys. When he got to the Bates home, the first key he tried opened the trunk of the salesman's car, where Bates kept his sample cases. Quite pleased with himself, Kush drove back to Chicago and charged Pops with disorderly conduct, resisting arrest, and possession of burglary tools—to wit, the key to Bates' car trunk.

Judge Daly again threw the case out of court, ruling that police could not charge Pops with a crime because no crime had been committed. Indeed, the overzealous cops had busted Pops before he'd had a chance to see if the Bates key worked.

With the Koniecki burglary trial still hanging over his head, Pops decided to see what he could do to help his own case. He did what every clear thinking Chicagoan did when he had a problem: He went to see his alderman. Naturally he left several hundred dollars with the alderman as a symbol of his good faith.

The alderman phoned Koniecki and invited him to come in to the ward office for a chat. "Look, Pops is just a local character who didn't mean any harm," the alderman explained. "We don't want to cause the poor devil any trouble, do we?"

"Well, what am I supposed to do? I already told the cops I caught him in my garage," Koniecki said.

"When you get on the witness stand, just say that Pops was in the alley taking a leak, and you pushed him into your garage by mistake because you thought he was up to something else."

Instead of following the script when he was called on to testify in court, Koniecki developed amnesia. He told Judge Robert English, "I have been in the case too long. I have a heart condition and I fear for the safety of my wife and family. I don't want them involved."

English, one of the few Criminal Court judges that reporters did not suspect of being on the take, would have none of the game. He threatened Koniecki with contempt of court unless he explained how he happened to bring about

Panczko's arrest. Koniecki then reluctantly told the jury that he was awakened by his burglar alarm, looked out the window and saw Panczko standing outside his garage. He said he and his son forced Pops into the garage, where they held him until police arrived.

Bieber and Devine argued that there was no evidence of guilt, if indeed Pops had not originally been found in the garage.

The jury of nine women and three men saw it their way, too. They deliberated for one hour and forty-five minutes before bringing in a verdict of innocent. Pops leaped to his feet and yelled, "Tank you, ladies and gentlemen. I know I shouldn't shout like dis but I'm excited."

State's Attorney Benjamin S. Adamowski was not excited, but appalled when he heard the verdict. He promptly sent his assistants back before the grand jury and had Panczko indicted for possession of a burglar tool—namely the ninety-eight-cent screwdriver he was holding in his hand when Koniecki and son took him into custody.

Pops was arraigned on the charge, and released on bond pending trial. Police, totally frustrated at Panczko's charmed life, put a twenty-four-hour tail on him, hoping to catch him in the act of breaking the law and finally making one of the charges stick.

"I can't work. I can't do nuttin'. Da cops are tailing me day and night," Pops complained to reporters, while relaxing one afternoon on the front steps of the Criminal Courts building, where he had just won a continuance of the latest charges against him.

"Aw, Pops, you're getting paranoid. Nobody's tailing you."

"I ain't either. See dat car parked across da street wit' two guys in it? Dere cops. Dere watchin' me. Get a load of dis!"

As the reporters watched, Panczko sprinted out into California Boulevard and clambered aboard the tailgate of a passing produce truck heading south. Sure enough, the car containing Detectives Gene Irvin and Robert Pettler made a U-turn and took off after the truck.

Taking a quick inventory of his surroundings, Pops determined he was riding with a load of onions. Reaching into the gunny sack he was sitting on, he extracted an onion and hurled it at the pursuing police car. Then he threw another, and another, bouncing Bermudas off the cops' hood and windshield as they hit the siren and pulled the truck over to the side.

"What's the trouble, officers? I wasn't going too fast, was I?" asked Frank Landato, the driver.

"You didn't do a thing," Irvin told him. "We're interested in your passenger."

"Passenger? All I got back there is a load of onions."

"Take a look."

"Well, I'll be damned. Who's he?"

"You've just been hijacked by Pops Panczko."

Indeed, Pops was put in handcuffs and charged with attempting to hijack a load of onions.

"I never took no onions," he scoffed. "I just figured I'd flip a ride to Cicero Avenue and catch me a bus. Look, here's fifty bucks. It's all I got on me, but lemme go and I'll give ya anudder fifty later."

The detectives added a charged of attempted bribery. When he was taken to detective headquarters and searched, they found he was carrying a pocketful of lead slugs for pay telephones.

As soon as Bieber got Pops out on bail, the surveillance resumed. Pops was sipping beer in a saloon at Chicago and Fairfield Avenues several days later when he spotted a battered old jalopy parked at the curb with two men in it. "Jeez," he mumbled. "Who do dey tink dere kiddin'?"

Pops went to the phone, dropped a slug in the coin slot, and made a brief call. Then he returned to his table and ordered another beer.

Within minutes the air was filled with the scream of sirens, and the street outside the saloon was jammed with squad cars and motorcycle cops. Police surrounded the jalopy and ordered the two shabbily dressed men who had been sitting in it to come out with their hands up. It seems an anonymous citizen had telephoned police and reported the two suspicious looking characters.

By the time the two detectives in disguise had convinced the horde of lawmen that they, too, were police officers, Pops had drained his beer and ducked out the back door. What he really wanted to do was walk out the front door and give the cops the finger, but there's no sense pushing one's luck.

It was in his best interest to keep a low profile, at least until the screwdriver trial was disposed of.

A jury of eight men and four women was selected to hear the case in the court of Judge Burton M. Bergstrom. Bieber and Devine looked like the cats that swallowed the canary as they pulled up their chairs alongside Pops at the defense table, opposite prosecutors Lewis Gaines and Robert Conley.

"Your honor, the defense would like to request Mr. Gaines to read the indictment to the jury," Bieber announced loudly.

Bergstrom raised his eyebrows and said, "Request granted."

Gaines, somewhat confused by the unusual move, read the indictment in which Joseph Panczko was charged with possession of a burglar tool—"one screw driver."

"Er, would you please read that last part again?" Bieber requested, cupping one ear as if he was hard of hearing. "Exactly."

Gaines wrinkled his forehead and studied the indictment. "One screw drive," he mumbled.

"Thank you, Mr. Prosecutor," Bieber oozed. "Now, the first thing we gotta do is find out what a 'screw drive' is."

"I think a 'screw drive' is the mechanical term for the drive rod for the propeller of a ship," offered Devine, rising to his feet.

"Your honor, this is just a typographical error on the indictment," Gaines stammered. "It obviously should say screw driver."

"If the defense wants to move for a mistrial, I will sustain the motion," Judge Bergstrom encouraged. "I must admit I'm beginning to get a little confused."

"Your honor, the defendant demands that he be tried on the charge for which he was indicted," Bieber insisted.

"I've done some extensive research on the subject," Devine interjected. "The dictionary defines 'screw drive' as a verb, meaning: To drive in, as does a screwdriver. Pops is either charged with possessing the mechanism for turning the propeller of a ship, or with possessing a verb." Now Panczko looked confused.

"For God's sake! It's a simple typographical error that doesn't mean a thing," argued Gaines.

At this point Bergstrom had to bang his gavel to quiet the spectators, who were rolling in the aisles with laughter, while doing his level best to suppress his own. "I am continuing this matter until tomorrow," he declared. "When court resumes I will expect the prosecution and defense attorneys to have resolved this problem."

Bieber and Devine agreed to let the indictment stand, figuring they could use the typo as grounds for an appeal, in the unlikely event the jury found Pops guilty.

Prosecutor Gaines called Edward Koniecki, who testified that he was in the garage when he heard the door slam. "When I turned on the lights, I found that my son had Mr. Panczko in custody," he said.

Since witnesses are not permitted to sit in on one another's testimony, Dennis Koniecki was unaware of what his father stated. He told the jury that he entered the garage to find Panczko lying on the floor, guarded by his father.

Embarrassed, Gaines announced that he would recall the elder Koniecki to the stand "to straighten out some small discrepancies." Bieber and Devine strenuously objected, and Bergstrom agreed to let the jury sort out which story they were going to believe.

The prosecution then called Police Officer Stephen Agin, the wagonman. He testified that Panczko was lying on his right side, on the garage floor, holding a screwdriver aloft by its blade in his right hand when he pulled up at the scene.

Agin's partner, Rodney Longdon, offered yet another version. "Panczko was sitting in a crouched position, with his knee in the air, holding the screwdriver by its handle, near the floor," he told the jury.

Longdon was followed on the witness stand by a uniformed police officer. Gaines was about to question the policeman when he took a good look at him and said, "Hey, this isn't our witness." The officer, who was never introduced, left the courtroom without anyone explaining what he was doing there.

The trial was thrown into an uproar the following morning when one of the jurors, Richard Moll, sixty, advised Judge Bergstrom that someone had mailed him an envelope full of newspaper clippings detailing Panczko's life of crime.

"Nobody but the defense would pull a stunt like that," Gaines exploded. "They're just trying to get a mistrial."

Judge Bergstrom, seeming only too eager to get the comedy of errors off his back, turned to the defense lawyers and asked, "Do you have a motion to file at this time?"

"No, your honor," Bieber answered innocently. "We don't want no mistrial. We think the state did this so they could get a mistrial."

At long last the case went to the jury, which simply had to decide whether Pops had been caught inside Koniecki's garage, or in the alley; was empty handed, was clutching three hundred dollars, or was holding a screwdriver by the point, or by the handle; as he lay on the garage floor on his right side, or sat with one knee up in the air.

To almost everyone's amazement, the jury found Panczko guilty of possessing a burglar tool—on the same occasion in which a previous jury had found him innocent of burglary. Bieber was baffled. "How could the screwdriver be a burglary tool if the other jury already decided he wasn't doing a burglary with it?"

Pops remained free on bond pending sentencing, while Judge English, who had presided over the earlier trial, took care of some unfinished business. English ordered the arrest of Edward Koniecki, declared him in contempt of court, and sentenced him to one year in jail for giving conflicting testimony in the screwdriver case.

Koniecki, the ill fated hosiery salesman, was dumbstruck. "I catch a guy in my garage and I go to jail. What in the hell's is going on here?"

Reporters watched with satisfaction as Koniecki was marched off to jail. He got what was coming to him, they figured, for jeopardizing their free coffee and rolls.

But English wasn't through yet. He also hailed Pops into court for contempt because he had remarked to Police Officer James Corbett, within earshot of the jury, "You're trying to frame me wit' a screwdriver."

"Naw, I never said nuttin' like dat," Pops protested indignantly. "What I told Corbett was, 'When dis trial is over, I wanna frame dat screwdriver!'"

"Your tale is so fanciful as to be incredible," the straightlaced English scoffed. "I am sentencing you to one year in jail with Mr. Koniecki."

As always, Panczko's lawyers managed to get him freed on bond while they filed an appeal.

The next case to go to trial was the matter of hijacking the truckload of onions. That one was thrown out of court in short order after Landato, the truck driver, was unable to tell exactly how many onions Pops had taken, if any. Nor was he able to identify any of the onions thrown at the pursuing police car as positively having come from his load.

Now the matter of the screwdriver conviction came up before Judge Bergstrom for sentencing. For this one Bieber and Devine tried an entirely new approach. They challenged Bergstrom's jurisdiction, arguing that an order appointing him to the bench had never been entered in the court clerk's records downtown.

The hearing was delayed for several hours while the harried Gaines raced down to the Loop office of the Superior Court's Executive Committee to obtain a photostat of the committee's order appointing Bergstrom to Criminal Court.

True, the appointment had not been entered in the clerk's records, however the Superior Court panel contended its order did not have to be entered to establish Bergstrom's right to sit on the bench, since he had been appointed by Governor William G. Stratton to fill a vacancy left by the death of another judge.

Once it was finally established that Bergstrom was indeed legitimate, Panczko was brought back before him to be sentenced for possessing the much discussed screwdriver.

In order to show that Pops was a hardened criminal who deserved a long prison stretch, Gaines brought in Panczko's parole officers, Sam Bonafede and William Evangalista. To the prosecutor's dismay, both testified under cross examination that Pops was one of their best parolees, who stayed home nights like he was supposed to while under their supervision.

Gaines objected to his own witnesses heaping praise on the convicted felon, but the judge pointed out that it was the prosecution that had brought them in to testify. After the furor subsided he handed Panczko a relatively light sentence of three to four years in prison as an habitual criminal.

Pops still did not go to jail, however. He remained free on bond while Bieber filed an appeal. Several months later the Illinois Supreme Court set aside the conviction for possession of a burglary tool, and reversed the conviction for contempt of court.

Pops Panczko was a free man!

Of course, all of Bieber's legal shenanigans did not come cheap, and Pops was forced to go to work immediately to get money to pay his bills. He hopped into his Oldsmobile and drove directly to the Merchandise Mart, in search of a jewelry salesman.

Pops parked the car on Orleans Street and went inside to look for a mark. When he came back out, the Olds was gone.

"What the f . . ."

There was only one thing to do, and it was really embarrassing. As he hiked over to the Eighteenth District Police Station on Chicago Avenue, Pops formulated a plan so the coppers wouldn't laugh at him. He would go on the offensive.

"Somebody stoled my car!" he shouted as he angrily barged into the familiar station. "What's dis city comin' to? It's gettin' so ya can't leave yer car for ten minutes witout some lousy teef takin' off wit' it!"

"Pops, for chrissake, calm down and tell me what this is all about," an amused Sergeant Patrick Bimmerlee said, directing him to a chair. "You say somebody stole your car?"

"Yeah. I parked out in front of da Mersh and went inside on business. I wasn't gone ten minutes when I come back and my car was gone."

Bimmerlee got a stolen auto report form and told Pops, "Settle down and give me the details."

"It's a 1958 Oldsmobile, four door sedan," Pops related. "White and charcoal colored. Equipped wit' a burglar alarm."

"Equipped with a burglar alarm?" Bimmerlee repeated, somewhat surprised.

"Yeah," Panczko said sheepishly. "But I forgot to turn it on."

Pops did not bother to tell Bimmerlee that he had also left the keys in the ignition, in case he had to make a quick get-away.

He gave two patrol officers twenty-five dollars to drive him around the neighborhood in their squad car, but his Olds was nowhere to be seen. They brought him back to the station and he called a cab to take him home.

Three days later Jack Regan, a young soldier home on leave, appeared at Panczko's door. "Do you own a '58 Olds?" he asked.

"Yeah, somebody swiped it. Do ya know where it is?"

"Yes, sir. It's in a no parking zone at Damen Avenue and Twenty-first Street, and neighborhood kids are jumping all over the roof."

"Howdja know it's my car?"

"I found some parking tickets with your address under the sun visor."

Pops pulled out his wallet and handed Regan twenty-five dollars. "Dis is a reward," he explained. "Ya know, I was almost a soldier myself once."

Pops called a cab and went to pick up his car, which by now had five parking tickets stuffed under the windshield wipers and footprints all over the roof. He drove a half a block and it stalled. Unable to get it going, he called a wrecker and had it towed to a gas station at Damen and Superior Street, where he knew Bill, the owner.

"Pops, somebody put sugar in your tank," Bill said, shaking his head.

"Kin ya fix it?"

"Gotta drain the tank and clean out the fuel line. It'll cost you a hundred bucks."

"Go ahead."

Bill got the car running, but not for long. The following day it stalled again. Same problem. Somebody was trying to keep Pops off the street, and he had a pretty good idea who it was. It kept him awake at night. "Some people count sheep. I count cops," he mused while lying in bed.

After getting the tank drained again, Pops put a locking gas cap on the car. This stymied whoever was sugaring him, but only brought on new problems.

The next morning, as he was getting dressed, he heard a series of popping sounds. When he went out to his car to drive to the bakery for his morning rolls, he discovered that someone had shot the vehicle full of holes. The windshield was blown out, the rear window was blasted, and there were bullet holes in the doors and trunk lid.

Pops took the car to his insurance man, who shook his head in disbelief and wrote Panczko a check for the damages.

Pops didn't bother to fix the car. He cashed the insurance check and sold the vehicle, "as is," to a neighborhood priest who frequented the same gas station he did.

After replacing the windows, the priest reveled in driving around in the bullet-riddled Oldsmobile. "This car used to belong to a famous gangster, but now it's in the hands of the Lord," he told his parishioners. There was supposed to be a hidden message there for them to grasp.

Pops, meanwhile, used the proceeds from the auto sale to pick up a used jalopy. For a test run he drove it over to the candy store at Grand and Noble, where he sat in at the ongoing card game. When he got ready to go home, all four of his tires were flat.

Pops contacted a police officer with whom he was on speaking terms. "What the hell's goin' on around here, O'Malley? I never had so many problems."

"They want you off the streets, Pops," the cop told him. "Who do you think it was that stole your other car in the first place? They had you under surveillance when you parked in front of the Mart and left your keys in the ignition. It was the coppers who drove your Olds to the Southwest Side and left it in the no parking zone."

"What did I ever do to dem? I never hurt no cop."

"Pops, believe me. You do too much damage. You don't realize how much paper work you put the department through. They're out to destroy you."

As the cat-and-mouse game continued, Pops devised a new strategy. Once a month he applied for a new set of license plates, slightly altering the serial number of his car for each set. By the time word got around on the force and police were laying for his model car with a certain license plate number, he was driving around with a different set of plates.

The ruse served him no good a week later, however, when two uniformed officers in a patrol car drove down an alley and caught him coming out the back door of a women's fashion shop with an arm load of expensive dresses. The cops handcuffed him and put him in the back seat of the squad car.

"Hey, what's goin' on? You guys know me."

"We've got you cold bang, Pops."

"I'll give ya a tousand dollars."

Silence. The arresting officers were thinking it over.

"Move da car. Move da car," Pops urged from the back seat.

"What the hell for?"

"Because if any more cops come, my bill will go higher. I'm out on bond. If you guys bust me, I'm on the way to the penitentiary. Den nobody gets nuttin'. Take it or leave it."

The police car pulled out of the alley and onto a side street. "Okay, Pops, give it to us."

"I'll meet ya at twelve o'clock tomorrow noon at Western and Chicago, in da restaurant on da corner."

"You ain't got the money on you?"

"Hell no. Who walks the streets at night wit' a grand in his pockets?"

"Well . . ."

"C'mon. All da years dat ya know me, have I ever cheated a cop? Tomorrow. I'll be dere. Twelve noon."

The two patrolmen gave Pops a pass. The next day, true to his word, he was in the restaurant at Western and Chicago Avenues when they came in, wearing civilian clothes, and ordered coffee. Pops slipped them the thousand bucks. They pocketed the money, drank their coffee and left—sticking Pops with the tab.

CHAPTER 21

PEANUTS COMES HOME; POPS GOES BYE-BYE

The high point of 1960, from the Panczko point of view, was Peanuts' release from the Tennessee state prison. The three thieving brothers would soon be together again.

Their legit brother, Frank, and his wife, Adeline, were waiting outside the gates in Nashville at 7 o'clock on a June morning as Peanuts walked out into the sunlight, shading his eyes. The warden walked out with him, one hand on Peanuts' shoulder, like the two were old friends.

"Now that you're on the outside, tell me PanZeeKo, what's goin' on in there?"

"Whadya mean, warden?"

"Well now, I don't mind confidin' in you. I'm a little bit alarmed over some rumbles we been gettin' about weapons being smuggled in to the inmates. You've been a trusty, and chairman of the inmates grievance committee and all. I figure that if anyone knows what's coming off in there, it's you."

"Warden, I don't know nothin' about nothin'," Peanuts told him. "It's been nice knowin' ya."

With that he climbed into the back seat of his brother's car and urged, "Let's get outa here."

"Don't you wanna stop for breakfast or anything?"

"Yeah, but not until we get outa Nashville. I never want to see this town again. No way! Never!"

They drove on up to Clarksville, just below the Kentucky border, before they stopped. Then the trio continued non-stop back to Chicago. Frank and Adeline spent most of the trip lecturing Peanuts on the folly of a life of crime, and the new opportunity he was getting to turn his life around.

"Frank, Adeline, you don't have to say nothin'," Peanuts assured them. "This boy's learned his lesson, that's for sure. As soon as we get back home I'm going to find a job."

Actually, as soon as they got back home he pulled a job. The first thing Peanuts did on planting his feet back to the old neighborhood was connect with Lover Boy Mendola. The two of them then drove out to Oak Park, where they broke into a warehouse and made off with 12,000 Sunbeam electric shavers.

Peanuts bought a new red Chevrolet with his proceeds of the score. He also took a new wife, and rented a small apartment in the western suburb of Bellwood.

Norma, an attractive divorcee with two small children, was originally from Knoxville. Her brother-in-law was Mendola's cellmate in the Tennessee prison, and as soon as he got out, Mendola looked her up. She was working as a waitress at the time. Mendola introduced her to Peanuts. Having had no association with the opposite sex in nearly nine years, he couldn't wait to get married.

As he had with Lauretta, Peanuts spent more time with his buddies at the ballpark than he did at home.

And when he wasn't enjoying a ball game, he was out on a score. Where he used to leave Lauretta home, however, he now made Norma an unwilling accomplice on some of his capers.

With Lover Boy as a partner, Peanuts was stealing almost full time. In addition to burglarizing three or four men's clothing shops a week, they were knocking off currency exchanges by breaking through the back doors with a battering ram he had mounted on the front of his car.

They were making as much as $80,000 on a score, but Peanuts blew it almost as fast as he could count it, betting as much as $20,000 on a single baseball game.

He had one particularly close call when he and another partner, Irish Murray, hit a currency exchange on Lincoln

Avenue shortly after nine o'clock one morning, right after the Brinks truck had made a big cash delivery. What they did not know was that an off-duty policeman was drinking in a saloon next door when the alarm went off.

As Peanuts and Irish made a run for it, the cop came out shooting. Their souped-up 1940 Ford get-away car took three hits as the bandits sped off, but neither man was injured.

After that Peanuts and Lover Boy decided to go into the cartage business. Unloading trucks, of course. Not hauling. They cruised the rail yards, and when they spotted a semi-trailer with a load of clothing, television sets, cigarettes or pharmaceutical products, they hooked up to it and drove away. When the owners found the trailer on a side street the next day it would be empty.

They often worked with a fellow thief, Charlie Sexton, whom they used as somewhat of a human divining rod. "Charlie, he can smell a load of cigarettes a mile away," Peanuts boasted.

The trucking companies fought back, however. Peanuts and his pals soon discovered the trailers had their wheels booted, so they could not be towed away, or found security men patrolling the loading docks.

No problem. Peanuts switched to truck stops. Driving a semi of their own, he and his cohorts would pull into a highway truck stop and watch a driver when he went in to grab some lunch. While the driver was eating, they would back their own trailer up flush against the rear of the unattended semi, cut the lock, and transfer the load. They would be gone before the driver returned to his rig and went on his way, often not realizing he had been cleaned out until he got to his destination.

Peanuts never pushed a good thing too far. Once truck drivers began getting cautious, he switched to jewelry sales-man. In one instance, he had followed a salesman from his home in Wheaton to the post office, where the man had placed his sample case in a lock box the night before.

Peanuts had a red flasher light on the dashboard of his car, a spotlight, and a siren, which he plugged into the cigarette lighter. As the salesman drove away from the post office, Peanuts put on a policeman's cap, complete with badge, plugged in the siren, and motioned for the salesman to pull over.

"Okay, guys. He's gettin' outa the car. Go! Go!"

Frank DeLegge and Mike LaJoy, who were crouched down in the back seat of Peanuts' car, jumped out and grabbed the startled salesman before he realized he wasn't being placed under arrest. Pushing him aside, the two men got into his car and drove off. Peanuts took off after them, with his red light flashing, leaving the salesman standing in the road.

The men drove six blocks to an isolated spot, where they ditched the salesman's car after removing his sample case, containing approximately $100,000 worth of gems.

The M.O. was so successful that the boys used the same trick to hijack a truckload of Alberto VO-5 hair cream from near the Alberto-Culver plant in Melrose Park.

When their souped-up Ford getaway car became too well known, Peanuts and his partners switched to a four-speed Pontiac as a work car. That might have thrown police off the track a little, but they all knew Panczko's personal car, the bright red Chevrolet, on sight.

He parked the Chevy a block away one night when he, Mendola, and a few of his regulars knocked off an air conditioner store on Lincoln Avenue. They loaded the units aboard a truck and headed for a garage at Augusta Boulevard and Western Avenue, with Peanuts and Mendola leading the way in the Pontiac. As they pulled into an alley behind the garage they spotted several squad cars lying in wait.

"Hang on," Peanuts yelled, as he hit the gas and took off with tires squealing. Police hit the red lights and sirens and took off after the Pontiac. Mendola monitored police calls on the radio, warning of possible road blocks ahead, while Peanuts kept one eye on the rear-view mirror and the other on the road. An expert wheelman, Peanuts eventually broke away from their pursuers at Central and Chicago Avenues, on the Northwest Side.

"We lost 'em," Peanuts told Lover Boy. "Let's go back and pick up my Chevy and get the hell home and go to bed."

It was almost daylight as they pulled up to the red Chevy on Lincoln Avenue. Peanuts could tell as they approached that all was not well.

"Look how low my car's riding," he told Mendola. "What the hell's goin' on here, Guy? Aw, shit. Lookit! Them fuckin' coppers let all the air outa my tires." That wasn't all. Once he had pumped up all four tires he still couldn't go anywhere. Detective William Hanhardt's burglary investigators had also removed the Chevrolet's distributor cap. It was their way of letting Peanuts know they were onto him, even though he hadn't been caught with the goods.

In no time at all Peanuts was rolling in more money than he was able to gamble away. He used some of the surplus to buy a $30,000 bi-level home with attached garage at 654 Winston Dr., in west suburban Melrose Park. He also figured it would be wise to get rid of his distinctive red Chevy, much as he loved it. He traded it in on a lime green Cadillac.

By now police had deduced that the rash of thefts from clothing stores, currency exchanges and semi trailers had coincided with Peanuts' release from prison, and placed him under heavy surveillance. It took Peanuts approximately the same amount of time to deduce that the cops were suddenly watching every move he made, and probably had his phone line tapped.

This called for a new strategy. He had a second telephone installed in the family room of his home, and entrusted the unlisted number to only a handful of his most faithful friends, such as Marty Gariti, Snuffy Ryan and Polack Bruno. He also brought Norma into the act, recruiting her to play a role she did not relish.

Whenever any of the boys had a job lined up, one of them would call Peanuts on his private line and say, "Tell your wife to go out for some milk." That was to throw off anyone who might be eavesdropping.

Peanuts would then slip into the attached garage and climb into the trunk of his Cadillac, and pull the lid shut after him. Norma would open the garage doors, get into the Caddy under the watchful eyes of the surveillance team, and drive over to the Winston Plaza shopping mall. Her orders were to leave the car in the parking lot and spend the next hour or so in the stores.

As soon as Norma left the car Peanuts' pals would pull up in another auto, let him out of the trunk, and he'd go off with them on a score, wearing plastic face masks. When Norma returned at the appointed time, he'd be back in the trunk with his share of the loot as she drove home and parked the car in the garage. From the vantage point of the surveillance team parked just down the block, Peanuts had never left the house.

The cops had their suspicions, however, after one particularly rewarding haul. A mechanic for the Brinks armored car company tipped off the gang that a $40,000 cash delivery was going to be made to the Sears warehouse in Franklin Park.

Norma drove to Winston Plaza and parked in the lot as instructed. Peanuts' pals let him out of the trunk, and they drove to nearby Franklin Park, where they donned their plastic masks and relieved the Brinks guards of the $40,000 in payroll money.

The next morning Peanuts couldn't resist putting on his Bermuda shorts and puttering around the yard under the watchful eyes of the surveillance team. Seeing him outside they drove up to the front of the house and called him over to the curb.

"What?" Peanuts demanded defensively, squinting into the car window.

"That Sears score yesterday," one of the cops said. "It's got your name written all over it. The guys who did it wore plastic face masks. That's your M.O., Peanuts."

"So?"

"We were watching, and you never left the house. Otherwise, I'd swear you pulled it off."

"Yeah, well, I guess it's a good thing you guys were here," Peanuts said. "You're my alibi, right?"

"Just keep one thing in mind, Panczko. We'll be on you, day and night."

"Thanks for the warning. I'm keeping my nose clean," Peanuts replied. "Have a good day."

Like so many of Peanuts' scores, the Sears heist was never solved. The inquisitive police had their man, but they didn't know it.

Things were heating up around Chicago, however, so Peanuts figured it was once again time to shift his operations farther afield, where every cop wouldn't recognize him on sight. He decided to try his luck in Minnesota.

Two of his regulars, Marty Gariti and Snuffy Ryan, had done time with an ex-con named Tony Legato, from the Minneapolis-St. Paul area, where his father was a police sergeant. Tony had often said, "Come on up. They got payrolls every Friday that'll knock your eyes out."

"Why don't we take your pal, Tony, up on his invitation?" Peanuts suggested. "Give the Chicago coppers a rest."

Good idea!

So they drove up to Minneapolis, where Legato had several jobs already cased for them. "We don't have currency exchanges in the Twin Cities like you got in Chicago," he explained. "The taverns all load up on dough every Friday, and people come in after work and cash their paychecks and have a few beers."

Peanuts and the boys checked into a motel near the University of Minnesota campus, where they could lie low until it was time to go to work. On Friday they stole a car and parked near a busy bank. When a saloon keeper came out with a loaded money bag, they followed him to his bar, put on their plastic face masks, and relieved him of the money when he got out of his car. Then they would ditch the stolen auto and drive back to Chicago in their souped-up getaway car.

It was the easiest money Peanuts ever made. The tavern owners usually walked out of the bank with anywhere from $30,000 to $50,000, which meant Peanuts, Marty, Snuffy and Tony were averaging $10,000 each, and cash was one commodity they did not have to run through a fence. It was all theirs.

For the next half a year they kept their weekends clear to drive up to Minneapolis-St. Paul, lying in wait outside a different bank on each occasion. Police suspected the holdup men were from Chicago, and began to set up roadblocks. When Peanuts picked up roadblock reports on his police radio, he simply headed for a hospital or shopping center, which had a large parking lot. Then he and his accomplices would kill several hours, walking around or shopping, until the road blocks were lifted and they could head home.

Legato hit it right off with the boys, and returned to Chicago with them, as a regular member of the Panczko team.

While Peanuts was not averse to hitting the road to make a good haul, Pops continued to confine his activities to Chicago, where his luck was not always the best.

When he stopped in to kibitz a card game one afternoon he found police Lieutenant Anthony De Grazio sitting at the table with several known mob figures. Recognizing the burglar, De Grazio ordered him to leave.

"What for? I ain't doin' nuttin'," Pops protested.

"You're under surveillance," De Grazio said. "We don't need some asshole like you bringing any heat down on this place. Get the fuck out of here before I run you in."

"Hey, lieutenant, dey ain't watchin' dis place for Pops," Panczko argued, speaking of himself in the third person. "You're da one dat's hot. You're da one they're watchin'."

Pops was being argumentative, and wanted it known he was leaving under protest. He did not realize how prophetic his statement would be. A short time later De Grazio was kicked off the force after it was disclosed that he and his wife had toured Europe for thirty-nine days with Crime Syndicate chieftain Anthony J. Accardo and his wife, Clarice.

What De Grazio said was indeed true about Pops, however. The police were out to get him.

One evening, as he and George "Stogie" Fedore were about to relieve a fur salesman of his array of samples at

Austin Boulevard and Chicago Avenue, three police officers approached with their service revolvers drawn. Stogie jumped into their getaway car and sped off. Pops was left standing there wearing a sheepish grin on his face.

"All I got wit' me is a pair of lock pullers," he explained. "I'll give ya tree hunnert bucks if ya let me go. Ya know I'm good for it."

It was no deal. To Panczko's amazement, all three cops turned him down. They placed him under arrest and took him to the Austin District station on West Chicago Avenue. As soon as he was permitted to make a phone call, Pops dialed Bieber and explained his predicament.

"Don't say nuttin' to nobody, Pops. I'll be right out there," Bieber said.

The defense lawyer drove up in his shiny black Chrysler within the hour, wearing a crisp blue suit, off-white shirt, and his most engaging smile. After shaking hands with the desk sergeant, the shift captain, and every patrolman in sight, he conferred with his client.

"I'm starvin' to death, Georgie. See if dey'll let me go get somethin' to eat," Pops complained.

Bieber talked to Captain Andrew Aitken, the shift commander. "We haven't booked him yet," Aitken said. "We're going to let him stew for a couple of hours."

"He says he's hungry," Bieber said. "How about letting him go out and grab a bite somewhere? You know he'll come back."

"Yeah, I know he'll come back," Aitken agreed. "Panczko is good for his word. But I can't let him go. He's got to get booked and have bail set, just like everyone else."

It was a quiet evening, and Pops was the only prisoner in the bullpen. As he sat puffing on a Lucky Strike, he noticed that the lockup keeper had forgotten to turn the key in the lock after shoving him in. He had simply pulled the key out of the lock and hung it on a ring on the wall behind his desk.

As Pops pondered the unique situation, the lockup keeper got up from his desk and went into the adjoining locker room to get something out of his coat. While he was in the other room a gust of wind slammed the door shut with such force that the doorknob fell off.

Trapped in the locker room, the keeper began pounding on the door. "Help! Help! I'm locked in here. Somebody let me out!" he yelled.

Panczko to the rescue. Pops pushed open the unlocked cell door, picked the doorknob up off the floor, put it back on the door, and freed the lockup keeper.

"Hey! How the hell did you get out of your cell?" he asked in amazement.

"Ya forgot to lock me in," Pops explained.

"Shhhh," the guard said. "Don't say anything or I could blow my job."

"Ya don't have to worry," Pops assured him. "I don't never say nuttin' about nuttin'."

"Yeah, but you could have taken off," the jailer said.

"What for?" Pops asked. "Everybody knows me."

A short time later he was taken to a second floor booking room, where two of the arresting officers were typing up their report.

"Jeez, I ain't had nuttin' to eat yet," Pops complained. "I got twenty dollars here. How about getting some coffee and sandwiches or sometin' for all tree of us?"

The cops hadn't eaten, either, and it was getting close to midnight. One of them took the twenty and drove over to a nearby restaurant, while the other sat hunched over the typewriter, pecking away with two fingers, with his back to the prisoner.

The evidence against Pops—his own personal lock puller —rested ominously on the table before him.

"Is it okay if I open a window and get some air?" Pops asked.

"Yeah, go ahead. Just don't bother me. I want to get the hell out of here."

Pops raised the window, took a deep breath of the night air, picked up the lock puller, and deftly tossed it out into the darkness. As he stood nonchalantly at the opening, he saw a policeman going off duty pick the lock puller up off the ground and toss it into his car.

"Dere goes da evidence," he smiled to himself, as the cop's tail lights faded into the night.

The other officer returned with the coffee and sandwiches, and handed Pops his change. "Na, keep it," Pops shrugged generously. "You been good to me."

While he and the arresting officers enjoyed a midnight snack, the one at the typewriter finished with his report. "Take Pops back to his cell and put a tag on those pullers," he told his partner.

"What pullers?"

The two cops looked at Panczko. He gave them the most innocent-as-a-babe look he could muster.

"All right, Pops. Don't try to pull a fast one on us. Where the fuck are those lock pullers?"

"I dunno what yer talkin' about," he shrugged. "You had maybe fifteen coppers walkin' in and outa here. Maybe one of dem took 'em."

Pops got down on his hands and knees with the two cops, looked under the desks, in the waste basket and even out in the hallway. The incriminating evidence was gone. Joseph Panczko had once again outsmarted the law—he thought.

"Wait a minute," one of the cops said. "I'll be right back." He went downstairs to the evidence room, found another lock puller, brought it up and tagged it as evidence.

Much to his chagrin, Pops recognized the device. It was an old one of his that police had confiscated as evidence during a previous arrest. He had been hoist by his own petard.

"Hey, any time youse guys get tired of bein' cops, you can work wit' me," he said begrudgingly. Ingenuity like that had to be admired.

When Pops told Bieber what happened, after being bailed out, the lawyer shook his head and said, "I think they got ya, Pops. These guys can't be paid off. They want ya off the street. I tell ya what, Pops. Why don't ya clear the books? Do a year and a day on this one, and they'll be off your back."

"Whatever ya want me to do, Georgie. You're da boss."

When the matter came up in court, Bieber cut a deal with the prosecution to drop the charge of possession of burglar tools, in exchange for Panczko's guilty plea to attempted bribery of a police officer.

As part of the plea bargain agreement, Judge Erwin J. Hasten sentenced him to a year and a day. He served six months at Stateville, and six months on the State Prison Farm at Vandalia, shoveling coal and picking strawberries.

Actually, Pops was grateful for the rest.

CHAPTER 22

PEANUTS GOES HOLLYWOOD

By 1962 Peanuts had clearly gone big time, with Chicago serving as home base for his ever widening network of thievery. His success in Minneapolis convinced him that there was plenty of money to be made in far-flung communities where his face would not be readily recognizable by every cop who passed him by.

Steve Tomaras had just returned from a visit to Beverly Hills. While most travelers to California might think of Beverly Hills as the home of movie stars, the seasoned Tomaras had come back with a somewhat different conception of the glitzy community.

"They keep a nice window out there," he told Peanuts enthusiastically.

"Who's they?" Peanuts inquired.

"A big jewelry store on Wilshire Boulevard," Tomaras explained. "The window's so full of diamonds, you'd think they were growing in there."

"Jeez, I'd like to see that," Peanuts said, licking his lips. "It's a great town."

"I hit the same store a couple of years ago," Tomaras said. "Now they got bullet-proof windows, and they figure the stuff is safe in there."

Tomaras gave Peanuts the address of the store. The next day he and two of his friends, John and Jerry, packed their suitcases and headed for the West Coast with high expectations. John drove out in his new Olds 98, while Peanuts brought along the souped-up, four-speed getaway car.

They had no trouble locating the jewelry store on Wilshire Boulevard. The window full of diamond bracelets and rings was there, just like Tomaras had promised, waiting to be harvested.

Pretending to window shop, Peanuts tapped innocuously on the glass with his diamond ring. "Jeez, it's a strong one," he remarked. "You'd need a sledge hammer to break it. Look at all those fancy diamonds."

"We got a sledge hammer," John smiled, raising and lowering his eyebrows.

"Okay, here's what we'll do . . . . . ." Peanuts said.

The next morning they stole a car and brazenly double-parked in Wilshire Boulevard, directly in front of the jewelry store. The idea was that any witnesses would give police a description of the stolen auto when they made their get-away. They would then abandon the get-away car and transfer to their own souped-up car, parked around the corner with phony license plates, and drive off unnoticed.

Peanuts remained behind the wheel as John and Jerry walked up to the reinforced plate glass window and attacked it with a sledge hammer. The fact that there were customers in the store did nothing to distract them from their chore.

Several people inside started screaming and running for the door as the heavy window shattered with a resounding crash. John calmly whipped out a handgun and ordered, "Get back in there," while Jerry reached in through the broken glass and scooped out the rings.

The entire operation took less than twenty seconds. The two men jumped back into the car, and Peanuts hit the gas. He spun around the corner, where he screeched to a halt and let his two partners off at their work car. Then he drove down a side street and abandoned the stolen auto.

When he got back to the getaway car, however, John and Jerry were nowhere around. "What the hell???"

Alerted by the store's alarm, a police car had come barreling down the street right after Peanuts had let them off, so the two of them walked right past the get-away car and into the nearest house, as though they lived there. Neither man said a word as they hurried past the startled occupants, let themselves out the back door, crossed the alley, and ducked on through the next house.

By the time Peanuts had circled the block in the back-up car, his two partners had just come out of the second house and were waiting at the curb. "What the hell are you guys doin', payin' social calls?" he asked. "Lemme see what we got."

Jerry displayed half a dozen rings and bracelets. As the trio headed toward Van Nuys, where a friend who knew a fence would hide them out, a news report on the radio quoted the jeweler as estimating his loss at $200,000.

"He must be talkin' wholesale," Peanuts laughed. "Look at this here." One of the rings, sporting a thirteen karat diamond, bore a $125,000 price tag. Another, labeled fifteen karats, was listed at $160,000. A smaller ring carried a $90,000 tag. "We got three, four hundred grand worth right here."

Much to their disappointment, the fence in Van Nuys offered them a lousy forty thousand dollars for the entire lot, sight unseen.

"Forty grand? You're only givin' us ten per cent," Peanuts complained.

"That's my offer. Take it or leave it."

"Stick it up your ass," Peanuts declared. "We can get twice that much back home."

The fence shrugged his shoulders. He was not nuts about dealing with the Chicago hoods in the first place. As soon as he left Peanuts got on the horn to Moishe Baer, a friend who owned a restaurant in Chicago. "Moish," he told him. "Get hold of Hornstein, will ya? I ain't got his number with me. He's on Sheridan Road. Ask him to give me a call out here."

Irving Hornstein called Peanuts at the Van Nuys number he had given Baer. Hornstein, a jewel buyer, knew that Panczko would not be trying to reach him unless it was worth while. "We got one ring here worth a hundred and twenty-five grand," Peanuts told him. "Another worth a hundred and sixty. Irv, you gotta see it to believe it."

"I would like to take a look for myself," Hornstein said. "You boys just sit tight. I'll be right out."

Hornstein hopped a plane for California. While waiting for him to show up, Peanuts, John and Jerry each took one ring for himself. When Hornstein arrived they laid the rest out for him to examine with his jeweler's eye piece. "Very nice. Very nice," he said appreciatively. "I can let you have sixty thousand."

"No way," Peanuts argued. "Eighty grand, Irv. You can peddle it for a couple of hundred thou. Easy."

"Seventy. That's the best I can do," Hornstein said.

"Seventy-five," Peanuts countered.

"You drive a hard bargain," Hornstein replied. "I must be nuts but, okay, seventy-five. But I'm not getting on any plane with this hot stuff. You get it back to Chi. Then we'll do business."

Peanuts was too smart to take the stolen goods back with him, either. He offered one of the bracelets, worth approximately fifteen thousand, to the wife of the friend they were staying with, if she would fly the goods to Chicago. She was only too happy to get aboard the plane, posing as a rich woman, her purse loaded with jewelry.

Jerry flew back on the same plane with Hornstein, so they could keep an eye on their investment. Peanuts and John drove back non stop in the Oldsmobile. California had been so good to them they had decided to leave the "work car" out there for future endeavors.

Back home, Peanuts met Hornstein in suburban Skokie, where Hornstein gave him a $25,000 cash down payment for the jewelry. "I'll have the other thirty-five for you in a couple of days," Hornstein said.

"Thirty-five? What the fuck are you talking about, Irv?" Peanuts exploded. "We agreed on seventy-five. Twenty-five and thirty-five—that's only sixty."

"Yeah, well, I've had a chance to look the stuff over a little better, and, ah, it ain't worth as much as I thought it was," Hornstein explained.

"Irv," Peanuts said icily. "It's me. Paul Panczko. Let's not play games. It could be dangerous to your health. I've never cheated you. Don't try to stick it to me. Okay? You looked at that stuff pretty good the first time, and knew goddam well how much it's worth when you offered seventy-five Gs. You ain't goin' to end up in the poor house on this deal."

"Yeah, ah, ha-ha. I'm just tryin' to make a living. You're right, Peanuts. A deal's a deal. I was just kidding. Seventy-five is fair enough. Meet me by the movie theater on Milwaukee Avenue and I'll have the other fifty grand for you in three days."

Hornstein proved a man of his word—thanks to some gentle prodding—and Peanuts and his two pals each cleared $25,000 on the deal, plus the ring each man kept for himself. The Beverly Hills heist was never solved.

"It's like taking candy from a baby out there, Guy," Peanuts told Lover Boy Mendola, showing him the ring he had saved from the window. "Let's go back and get some more," Mendola suggested.

It was, for all practical purposes, a pleasure trip. Peanuts drove Lover Boy out to California just to show him how easy it was. He showed him the jewelry store they had knocked off, and described how the customers had scattered when Jerry and John laid the sledge hammer into the bullet-proof window. Then the two of them stole a car and simply drove around, looking for a way to "make expenses," before they returned home.

"Jeez, will ya look at that!" Peanuts exclaimed, as they cruised slowly through the giant outdoor Farmers Market. A stunningly attractive young woman had just emerged from a supermarket, pushing a baby carriage.

"Yeah, what a looker!" Mendola agreed.

"Not her, you jerk, her finger," Peanuts said. "That's maybe a seven, eight or ten karat ring she's flashing there."

"How d'ya know it ain't junk?"

"I can see good stuff when I see it."

"Wow, just what we're lookin' for," Mendola agreed. "Slow down a little."

Peanuts slowed to a crawl. As they drew abreast of the woman Mendola jumped out of the car, waving his gun, and shouted, "C'mere!"

The frightened woman let go of the baby carriage and backed away. Without missing a beat, Mendola scooped the infant out of the carriage and threatened, "I'll shoot the kid!"

"No, no, no. Please. Don't hurt my baby," the woman pleaded.

"C'mon back and take off that ring," Mendola told her.

"I can't get it off!" she exclaimed, tugging at her finger.

"Shoot da finger off!" Peanuts yelled out of the car window. This job was taking too long.

"Oh, no," the woman begged. She put her finger into her mouth, wet it, and pulled the ring off with her teeth.

"Thanks, lady," Mendola said, as she handed him the ring. "I wasn't really gonna hurt the kid."

"Let's go! Let's go!" Peanuts yelled.

"Hey, you didn't really want me to shoot that broad's finger off, did you?" Mendola asked as they sped away.

"Hell, no," Peanuts said. "Ya just gotta give 'em a little bullshit, ya know? Ya got the ring, didn't ya? Don't ask questions."

Peanuts knew his diamonds when he saw them. The $30,000 he and Mendola got for the ring more than paid for the trip.

"Jeez, I almost forgot how easy it is out there," he told his regular crew when he got back home. "Anybody wanna go back and do it again?"

"You mean another jewelry store?" Jerry asked.

"Why not?" Peanuts suggested.

"Why not?" agreed John.

Peanuts, Jerry and John piled into the Olds 98 and headed once again for the West Coast. Once they had reached Beverly Hills they had no trouble lining up another swank jewelry store on Wilshire Boulevard. This one did not have a bullet-proof window like the last one, however the owner cleaned the goodies out of the display area every night and stashed them away in his safe. That made it easy. They wouldn't even have to break the glass.

Pretending to be a customer, Peanuts cased the store. To his utter amazement, the front door was not locked with a key. The owner simply locked the door from the inside by turning the knob, like on the inside of a bathroom door. When he was through for the day, he just slammed the door behind him.

"I can't believe it," Peanuts told his partners. "All we gotta do is walk in and help ourselves. These fruitcakes out here are just waitin' to get knocked off."

At closing time, as Peanuts, Jerry and John watched from a discreet distance, the owner turned the knob and locked the front door from the inside. Then he meticulously cleaned the jewelry out of the display window and placed everything on two large trays, intending to put them into the safe.

That was not to be, however. Peanuts and his "three minute" boys appeared from nowhere, punched a hole in the glass door with a brick, reached in and turned the knob, unlocking the door from the inside. The astonished merchant stood there with his mouth agape and two trays of rings, diamonds and watches in his hand as the trio walked in.

"Gimme those trays," Peanuts said, grabbing them out of the stunned jeweler's hands. "Thanks, pal." Before the store owner fully grasped the nightmare, the three thieves were back in their car on Wilshire, and had crossed over into L.A.

Again, the take was more than $300,000, and they had no trouble fencing it for $60,000, after carefully selecting a few rings for themselves, of course.

Before heading back to Illinois the trio decided to make a few jewelry salesmen, since the stores were now on the alert. Once they spotted a salesman they would make a key for his car, and take the sample cases out of his trunk when he went to lunch.

"Remember one thing," Peanuts advised his cohorts. "Everybody goes to eat. We just wait until they're hungry, and their diamonds are ours."

It was not long before the salesmen, too, were on the alert. One of them tried to outwit the boys with a sophisticated alarm system, that would go off if any door or the trunk lid of his car was opened. He tucked his samples neatly in his trunk when he went off to eat, secure in the knowledge that he was electronically safe. And safe he might have been from your run-of-the-mill California thief, but this man was matching wits with a Panczko.

Peanuts smashed the back window out of the car. After wiping away the glass, the smallest member of his crew shinnied in through the opening, started the engine, and drove off, without ever activating the alarm. They took the vehicle to a secluded area near the Los Angeles International Airport, where they popped open the trunk and removed the jewelry, letting the siren wail all it wanted to.

The take amounted to several hundred thousand dollars. None of the jewelry store heists or salesman thefts was ever solved, and Peanuts decided to bid good-bye to the Home of the Stars while he was still ahead. He shifted his operations to San Francisco.

"Frisco's a great town," he told Mendola. "I once grabbed a lady with a big diamond ring there. She owned a restaurant on Fishermen's Wharf. Great town."

Just as he shifted operations, Peanuts would regularly rotate gang members, so nothing would ever be the same in case police were trying to work out some sort of a pattern.

On one memorable trip to San Francisco, he, Mendola and Joe Rossi spotted a jewelry salesman emerging from an exclusive hotel on Market Street. "I know that guy," Peanuts exclaimed. "I seen him in L.A. He's sharp. He takes his sample cases everywhere he goes. He holds 'em between his legs when he's eatin' lunch."

As always, no problem. After jotting down the salesman's license plate number, Peanuts got his identity from the motor vehicle department, called the dealer who had sold him the car, and in no time had his own set of keys to the victim's auto.

"Like candy from a baby," he told Mendola. "Why don't the guy just give us his samples and save everybody a lot of trouble all the way around?"

They followed the salesman when he went to lunch, taking his samples with him. Then he called on a local jeweler. While he was in the store Mendola, the smallest of the trio, let himself into the salesman's car with a spare key and crouched down on the front seat. When the salesman came out of the store he opened his trunk, carefully placed his sample satchel inside, and slammed down the lid.

The instant the trunk slammed shut Mendola turned the key in the ignition, pulled himself up behind the steering wheel, and drove away. "Atta boy, Lover Boy," Peanuts cheered, as he and Rossi took off after the car in their own auto, leaving the stunned salesman standing in the street with his keys in his hand.

He had just been Panczkoed.

In the early 1960s, thanks to Peanuts and his pals, there was an almost steady flow of riches from California to Illinois.

Pops, of course, couldn't wait to get his share once he did his year and a day. As soon as he got out of stir he bought a car under an assumed name and went back to work.

The problem was, Pops still didn't have a driver's license, and every cop in town knew it. He drove down to the state capitol in Springfield to try to rectify the situation with the Secretary of State's office. An employee of the office pulled his file, glanced through it, and shook his head. "Sorry, Mr. Panczko, but your file's been flagged."

"I'm flagged? What's dat mean?"

"It means that this office is under orders not to issue a driver's license in your name."

So Pops drove back to Chicago, without a license. The cops had a good thing going. Every time they spotted him behind the wheel they shook him down for driving without a license, while at the same time somebody had fixed it so he couldn't get one. He'd just have to take his chances.

Pops, Stogie Fedore and Frank Forst found a general merchandise store at Madison and Halsted streets that specialized in watches. "Jeez, dere must be two tousand watches in dere," Pops mused. "Let's clean 'em out."

"When d'ya wanna go?" Stogie asked.

"How 'bout Saturday morning?" Pops suggested.

"Okay, see ya then."

On Friday night Pops went looking for Fedore to map out final plans for the hit. He couldn't find him anywhere. He asked around, but no one had seen Stogie. On Saturday morning, while Pops was getting his gear together for the job, he heard on the radio that someone had burglarized the store the night before and made off with more than a hundred thousand dollars worth of watches.

"Dat son of a bitch!" Pops fumed. "He couldn't wait for me. An' it was my idea."

On a pretty good hunch he drove over to Lawrence Sylvester's. Sure enough, Stogie was there, dealing with the fence. There were hundreds of watches laid out all over the floor, and Sylvester was taking inventory.

"You son-of-a-bitch," Pops said, grabbing Stogie by the front of the shirt and punching him in the mouth. "I found dat joint! I case it, and you made it, you crook."

"Pops, Pops, stop hitting me," Stogie blubbered. "I got your end. I got your end for you."

"Yeah? Where's my end? I don't see no end."

"It's in a bag, sitting in my yard. Honest to God."

After things calmed down, Sylvester paid Stogie ten dollars apiece for the stolen watches. Pops then followed Stogie home and, sure enough, there was a burlap bag in his back yard containing more than a hundred watches. Pops took the bag to a different fence and laid the watches out on the counter. "All brand new," he beamed. "What'll ya give me for 'em?"

"Hmmm. Twenty buck apiece for the whole batch," he said.

Pops took his money back to Stogie's house and waved it in his face. "Ya dumb shit. Ya gave your watches away for nuttin'. Next time let Pops do da thinkin'. Dis serves ya right."

On the way home Pops was pulled over by a motorcycle cop. "Whose car?" the cop asked.

"It's a friend of mine's," Pop answered.

"Let me see your license."

"You know I don't have no license."

The cop just stood there. Pops reached into his pocket, pulled out his wallet, and slapped fifty dollars into the lawman's hand. "Here's my license," he said.

As he drove off, Pops figured it was cheap at any price. If he hadn't slipped the copper fifty bucks, he would have been taken in to the station. Then he would have had to make bond and hire a lawyer, who would want a minimum of five hundred dollars up front. Then, once they got to court, the lawyer would say, "I need another three hundred for the judge, and he'll throw the case out."

He figured a bust would cost close to a thousand dollars, plus the cops would impound his car, and he'd have to buy another one, because if they caught him driving his old one away from the pound, they'd arrest him again and charge him with phony registration of a vehicle.

At this point in his life, he had already abandoned five cars to the city auto pound. Paying a cop fifty dollars to let him go avoided an awful lot of red tape and expense.

Many of the police officers who were shaking Pops down for driving without a license were not otherwise on the take. They saw nothing wrong, however, in extorting money from a burglar. If they couldn't keep him behind bars, they reasoned, the least they could do was punish his wallet.

Pops was driving an old clunker, so as not to attract too much attention. He had stolen a new car in Skokie, and transferred the tires to his jalopy. He liked to have a good set of rubber between him and the road. He also had a burglar alarm on his car, and a siren that would turn on to clear the streets ahead in the event the cops were chasing him.

Life for Pops Panczko was an ongoing battle of wits with the law. Once, when he was in a holding tank after being arrested, the cops took the car keys out of his personal property envelope and had a duplicate set made.

They went by his sister's house one night, when everyone was asleep, and used one of the duplicate keys to turn off the burglar alarm on Pops' car. Then they opened the trunk and slipped a crowbar and large screwdriver into it.

The next day as he was driving down the street a detectives' car pulled him over. Figuring it was going to cost him the usual fifty bucks for driving without a license, Pops reached for his wallet. "We're going to have to search your car, Panczko," one of the detectives told him.

"Yeah, go ahead," Pops said. "I ain't got nuttin' wit' me."

The two detectives went directly to the trunk, opened it, and took out the crowbar and screw driver. "What are you doing with this, Pops?" one of them said. "We're taking you in for possession of burglar tools."

"I don't know nuttin' about it," Pops protested.

"Drive to the station, Pops. We'll be right behind you, so don't try anything."

Fuming, Pops drove for about five blocks, then pulled over to the curb. The unmarked police car pulled alongside. "How much'll it cost me?" Pops yelled through the open window.

"Five hundred."

"I'll give ya tree hunnert," he said.

"Go to the station."

Wearily, Pops got out of the car. "Okay, I'll give it to ya," he sighed. "Follow me to my house."

The two detectives followed him home, collected the five hundred dollars from his kitty, and left. From that day on, whenever Pops was arrested, the first thing he did when he got out on bond was stop at a locksmith's and get the locks on his car changed.

It cost him forty dollars a shot, which was a lot cheaper than five hundred.

He also had the car repainted, applied for a new set of license plates under a phony name, and parked the car several blocks from his house. This worked for awhile, since the cops were still looking for the old car. They finally deduced, however, that he was playing under a new set of rules.

As he left the house at 5:30 one morning, he did not notice that the place had been under surveillance. It was still dark as he walked the several blocks to where his car was parked at School Street and Crawford Avenue. He was just opening the door to get in when a blinding spotlight caught him right in the face.

"Police officer," a voice said loudly. "What are you doing by that car?"

"It belongs to a friend of mine," Pops said.

"Let's see your driver's license."

"I ain't got a license."

"What's your name?"

"Joe Panczko."

"So, you painted your car and got new plates, eh Pops? Sure looks good. I'm sorry, but I'm gonna have to take you in."

Pops started adding up what it would cost him—another car to the auto pound, just after he spent fifty bucks for a tune-up, five hundred for a lawyer, three hundred more to put in the fix, plus he'd have to get another car, new tires, a paint job, new plates . . . .

"I'll give ya tree hunnert bucks for a pass," he said.

"Won't do you no good, Pops. There's three more squads laying for you."

"Where?"

"They're around here somewhere."

"I don't see no more cars. Tree hunnert!"

"Sorry, Pops. No deal."

"What do ya want for a pass?"

"A thousand."

"A tousand? You gotta be crazy!"

"Well, let's go to the station."

"Okay, you win. Follow me to my house."

Pops had a nest egg of twenty-five hundred dollars squirreled away for "fall money." He dug into his cache and gave the cop a thousand. "Be careful, Pops," the cop warned, as he pocketed the money. "There's other cops around here, just laying for you."

Two weeks later, as Pops was taking a pair of trousers to the cleaner's, he was pulled over by another unmarked squad car. The detective behind the wheel called him by name. "Pops, let's see your driver's license."

"You know I ain't got one. Why ask?"

"Let's go, Pops. Follow us to the Albany Park station."

"Aw, jeez! I'll give ya tree hunnert bucks, okay?"

"A thousand, Pops."

"A tousand?"

"You ain't got no choice."

The detective followed Pops home and collected his thousand dollars. By now Pops was starting to figure things out. The first cop had told his friends that Pops was good for a thousand bucks. "He'll offer you three hundred, but he'll come up with a thousand. He doesn't want to go to jail."

It looked like the days of the fifty-dollar shakedowns were a thing of the past. This was starting to get expensive. Pops parked his car in front of his house on Iowa Street and left it there. Whenever he went out on a job, he ducked out the back door and had a friend pick him up on the next street.

This couldn't go on forever, though. He needed his wheels. He went to the Secretary of State's branch office on Chicago's West Side and applied for a new driver's license. As expected, the payroller on duty pulled the file and shook his head. "Sorry, pal. You've been flagged."

"How much to take da flag off?" Pops asked earnestly.

The employee moved closer. "It would take a lot of doing," he confided.

"How much doin'?"

"Well, it would take three hundred for me . . ."

"Okay."

". . . and I'd need to take care of my supervisor, and then there's the people in the Springfield office. I'd have to spread some around."

"Yeah, well, I gotta have a car for my work, see? So just gimme da bottom line. How much will it take?"

"All together, I could take care of it for you for eighteen hundred."

"You got it."

Pops slipped him the money, and the clerk handed him an application blank. "Fill this out, have your picture taken over there, and pay the cashier seven dollars," the clerk said.

Pops left the facility with a new driver's license in his pocket. It was as though a thousand tons had been lifted from his shoulders. He knocked off a men's clothing store that very night, and used the proceeds to buy a new car, in his own name.

Several days later a police officer spotted him and waved him over to the curb. "I'm gonna have to run you in for driving without a license," the cop said.

"Whaddya mean? I got a license," Pops protested.

"Bullshit. Let me see it."

Pops handed him his driver's license.

"Where the hell did you get this?"

"Ain't I entitled to it? It's been twelve years already. Dey give it back to me."

"Get out of the car," the cop ordered.

While Pops stood with his hands on the roof the cop searched the car. There was nothing under the seats, nothing in the trunk. Incredibly, everything appeared to be in order, including the new driver's license.

"Get the hell out of here," the cop frowned.

Pops gave him his very best grin, got back into his car and drove away, carefully obeying the speed limit. It was the best eighteen hundred bucks he'd ever spent.

CHAPTER 23

GO EAST, YOUNG MAN, GO EAST

With Pops once again keeping police hopping on the home front, Peanuts looked around for new and untapped horizons. He had already ventured north, south and west. There was only one point of the compass he had not explored. He and his boys piled into their souped-up car and headed east.

Baltimore became the first place he ever actually used a weapon on the job. Up until now, Marty and Snuffy had been the main pistol wavers while Peanuts acted as the wheelman. In Maryland, however, things took an unexpected turn that called for drastic action.

Peanuts was double-parked in front of a jewelry store in a stolen car, with the engine running. His two associates were inside the shop, cleaning out the showcase. All were wearing plastic masks with smiling faces. Their real get-away car was stashed several blocks away.

As Peanuts waited for his partners to come out, a motorcycle cop came putting by with a long stick tipped with a piece of yellow chalk. He was marking the tires of cars lined up along the curb in a fifteen-minute parking zone. The cop paused for a moment and tossed a glance toward the double-parked car. The man behind the wheel stared back at him, with a fixed, plastic smile.

This did not look kosher. The cop put down his kick-stand and walked over to the car, leaned into the window, and inquired, "Whatya doing?"

Peanuts had a .38 caliber snub-nosed revolver setting on the seat next to him, in case of emergency, and this certainly fit the definition. He grabbed the gun off the seat, pointed it at the policeman's chest, and ordered, "Stand right there."

The lawman wasn't about to argue. As he stood stiffly next to the car, Peanuts reached out the window, flipped open the flap, and fished his service revolver out of its holster. He put the officer's gun on the seat beside him, and kept his own weapon levelled at his chest. The cop remained frozen to the spot.

The boys inside the jewelry store, meanwhile, had cleaned up their work in less than a minute. They were about to duck back out when they glanced through the shop window and saw the police officer standing beside their car, seemingly engaged in conversation with Peanuts.

Peanuts waited. The cop waited. He didn't have a choice. The two plastic faced men inside the store waited, holding customers and employees at bay. Sensing what the hang-up might be, Peanuts—holding his gun on the cop with one hand—waved to them with the other and yelled, "Come on, for chrissake!" On receiving his signal they warily made their way to the car and got in as Peanuts drove off, leaving the policeman standing in the road, with an empty holster.

"What took you guys so long?" Peanuts asked as they ate up the three blocks to their getaway car.

"You were talkin' to the cop, for chrissake. Did you expect us to run up and say 'Here we are, let's go?'"

"Jesus, didn't ya see what happened there? That's the first time I ever put a gun on anybody who had a gun on himself. I'm sure glad I didn't have to use it."

"Would you have shot the son-of-a-bitch?"

"Hell no. Guns are for gettin' people's attention, not shootin' 'em."

"How come your brother, Pops, never carries a gun?"

"'Cause Pops is nuts. If I didn't have that .38 just now we'd all be in the shithouse. You know that, don'tcha?"

Back home, Pops was busy as a bumble bee in a rose garden. Working solo, he had just emptied a car load of cloth coats on the North Side, and was heading west on Grand Avenue with the haul. As he crossed Rockwell Street a motorcycle cop pulled him over for speeding.

"I couldn't be, which I am always careful about dat," Pops explained to the officer.

"Let's see your license."

Pops handed it to him, relieved that for once in his life he wasn't going to get shaken down for driving without a license. The cop examined it, handed it back to him, and peered into the car.

"Where'd you get all those coats?"

Pops was sticking the license back into his billfold. As he withdrew his hand he fished out a five dollar bill. "Officer, here's five dollars," he said. "Gimme a break. I just got a job, see? An I want da boss to see how fast I could make a delivery for him."

The cop pocketed the five dollars. "Okay, deliver your stuff, but take it easy."

"Tank you, officer."

Pops slipped the car into gear and drove directly to the fence, where he disposed of the coats before their rightful owner knew they were missing. Two weeks later, by sheer coincidence, the same motorcycle cop pulled him over again. This time Pops had fifteen men's suits laid neatly across the back seat.

"You again?" the cop said, as Pops extended his hand with a five dollar bill between the fingers. The patrolman looked into the car, saw the suits, and smiled. "Go ahead," he said, rejecting the bribe. "This one's on me."

"Gee, tanks again, officer. I owe ya."

"Yeah," said the cop. "From now on you'll be working for me."

The implication was clear. Pops would be able to operate in this cop's territory without fear of arrest, but it was going to cost him. That was okay. Cutting a cop in on the take up front would be cheaper than paying Bieber and fixing a judge.

Besides, Pops had hit upon a new money-making scheme that was almost legit. He would buy or steal cheap jewelry, and then tag the items with higher prices before disposing of them.

In one instance, he actually purchased a batch of four dollar rings, put a twenty dollar price tag on each one, and peddled them for fifteen dollars apiece. He disposed of a case of watches in the same manner. His reputation as a big time thief only enhanced the operation, since his customers figured they were getting a good deal on stolen goods.

At the same time, Pops was enhancing the reputation of some of the cops. Whenever he pulled a job, which they were certain bore his trademark, but they couldn't prove it, someone would give him a phone call.

"Look, Pops, that fur salesman that got ripped off last night . . ."

"I don't know nuttin' about no fur salesman."

"Right, Pops. But where would you say we might find the gaffer's car?"

"I tole ya, I don't know nuttin' about no furs."

"Nobody's asking about any furs, Pops. The guy's car. Where the fuck is it?"

"His car? Gee, I dunno. Maybe it's parked over by Franklin and Erie Streets."

"Thanks, Pops."

Police would then check the neighborhood and find the salesman's automobile—right where Pops hinted it might be. At least, then, they could contact the unfortunate victim and tell him, "Whatever you had inside it is gone, but you'll be glad to know we recovered your car for you." And the salesman would be grateful to the police for getting his wheels back under him.

Peanuts, meanwhile, was putting miles on his lime green Cadillac. After the close call in Baltimore, he and the boys high-tailed it back to Chicago where they laid low until the money ran out. Now he was on the road again, heading back east with Joe Rossi and Lover Boy Mendola.

"I hear they got gold refineries in Newark, New Jersey," he told his partners. "That's where they melt the gold into rings and stuff for the jewelry stores. Ya know what I mean? A Railway Express truck picks up the casings for all the jewelry places that make rings. All we gotta do is stake out a high class jewelry store until we see a Railway Express truck make the drop-off. Then we follow the truck to the gold factory."

It sounded too good to be true, and it was.

Peanuts and the boys found a jewelry store and parked across the street to begin the waiting game. Just like Peanuts' tipster had promised, a Railway Express truck eventually pulled up to make a delivery. The driver wore a holster with a sidearm, which meant he was hauling a valuable cargo.

"That's our guy," Peanuts said. "Look. He's carrying a gun."

"Oh, oh. What's this here?" Mendola interrupted.

A car had pulled alongside of them and ominously slowed down. As the trio tried to look innocent, the car's occupants, two clean-cut men in three-piece suits, gave Panczko, Rossi and Mendola the once-over.

"What's this here?" Peanuts repeated, eyeing the car. "I'll tell you what's this here. If those guys ain't FBI, my name ain't Peanuts." He turned the ignition key and slowly eased the car away from the curb, making sure to stay well within the speed limit as he proceeded down the street.

"What now?" Rossi asked.

"Back the fuck to Chicago," Peanuts explained. "No way are we going to pull a job if the FBI already made us."

It was one of the very few out of town ventures in which Peanuts returned to Chicago empty handed. Caution was the better part of greed. Three weeks later the trio piled back into the garish Cadillac and drove back to Newark for a second chance. This time, however, they observed every possible precaution.

They crossed the toll bridge into New York and left the Caddy in lower Manhattan, where they stole a less conspicuous car and drove back to Newark. The jewelry store was right across from the U.S. Post Office, which explained the presence of the FBI men. The local FBI headquarters was in the post office building.

"That joint is ripe to make," Peanuts observed. "They don't figure nobody's gonna hit 'em, right across the street from the FBI. That's the safest place in town. Whaddya say?"

"Let's take a look."

Parking the car, the trio walked up to the front of the store and studied the display window. Every ring, watch or bracelet was clearly marked with a price tag. Totaling the amounts that were visible on the tags, Peanuts figured the window alone contained more than $150,000 worth of goodies.

"It looks pretty good to me," he said. "Let's make the store."

They patiently bided their time, and watched from across the street as the jeweler gingerly removed each item from the window at closing time, arranging them one by one on display trays in a box, which would go into his safe.

"Let's make our move," Peanuts said.

His partners got out of the car and casually approached the store, as the jeweler was tucking away the last of the gems. Peanuts, seated inside the car to muffle the sound, leveled a .22 caliber pistol at the heavy glass window and squeezed the trigger.

There was a sharp crack as the bullet slammed into the heavy window, causing the glass to crystallize and turn white. The stunned merchant froze. He'd been completely taken by surprise. Before he could recover his composure, Peanuts' partners were in the store, relieving him of the display trays at gunpoint.

Less than fifteen minutes later they were back in Manhattan, where they abandoned the stolen auto, transferred the loot to the gaudy green Cadillac, and motored back to Chicago.

There they enthusiastically delivered the goods to a fence, who paid the brazen trio $15,000 apiece. "I almost feel guilty," Peanuts said, as he counted his share. "Like taking candy from a baby."

CHAPTER 24

![black bar]

THE POMPANO
BEACH BOYS

During the nine years that Peanuts spent picking cotton and digging coal in Tennessee, his old partner from the Union Station suitcase caper, Chester Gray, had done quite well on his own, married the daughter of a prominent Chicago trucking magnate, and retired to Pompano Beach, Florida, where he opened an art gallery.

In late January of 1962 Peanuts, on the lam from a bitter Chicago winter, hopped a plane for the Sunshine State, where he figured to do a little business himself.

He and a partner, 38-year-old Richard Kay of Three Oaks, Michigan, checked into the Treasure Island Motel at Miami Beach. They were joined in early February by Tony Legato, 25-year-old John Patrick Johnson of Chicago, and 36-year-old Edward Cook of the Chicago suburb of Oak Lawn,. Once the boys had gotten their bearings, Peanuts rented a car and drove up to Pompano Beach, a coastal town of 55,000, just north of Fort Lauderdale, hoping to renew old acquaintances.

"Peanuts, jeez, it's good to see you. You look great," Chester bubbled, pumping his hand.

"It's good to be here," Peanuts said. "I was freezing my buns off in Chi. Some of my friends, they said, 'Go see Chester.' So here I am. Just don't touch me. I'm so sunburned

I feel like a Florida lobster. I've been hearing a lot of good things about ya."

"Yeah, well, there's a lot of opportunities down here, Peanuts."

"Do you think you can line me up with something?"

"There's places that are just begging for your touch, Peanuts. You came to the right man."

The first score Chester set up was at an ultra swank jewelry store in Palm Beach. The scheme called for Peanuts, all decked out as a chauffeur, to sit behind the wheel of a Cadillac limousine parked in front of the shop while his partners went in and cleaned out the display cases. Before Panczko could get fitted for his uniform, however, Chester came up with an even better mark—the Leonard Taylor Jewelry Store at 22 Ocean Center, just one block from the Atlantic Ocean in downtown Pompano Beach.

Taylor's was every jewel thief's dream. The logistics of the caper were challenging. "There's only one road out of town. That's the state highway, A1A, and if the cops block it, we're dead," Peanuts speculated. "So, how are we gonna do this now?"

"Take a boat," Legato volunteered.

"Absolutely. We use boats," Peanuts declared. "The coppers will be watching the road, and we'll be putt-putting away like a bunch of pirates, right under their noses!" The get-away script, it would turn out, could better have been written by the Three Stooges.

It started out as one of the best planned jobs, ever. On Saturday, February 11th, Panczko and Legato rented two outboard motor boats at Pier 66 in Fort Lauderdale under the name of John Kennedy. After gassing up they cruised up to Pompano Beach and tied up at a private club, where their partners were waiting for them in the rented car. Returning to Fort Lauderdale, they stole another auto, put phony license plates on it, and motored back to Pompano Beach in a slight rainfall. It was all systems go.

At 2 p.m., five sporty looking gents wearing white golf caps and Italian style sun glasses, pulled into a parking space directly in front of Taylor's, which was located in a small shopping mall with an ocean view. Between them they carried five loaded pistols, three two-way transistor radios, a large supply of ammunition, and five sets of handcuffs. Peanuts remained in the car as his four partners, wearing clear plastic face masks, marched into the exclusive store.

As it turned out, they did not need the handcuffs. There were only two people inside at the time, Joseph Tarnove, the 38-year-old manager, and Jesse C. Edwards, the porter. The bandits herded them at gunpoint to a storeroom, where they bound them with telephone wire.

While they were wrapping up Tarnove and Edwards, an iron grillwork gate separating the back room from the public area of the store slammed shut, locking the four gunmen in with their prisoners. Taking a ring of keys from Tarnove, they tried for ten minutes to unlock the gate, without success, until the store manager finally obliged by telling them which key to use.

Then they spent the next twenty minutes, methodically looting the store of diamonds, rubies, emeralds and other gems, shimmering in their settings of gold, silver and platinum.

"Look at this little dandy," said Kay, as he flipped an emerald ring, bearing a $34,000 price tag, into a suitcase he was carrying. Some of the jewelry items bore claim numbers and people's names, indicating they had been brought into the shop for repair.

Mistaking the smiling faces on the plastic masks as those of people who were happy in their work, several passers-by smiled and waved at the thieves as they busied themselves, cleaning out the show window. The thieves waved back, and continued with their work.

By the time they had virtually cleaned out the store and prepared to make their retreat they hit their next snag. The inside door would not open. The shop was equipped with an electronic safety lock, and they could not get out. They did not realize that the jeweler, seeing them approach, had pushed a hidden button and buzzed them into the shop. Picture the scene:

Peanuts' sunburn is killing him. He is poised uncomfortably at the wheel of the stolen get-away car, revving the engine, and his partners, holding pistols in one hand and suitcases full of jewelry in the other, are standing there, looking at him through the window. Peanuts looks apprehensive. His partners shrug their shoulders. Finally Legato figures out what's wrong. Racing to the back room, he grabs Tarnove, the manager, presses the gun to his head and says, "Push the fucking button!" Tarnove reaches under the counter, presses a button, and buzzes the bandits out.

In their haste to depart, the four gunmen nearly knocked down a passer-by, who was standing on the sidewalk in front of the store. The stunned spectator stood and watched in amazement as Peanuts inadvertently slipped the car into reverse, nearly knocking down one of his partners, who was running around the rear of the car to get in from the other side.

"It's about time," Peanuts fumed as they piled into the auto and pulled off their funny faces. "I thought maybe you guys went to lunch or somethin'."

He depressed the gas pedal to ease the car away from the store. At that precise moment, however, another vehicle pulled into the parking space behind him, and wedged him in. It took another full minute of frantic maneuvering to get the car out into traffic, with Peanuts doing his best to keep his cool. He took off slowly. No sense attracting attention. He casually guided the auto across the Intercoastal Waterway bridge and down to the end of the beach. To all outward appearances, the car carrying the richest jewel heist in American history contained nothing more than a group of white-capped duffers, returning from an afternoon on the golf course.

They abandoned the car at the end of the pier, where they scrambled aboard the two waiting boats with their loot.

Peanuts and Legato took the first craft, while the others got into the second. Then they encountered another hitch.

The motor on the first boat kicked off like gangbusters when the starter cord was pulled, and Legato was ready to give her the throttle, but Cook, Johnson and Kay were having problems with the other boat. In their anxiety to make good their escape, they had flooded the motor, and it refused to start.

"Tony, swing around and we'll trow 'em a rope," Peanuts yelled. "We gotta get the hell outa here before the coppers figure out that we're not on the road."

Legato brought the boat around and eased alongside the disabled craft, while Peanuts tossed his partners a line. As soon as they had made it fast, Peanuts yelled to Legato, "Okay, let's go."

"Legato shoved the throttle forward, the bow of the boat lifted out of the water, and it surged ahead. Snap! Twang! "Aw, Jeezus Christ," Peanuts cursed in frustration. "Now the goddam rope broke."

Time was getting short. By now the alarm had been given, and police had the road out of town blocked. Yet the bandits still hadn't pulled away from the pier. Kay leaped into the water, fully clothed, and retrieved the end of the line trailing from Peanuts' boat. Soaking wet, he clambered back aboard the second craft and stood in the bow, holding the tow line.

"Let's go! Let's go!" Captain Peanuts commanded, as the two small boats pulled single-file away from the dock. Cook, still jerking the starter cord, eventually got the stalled motor to kick over. There was a cloud of gasoline-smelly smoke as it started to sputter, and finally broke into a throaty roar. The two boats now sped together into the channel, leaving Pompano Beach in their somewhat haphazard wake.

Two women, boat-watching from a bridge over the canal, looked on in amusement as the two small crafts zoomed under the bridge and headed out to sea. One of the women would later identify Peanuts as the man with the "red, sunburned face."

The derring-do robbers covered the nine miles from Pompano Beach to Fort Lauderdale at top speed, holding on for dear life as the bottoms of the small boats slapped against the waves. At Fort Lauderdale they tied up to the rental dock, switched to another stolen car and drove the remaining twenty-three miles to Miami Beach.

Back at the Treasure Island Motel, they dumped the contents of the suitcases out on the bed. In all, they counted 521 pieces of jewelry glittering up at them from the bedspread.

Peanuts laid aside an $18,000 ring as each man picked one item as a bonus for himself. Then they removed the jewelry from the boxes, picked off most of the identifying price tags, and discarded the tags and boxes in the fast-flowing causeway outside the motel.

As they were rolling the jewelry in beach towels, and carefully packing everything into one suitcase, Chester drove up and banged on the motel door.

"It's all over the radio," he said. "What happened?"

"Chester, we're still getting things together here. Come back later," Peanuts said, trying to head him off.

"I came for my end," Chester pressed. "It says on the radio you guys got nearly two million bucks worth."

"Dammit, I told ya, come back later," Peanuts said. "You'll get your end—10 percent for setting it up. Don't worry, for crissakes."

Indeed, Tarnove had taken inventory and determined that the thieves had actually made off with $1,750,000 in gems. Peanuts, the kid brother of the Panczko clan, had engineered the biggest jewel heist in U.S. history. In terms of today's money, the loot would total more than seventeen million dollars.

Peanuts finally sent Chester on his way while he and the boys continued putting things in order. But Chester was not to be dissuaded. A short time later he was on the phone. "I'll meet you guys at Pumpernickel's," he said.

"You got a legit car?" Peanuts asked him.

"Yeah."

"Well, come by and pick us up then. We don't wanna be seen driving anywhere, in case somebody made us."

Chester picked the five jewel thieves up and they drove together to the popular cocktail lounge, where they discussed their next move.

"Jeez, we had this score mapped out like clockwork, but none of us figured what to do once we pulled it off," Peanuts pointed out. "We forgot all about that."

"Maybe I could move it for you," Chester suggested.

"Naw. You're a known thief like the rest of us. None of us can take a chance at getting stopped, and having the stuff in the car with us. I think I got an idea."

Peanuts called two friends, Mary Blanton and Betty Jean Moody, both thirty-one, and asked them to meet him and the boys at Pumpernickel's. Chester also made a few phone calls. When the women arrived, Peanuts asked for a ride back to the motel, where he had stashed the loot in the trunk of the rental car. His plan was to pay Blanton and Moody $1,000 to drive up to Chicago with the suitcase containing the jewelry, figuring police would not be suspicious of two women riding alone. He and the boys would fly on ahead and be waiting for them when they arrived.

Peanuts, Cook and Kay got into the women's car to ride back to the motel with them, while Legato and Johnson remained at Pumpernickel's with Chester. They had not driven one block before they heard a siren, and someone shouting, "Pull over! Pull over!" They suddenly found themselves surrounded by more Miami Beach police officers and FBI agents than an Eliot Ness movie.

As Panczko looked at the flashing Mars lights, hopelessly trying to figure a way out of the mess, an FBI agent leaned into the car window and said, "Hi, Peanuts. Introduce me to your friends."

The bust came as a total surprise, and proved Peanuts had made a wise decision in not carrying the stolen goods around with him.

The three men and two women were taken to the Broward County jail in Fort Lauderdale, where they were questioned by Wesley G. Grapp, special agent in charge of the Miami FBI office.

"What am I supposed to have done? Do you mind telling me?" Peanuts asked indignantly.

"Where's the jewelry?" Grapp demanded, wasting no time in letting Peanuts know why he and his friends were in custody.

"Jewelry? What jewelry?" he said, wrinkling his brow. "C'mon. I ain't got all night. I don't understand what you're talkin' about."

After several hours of verbal sparring, Panczko, Cook and Kay were charged with armed robbery, auto theft, conspiracy, and consorting with known criminals, while the two women were booked as accomplices. At the time of her arrest, Mary Blanton had $1,000 in large denomination bills in her purse.

When Peanuts was permitted to make the customary phone call, he reached out for a Miami lawyer, Joe Varon, whose name he kept on file for emergencies. The attorney showed up a short time later and told Panczko, "They got the jewelry."

Stealing jewelry is not a federal offense, however FBI offices are routinely notified by other FBI divisions whenever known thieves converge on a given area. Thus, Peanuts sojourn to Fort Lauderdale had been no secret, and federal agents were already poised, waiting to lend local authorities a hand, in the likely event of a major crime. Even though Peanuts and his pals had outwitted the law by escaping by sea, the feds had a pretty good idea who they were looking for the minute the jeweler freed himself and turned in the alarm.

When Peanuts was asked to dump the contents of his pockets out onto a table, following his arrest, Grapp was particularly interested in a key ring. It contained an automobile key, which the FBI men were able to trace to a local car rental agency. Once they had a description and license number of the rent-a-car, they easily located it back at the motel. Using the key from Peanuts' key ring, they opened the trunk and recovered the suitcase full of jewels.

Grapp was ecstatic. He called a news conference to announce the arrests, and declared, "This is the largest recovery of stolen jewelry in the history of American crime!"

For the benefit of photographers, the FBI agents had laid out the loot on a black cloth draped over a four-by-seven foot table. The 521 glittering diamonds, rubies, emeralds and other gems covered the entire top of the table.

"Here. Do you want to see $100,000 worth of jewels in the palm of one hand?" Grapp teased wide-eyed reporters. He held up a $40,000 set of diamond earrings and two $30,000 diamond bracelets. "Paul Panczko is one of the most dangerous and professional jewel thieves in the United States," he added. "But we got 'em."

Indeed, the monumental theft—which would go into the Guinness Book of Records—paled all of Peanuts' many other accomplishments to date.

Panczko, Cook and Kay went on trial in November for the Pompano Beach heist, but the judge had to call a mistrial after the jurors failed to reach an agreement. Rumors were flying that one or more of them had been bribed, in true Chicago fashion, but nothing was ever proved, one way or the other.

The robbers remained free on bond until they were retried in March of 1963. And this time they were found guilty. Criminal Court of Record Judge Douglas Lambeth sentenced all three men to life in prison.

It was nearly a year later, while his Florida lawyer was filing motions of discovery, that Peanuts learned how the Feds had gotten onto him so fast in the first place. His dear friend, Chester, it seems, had been a government snitch.

Peanuts was told that some years earlier Chester had been arrested with a load of counterfeit money in Havana, where he had gone to gamble. He was starving in a rat-infested Cuban dungeon when American authorities offered to cut a deal with the Batista government to get him sent back home if he would agree to become an FBI informant.

Fearing he would never see freedom again, he took the bait, and the government had him hooked.

On the night Peanuts and his partners rendezvoused in Pumpernickel's, Chester blew the whistle on them.

"Can you beat that!" an astonished Peanuts said when his lawyer advised him how he'd been tripped up. "Chester, he gives us the score, and he got us busted! He sets up a meeting wit' us, and he's on the phone, callin' the 'G'."

"You guys aren't going to do anything stupid and try to get even, are you?" Varon asked.

"Nah, fuck 'im," Peanuts said, dismissing his ex-partner like a speck of dust. "We don't operate like that. It ain't our way. Chester, he did what he had to do. Who knows what you might do under those circumstances? But I'll tell ya one thing—you ain't gonna see me doin' business wit' him no more."

CHAPTER 25

HEY, MISTER, YOUR KEYS

Peanuts never served a day in jail for pulling off the history making jewel heist, despite the fact that he and his buddies had been caught with the carats. He remained free on $50,000 bond during both his trials, and while his conviction was being appealed. A higher court ultimately reversed the conviction because prosecutors had told the jury that Panczko, Cook and Kay were "known felons"—and that's a no-no. So they tried him again, and the third trial, like the first, ended ingloriously with a hung jury.

Three strikes and you're out. Florida prosecutors gave up on trying to put the bandits away. After all, they did get the swag back, and they could only hope the youngest Panczko brother would never darken their state again.

Peanuts, of course, had other plans. Through it all, he had remained active through necessity. He had not only lost nearly two million dollars in jewelry when the G-men found the key to his rented car, but he had the Florida bail bondsman and big-time lawyer fees to contend with.

For awhile he tried staying closer to home, but in his case, crime didn't pay. For one thing, before heading down to Pompano Beach in the first place he had stashed two trailer loads of television sets, worth $75,000, in a chicken house near Chicago Heights. But when he came back to fence them they were gone.

The FBI had discovered the cache, and arrested six of Peanuts' helpers in the process.

Then Peanuts, Guy Mendola and James D'Antonio were picked up on a phony traffic charge so police could question them about the $50,000 burglary of the Formfit Aluminum and Heating Company in Cicero, Illinois.

And in west suburban Melrose Park he was curbed by police while "running interference" for a stolen truck loaded with wash machines and a hot water heater. "What the hell are youse guys talkin' about?" he argued, when the cops demanded to know why he had zig-zagged in front of a squad car and cut them off. "Jeez, I just got confused by the sireen. I'm sorry, officers."

He neglected to tell them that his partner, Guy Mendola, had been behind the wheel of the truck. He and Mendola had been on the way downtown with a couple of stolen keys to U.S. postal boxes when they spotted the truck, unattended while its driver made a delivery, and decided to run off with it. What the hell?

Thanks to Peanuts' ability as a wheelman, Mendola had gotten away, but Peanuts suddenly had some fast talking to do. Which reminded him, he still had the stolen keys in his pocket. That could be dangerous. While Patrolmen Daniel Principe and Anthony Stellato berated him for getting in their way, he surreptitiously reached into his side pocket and let the keys fall to the ground.

"Hey, Mister. You dropped your keys."

It was nine-year-old James Kearney, a helpful neighborhood kid who had been playing nearby. He handed Peanuts the key chain.

"Oh, yeah. Tanks, kid," Peanuts scowled.

"Let's see your driver's license," Stellato said.

"Sure, officer." As he handed the policeman his license with one hand, he flung the keys off behind his back with the other.

"Panczko? You are Paul Walter Panczko?" Stellato asked, studying the driver's license.

"Yeah."

"Put your hands on the roof of the car."

As Peanuts was assuming the position, another kid ran up to the car.

"Stay away from here, Sonny," Principe told him.

"I was just bringing the man his keys. They fell out of his pocket again," ten-year-old Michael McGarr explained. Michael had been taught honesty. His father, Frank J. McGarr, was a federal prosecutor and later a U.S. District Court judge.

"Let's see those keys," said Principe, extending his hand. The youngster handed him a brass chain with two keys stamped "U.S. Mail."

"Where'd you get these keys?" Principe inquired.

"Me? I never saw 'em before."

"You just dropped 'em out of your pocket," the McGarr boy offered.

"No, no, no. That was just a gum wrapper."

"We're taking you in, Panczko."

Postal inspectors were called, and discovered that Panczko was carrying a set of keys that fit every mail deposit box in the city of Chicago. Since he did not work for the U.S. Postal Service, that was a federal offense.

And he wasn't the only member of his family in dutch with the law.

Butch had just been arrested for receiving stolen property, after he tried to cash in 6,254 stolen trading stamps for a black metal waste basket, a vanity chair, and a clothes hamper. The stamps had been taken in a burglary of a National Tea Company store. It was Butch's sixty-sixth arrest of record.

As for Pops—he continued to give police writer's cramp. And for the press it became a challenge to catalogue his endless litany of arrests without being repetitious. Hardly a day went by that there wasn't a story in one of the downtown papers about "Chicago's busiest burglar," "Chicago's perennial burglary suspect," "Chicago's hardest working burglar,"

"Chicago's most publicized burglar," "Chicago's leading burglar," "Chicago's veteran burglar," "Chicago's most celebrated burglar," "Chicago's most notorious burglar," "the city's most active and outspoken burglar," or "one of the top professional burglars in the country."

At one point Judge Benjamin Nelson ordered mental tests for Pops, being curious as to what made him tick. Dr. John E. Kysar, a psychiatrist who conducted the court-ordered examination, reported back, "Joseph Panczko is a sociopathic personality, who probably gets gratifiction out of being a famous burglar constantly persecuted by police. But he is not certifiable, nor is he amenable to treatment."

This merely proved what everyone already knew: Pops was far from crazy, but there was no known cure for his appetite for appropriating other people's property as his own.

And then there was the ninety-five miles-an-hour police chase through town in which Detective Eugene Irwen finally caught and curbed Pops' powerful eight-cylinder sedan. Both Panczko and Irwen had their sirens wailing to clear traffic and pedestrians out of the way, until the cop finally outmaneuvered his quarry. As Pops got out of his car with his hands up, he walked curiously over to the detective's pursuit car and asked, "Is dat an eight?"

"No, it's six," Irwen patiently explained. "I'm just a good driver."

"You must be nuts, chasing' people like dat," admonished Pops, shaking his head. "You probably got a wife and kids. Me, I got nuttin' to lose."

"You're gonna lose your freedom, that's what," the cop answered.

The chase story made the papers under the headline:

"POPS" NABBED
IN CHASE; IT'S
EMBARRASSING

With all this going on, Peanuts decided Chicago was getting too hot for him to work in. Too many cops were playing Catch-a-Panczko. It would be better to resume doing business out of town. So, he decided to head back to Florida—after pulling one last job to make expenses.

Peanuts and Frank DeLegge were coming out of the deli at Clark and Belden on Sunday morning when Peanuts, who always looked at a woman's fingers before he checked out her legs, nudged his partner in the ribs and said, "Look at the fuckin' rock!"

A middle-aged woman had just come out of the store wearing a diamond ring that looked like at least nine or ten carats. When she got into her car, bearing Massachusetts license plates, Peanuts and DeLegge tailed her to a high-rise apartment right near George Bieber's. While she was inside, Peanuts got on the phone and ran a license plate check. The car was registered to a physician from Boston.

In order to make sure it was her, Peanuts dialed the doctor's number in Boston. "Doctor Smith is in Chicago, visiting her daughter," the receptionist told him.

"This is officer Peterson of the Chicago P.D.," Peanuts explained. "The doctor's been involved in a little hit-and-run accident, and we need to know the name and phone number of the person she's staying with here." The receptionist obligingly gave him the daughter's name, address and phone number.

Peanuts then called the apartment and tried to make an appointment with the doctor. Somewhat irritated that anybody would bother her while she was on vacation, she told him, "I'm sorry, but I'm going back home tomorrow."

The next day Peanuts, DeLegge and Mike LaJoy were waiting at O'Hare International Airport near the Boston departure gate. "Here comes the old broad now," Peanuts said, as she approached, after checking her luggage aboard the plane. He quickly ducked to a telephone and had her paged. When the doctor answered the page he identified himself as Sergeant Cassidy, and told her that her daughter had been in an accident.

"Oh, my. I just left her, not a half hour ago," the doctor said.

"All right. You stay right there now," Peanuts instructed. "A detective will be there in a few minutes to pick you up. We'll take you to the hospital."

Frank DeLegge showed up a few minutes later, wearing a phony badge. "Doctor Smith?" he said. "Come with me, please." He escorted her to his vehicle, which happened to be a regular burglar's work car equipped with a police radio. The doctor got in, and DeLegge pulled away from the airport circle and headed south in Mannheim Road. After driving a short distance he pulled under a viaduct and stopped.

"There's something haywire with the car," he explained. What was wrong was that DeLegge did not know how to drive a stick shift, and he couldn't get the car out of first gear. He was rescued by Peanuts and LaJoy, who had been following in a stolen car. They ran up, pulled the ring off the frightened woman's finger, pushed her out of the auto, and sped away.

They drove straight downtown and offered the ring to Irv Hornstein. He appraised it at $30,000, and gave the boys $3,400 apiece for their afternoon's work.

Now Peanuts had enough traveling money to get back to Florida. He said so long to Norma and his two step-children, jumped into his Cadillac convertible and headed south with two assistants.

The day of their arrival in Miami will forever be imbedded in Peanuts' mind, as in the minds of so many other Americans. He and John D'Amato were in a pet shop, actually purchasing something. His partner bought an apricot poodle for his daughter back home and Peanuts, utterly overcome by his surroundings, decided he could use a pet monkey.

While he and D'Amato were in the shop, they heard over the radio that President John F. Kennedy had been assassinated. It didn't mean a hell of a lot to Peanuts. He had never voted in his life and, as a convicted felon, he never would. He didn't gave a damn who was in the White House. One politician was as bad as the other. The President's death, however, meant many places of business would be closed, forcing him to sit in his motel room with the monkey, watching endless reruns of the assassination and the subsequent shooting of Lee Harvey Oswald.

Actually, Peanuts had intended to bring the monkey home as a surprise for Norma's two kids. He bought a long chain for it, named it Chico, and walked it out to the car. The monk seemed to enjoy riding in the convertible, but every time Peanuts pulled up alongside another auto at a stop sign, Chico would jump into the other car. The occupants of the other car would be screaming as Peanuts yanked the chain and yelled, "Get over here!" Chico would jump back and defecate all over the seat.

Thanks to Chico, Peanuts had to carry a roll of toilet paper every where he went.

"This goddam monkey shits all the time," he complained to Frank DeLegge, his other partner. "What kind of a pet is that—shittin' all over the place? Monkeys do that a lot. Did ya know that? They don't tell ya that at the store. I shoulda got me a mutt. My brother, Butch, he's got a Doberman pinscher. Butch has a few beers and goes jimmying suit places and takes the dog wit' him. He goes in an alley, ties the dog to a post and pries open the door. If Butch hears the dog growlin', he walks away from the door, grabs the dog and pretends like he's just walkin' the dog down the alley to pee on telephone poles. Sometimes the cops see my brother and say, 'C'mon, Butch, we wanna take you in.' And they go to Butch's car and the dog, he almost eats the glass. The cops, they don't mess wit' Butch. Not when he's wit' that crazy dog. So what've I got? A monkey that non-stop shits."

"Yeah? What does Butch feed his mutt, anyway?"

"Pies, choice cuts of meat—whatever he can steal."

"How 'bout your monk. What does he eat?"

"Too damn much, if ya ask me."

At the end of two weeks Peanuts had all he could stand of Chico and his carefree bowels. He traded him in for a black poodle, which he named Sambo. The kids would love it.

The stay in Miami, of course, wasn't all walking the dog. Operating out of a swank hotel on Biscayne Boulevard,

Peanuts, Frank and John commuted regularly to San Juan, where they worked the gambling casinos. Not as gamblers, of course, but as highly selective jewel thieves.

Wearing tuxedos like the rest of the gamblers, they would circulate among the crowd in the posh San Juan casinos until they fixed on a woman with a glittering necklace or perhaps a ten or fifteen carat ring on one of her fingers.

More often than not her male companion also flashed a good sized rock on his pinky finger.

"Okay, let's keep an eye on 'em when they leave. See what room they go in," Peanuts winked at his partners. By experimenting with the door lock in their own room John, a world class locksmith, had fashioned a master key that would admit the trio to any room in the hotel.

"Then we give 'em a chance to go to sleep, take a shower, have sex or whatever," Peanuts continued. "Give 'em two, three hours. Do you know the hardest time that you sleep? It's just at daylight. That's when a person sleeps the hardest. We wait 'til that time. Just when it's getting a little light outside. That's when they're out. Then we go in, pick the stuff off the dresser and tiptoe out. Those people, they don't get up until eleven, twelve o'clock. By that time we're on the plane back to Miami."

Only once did any of their victims wake up while being relieved of their jewels. It was in the hotel in San Juan, while sacking the room of a couple in their late thirties. The woman was wearing black eye shades, which reminded Peanuts of horse blinders, so the sunlight would not disturb her sleep.

Something else disturbed her, however, and both she and her husband sat bolt upright in bed while the boys were looting the room. "Just sit there an' keep your traps shut," Peanuts cautioned the couple. "Nuttin's gonna happen, as long as you don't make no noise."

After pocketing the jewels, he and his partners tied the couple up with telephone wire, hung a "Do Not Disturb" sign on their door, and walked out. The score, like every other one they pulled in San Juan, was good for several hundred thousand dollars.

CHAPTER 26

KING SOLOMON'S MINES

Peanuts and his partners were becoming frequent fliers between Miami and San Juan, as well as Nassau, in the Bahamas, where they pulled off other lucrative capers. But it was only a matter of time, Peanuts figured, before the island cops would get wise. By checking flight manifests, a smart cop would eventually discover that the same three guys left town every morning after there was a hotel burglary.

The answer, obviously, was to blow town by boat. Not a scheduled cruise liner, which also kept passenger lists, but by a seaworthy craft of their own.

The more he thought about it, the more the idea inspired him. Just like those legendary swashbucklers of yore, he and his fellow buccaneers, John and Frank, would sack the towns and sail away to steal again another day. True, he'd been caught the last time he went boating at Pompano Beach, but that was only because someone had blown the whistle on him—not because of any flaw in his plan.

John lined up a fast boat. It was a powerful inboard that would make Nassau in four to five hours. Now they were in business.

The first two things Peanuts had noticed about Nassau was that the cops rode bicycles, and they did not carry guns.

He also noticed that King Solomon's Mines, the biggest jewelry store in town, had no burglar alarm. Furthermore, the owner left the jewelry in the display window all night.

Who would steal it, right? You're stuck on an island. You ain't going nowhere. Ha-ha!

"Here's what we'll do now," Peanuts suggested. "We'll stand by the door like we're bullshittin' or somethin', or lookin' at the jewelry in the window, and John, you go to work on the lock."

They went by one evening after closing and stood in the doorway like they were passing the time of day. While Frank and Peanuts shielded him from view, John pulled out a screwdriver and removed the tumblers from the lock, so they could make a key of their own. Then he put the lock back together and they left.

They returned at midnight Saturday, after the town had gone to bed for the weekend, and let themselves in. They would have the store all to themselves until Monday morning. They originally figured on just helping themselves to the jewelry, but down in the basement they discovered a large safe.

"Holy Christ," Peanuts said as he played the beam of his flashlight on the safe. "King Solomon's mines, for real! Maybe they got the king's jewels in there."

"Yeah, but how the hell are we gonna open it?" John puzzled. "We got no torch, no punches."

"Hey, I remember one time when we flew in, they had a torch at the airport," Frank recalled.

"We better go get the son-of-a-bitch," Peanuts said.

They let themselves out of the store, locked the door, stole a car, and headed for the airport. Sure enough, there was an acetylene torch and two tanks, right where Frank had remembered them. They loaded the unit into the car and returned to the shop.

Back in King Solomon's basement they took their time burning the safe open. It was hot, smelly, smoky work. Fortunately, there was also a small kitchen in the basement, where the employees apparently prepared lunch. The boys made some sandwiches, and cracked open several bottles of champagne. After a refreshing midnight snack they finished burning the door off the safe. To their dismay, there was no jewelry in it, but their disappointment was tempered by the fact that it was stuffed full of cash.

"Jeez, lookit all the English pound money," Peanuts exclaimed, holding several of the large bills up to the light. "There must be twenty, thirty thousand dollars worth here, or maybe twenty, thirty million. How much is pound money worth?"

The boys stuffed it all into a wicker picnic basket, along with some U.S. currency that the jeweler had apparently taken in from tourists. Then they went back upstairs, crawled to the front of the store on their hands and knees, and cleaned all the diamonds out of the show cases, along with nearly a thousand French watches bearing price tags ranging from $1,500 to $1,800 apiece.

Everything was packed neatly into the wicker basket. As an afterthought, they grabbed a bottle of champagne and laid it on top of the loot. In all, they had been in the store for more than three hours. It was time to get back to the boat dock.

The trio had barely left the store, however, when a black Bahamian police officer rode up on his bicycle and challenged them. "Hey, what are you gentlemen doing out here at three in the morning? The bars are closed already."

Peanuts' brain works fastest when he is under pressure. Fishing the bottle of champagne out of the basket and holding it up for the policeman to admire, he slurred, "Aargh, we been drinkin', ossifer. Here, have a li'l sip." His companions both nodded, with silly grins on their faces.

"I think you gentlemen had better get back to your hotel and sleep it off," the policeman smiled, shaking his head. "Please, get off the streets now. You should not be out here at this hour."

"Yeah, yeah, yeah . . . . OOO-kay . . . . Tanks, buddy. We're goin. Haw, haw, haw."

They went all right—straight back to Miami, where they fenced the loot with a Cuban for half a million dollars.

Peanuts and his cronies made two subsequent trips to Nassau, where they burgled other jewelry stores, which netted them about $10,000 apiece. Shortly after their last visit to the Miami fence, he was shot to death. The Panczko gang was dealing with people who didn't mess around.

Had Peanuts been born honest, he might have become an international financier. As it was, he decided to become an international thief. The farther he roamed from home base, the more challenging the adventure. Frank and John had been criss-crossing Europe, making "scores" in Spain and the Netherlands. But it was in Venezuela that they came upon the creme de la creme.

"They got this mine in Caracas where all the diamonds come from," they told Peanuts. "And from there they go to a jewelry company where they polish 'em all up. This place must have ten, twenty million dollars worth of diamonds. You want a certain kinda diamond, they got files to look at, they got so many of 'em. Six, eight, ten carats."

"I never heard of anything like that in my life," Peanuts said, wide eyed.

"So, what d'ya figure we do?" DeLegge asked.

"D'ya know how far that is? We get a boat," Peanuts said.

They were now talking ocean sailing in a big way, so Peanuts, Frank and John brought Buddy Bradshaw in on the deal. "Buddy, he knows somethin' about boats, but he wants to be a burglar like his dad," Peanuts said. "We need a guy who knows all about bulkheads and bilges and stuff."

In response to a want ad in the *Miami Herald* they found a used boat for $90,000. It had a shower, galley, four bunks, dual engines, and twin masts with sails to save on fuel. They gave the owner a $10,000 deposit and signed a phony name to the contract, which was the last he would ever see of them or his vessel. Then they lined the deck with 55-gallon drums of fuel, covered them with a tarp, and set out to sea.

It was just getting dark as they pulled away from the dock, and the automatic steering mechanism, which would follow a charted course, went on the blink. "So, now what do we do?" Peanuts asked. "We don't wanna stop, dat's for sure."

"We take turns at the helm," Buddy told him.

"Whaddya mean, take turns? I don't know nuttin' about da ocean. You got a road map, you can go down dis or dat highway, but I never traveled on da ocean before. It's a long drive."

"We go by Loran," Buddy explained. "You steer by beeps on the transoceanic radio. We each stand a twenty-minute watch."

It proved to be one of those trips that, if anything could go wrong, it would. They ran into a gale the first night out, which ripped one of their sails right down the middle. After putting in at Puerto Rico for repairs, Peanuts suggested, "Let's go find us some broads."

"How do we do that? We don't know anybody here," Frank said.

"Lemme talk to a cab driver," Peanuts offered. A short time later he returned to his crew and briefed them: "They don't call 'em broads down here. They call 'em muchachas. Mu-chachas. But when I said 'hookers,' he knew what I meant."

With the help of the cab driver, they found several hopeful muchachas at a waterfront bar. The general procedure, when engaging a hooker in this part of creation, was for her to accompany the customer to his hotel. But the seafarers were not staying at a hotel. "Let's take 'em back to da boat wit' us," Peanuts suggested.

"On the boat? What are we gonna do wit' 'em on the boat?" Frank asked.

"When we're through wit' 'em, we can trow 'em in da ocean," Peanuts said matter-of-factly. "They're just Puerto Ricans, ya know?"

The muchachas evidently understood more English then they had let on, because two of them refused to accompany the boys to the boat. Only one was willing to take the risk, but after getting a better look at her, they opted to return to the sea as bachelors.

After gassing up at San Juan, they sailed an "S" shaped course, past the Dominican Republic, and through the Windward Passage between Cuba and Haiti, then down to Caracas.

As they crossed the Caribbean they amused themselves by blasting away at sharks, which had come alongside the boat, with their .38s and .45s. "Will ya look at dat!" Peanuts exclaimed, as he emptied his gun at the creatures. "Da slugs just put little pin holes in 'em, and dey keep right on swimmin'."

At Caracas they tied up at the dock, stole a car, and went looking for a score. The streets were crowded with tourists from several cruise liners, and every block or so they passed an unarmed police officer, walking his beat or pedaling by on a bike. Their dreams of untold riches tempered by reality, they settled on a small jewelry store protected by an alarm under an overhead balcony. "All we gotta do is shut dat alarm off," Peanuts said.

They went back to the boat, got their tool kit, and an aerosol can of foam, which had been kept in the refrigerator. The plan was to drill a hole through the balcony floor, into the top of the burglar alarm. Then squirt the foamy substance through the hole, and neutralize the alarm. As they were drilling, however, the bit broke.

"Jeezus Christ, what next?" Peanuts asked in exasperation, wiping the sweat from his forehead. He would find out in a moment.

Suddenly the air was shattered with the shrill cry of "Banditos! Banditos!" It was a fat woman across the street, who had come out of an apartment and spotted the boys on the jeweler's balcony. "Banditos!" she screamed. "Banditos!"

Peanuts, John and Frank jumped off the balcony, got into the car and drove back to the boat, where Buddy was waiting. "That's it. I say, let's go home. We blew the score," Peanuts stormed in disgust. It was a most inglorious end to a very ambitious venture—but it was not over yet.

They had no sooner put back out to sea than one of the engines conked out. Then a storm came up and ripped both the sails right off the masts. Next the refrigeration unit blew. As the small craft was being tossed from one wave to another while it tried to stay on course with only one engine, Peanuts glared at Buddy and declared, "Dis is a real lemon boat you got us."

"May Day! May Day!" Buddy began to shout.

They all joined him in hollering "May Day!" at the top of their lungs, hoping to attract the attention of another boat before they went under. They were somewhere between Cuba and Haiti. "May Day! May Day!" they yelled. Then the remaining engine coughed and quit.

As the boat bobbed silently from side to side, Peanuts suddenly recalled that our country was not on the best of terms with Cuba. "Stop yellin' May Day!" he hollered. "Those goddam Cubans will come and arrest us. We gotta think of somethin' else."

"I just did," John said, drawing his pistol. He grabbed Buddy by the front of his wet shirt, put the gun to his frightened partner's head, and ordered, "Fix that fuckin' motor."

"I dunno what to do," Buddy protested.

"Get below and figure something, you son-of-a-bitch," John said, shoving him toward the hatch, still holding the gun to his head.

Buddy was another guy who could think fast under pressure. He took parts off one disabled engine and used them to repair the other. He finally got one of them going, and they somehow made it to the coast of Puerto Rico. The boat was a disaster, and they abandoned it on the spot.

They stole a car, drove to the airport, and took the first plane back to Miami. From there, Peanuts flew on to Chicago, where he was scheduled to stand trial for getting caught with those telltale mail box keys.

CHAPTER 27

AND SO, TO JAIL

It was a hostile hometown that Peanuts came back to—at least from the Panczko point of view. For starters, he was arrested for murder.

All decked out in sports clothes and sneakers, without socks, he was on his way home from a night of cabaret hopping when sheriff's police pulled him over for straddling traffic lanes on Mannheim Road, just south of O'Hare International Airport.

He was taken to the Milwaukee Avenue Station, where Niles police were waiting to serve him with a warrant charging him with the murder of twenty-six-year-old Terrence Zilligen, a television salesman for Sears, Roebuck & Company. Zilligen was shot in the head after he had tackled one of three masked bandits who had robbed the Sears store in Golf Mill Shopping Center of $20,000.

The bandits escaped in a stolen auto—which was Peanuts' regular M.O.

Five witnesses to the salesman's murder subsequently identified him as one of the three gunmen, based on his husky physique and the way he shuffled when he walked, although no one had seen the killer's face.

While Peanuts was free on bond on that charge, someone ambushed Lover Boy Mendola and killed him with five shotgun blasts as he parked his car in the garage of his home in suburban Stone Park.

Peanuts, Joe D'Argento and James D'Antonio were all brought in for questioning in the Mendola murder, since they were known to have been among his closest associates. On the advice of George Bieber, they gave police their names and addresses, but refused to say anything more.

George Bieber no sooner extricated Peanuts from those two messes than he was indicted by a federal grand jury on a charge of counterfeiting. Specifically, the government charged him with possessing and passing more than $32,000 in bogus ten-dollar bills. When Secret Service agents arrested him in his Melrose Park home they discovered "a wonderland of eavesdropping devices," that enabled Peanuts to listen in on conversations in any room of his house.

They also found three fully loaded .38 caliber revolvers, hydraulic jacks used to force open doors, a key code book for all General Motors cars, several hood-type masks with slits for eyes, clear plastic face masks, canvas gloves, bolt cutters, lock pullers, walkie-talkie radios, and a collection of jet black jackets, sweaters and top coats.

"Those are my work clothes," Peanuts explained, when asked about his black wardrobe.

He indignantly accused police and federal agents of unlawfully breaking down the door and storming into his home with submachine guns and shotguns. The G-men said they had to break in because Peanuts refused to open the door after they went to the trouble of phoning ahead to make sure he was home.

All this excitement was the last straw for Norma, who decided that marriage to a widely-known burglar was not her idea of connubial bliss. She obtained a divorce, leaving Peanuts free to face the latest round of charges against him as a bachelor.

He was out on bond on the counterfeiting rap when he went on trial for having those incriminating mailbox keys, after eighteen months of delaying tactics by Bieber. Since he was not versed in federal law, Bieber brought in another lawyer, George F. Callaghan, to handle the actual trial work.

It was the little guys versus the big guy—Peanuts now weighed 245 pounds—when the case finally unfolded before Judge Abraham Lincoln Marovitz, who in the interim had been elevated to the federal bench.

Twelve-year-old John Kearney, his feet dangling above the floor as he sat in the witness chair, told Marovitz:

"We were playing when we saw this man being chased by the squad. He stopped, got out and tossed his key ring into the grass. I saw my brother, Jim, get the keys and hand them to the man. He said, 'Hey, Mister. You dropped your keys.' The man thanked him and threw them into the grass again. I picked them up and handed them to the man and he again flung them away. Then Mike McGarr picked them up. We were getting sort of excited, so we gave them to the police."

John's brother, Jim, now ten, along with the eleven-year-old McGarr youngster, ten-year-old Vincent Geraci, and thirteen-year-old Lawrence Rollins all took the stand and corroborated John's testimony.

It took the jury eight hours of deliberating over two days before they were able to reach a verdict. They found Peanuts guilty of illegally possessing mailbox keys. It was just ten days before Christmas. Some present!

Although Peanuts' arrest record contained more than sixty entries, it was only the third time in his career that he'd been convicted.

A lesser man might have gone straight to jail, but Peanuts remained free on bond while Marovitz ordered a presentencing investigation.

"I don't know anything about this man except what I read in the newspapers," the judge declared. "But I am going to sentence him to the penitentiary. He could get ten years. I can tell you right now I am not going to grant him probation."

With the threat of ten years hanging over his head, Peanuts had to hustle to come up with the legal fees for, not one, but two expensive mouth pieces.

A Brinks mechanic had tipped off Marty, Snuffy and Polack Bruno about an armored truck that was ripe for the plucking. They felt it was a little too risky, so they passed the info on to Peanuts. With their help he had relieved a Brinks truck of $47,000 in June of 1963, so he was more than ready to do a follow-up.

He rounded up Mike LaJoy, Frank DeLegge and Joe D'Argento, and told them, "Let's make another money wagon." They were game. After tailing the truck for more than a week, they determined that it was most vulnerable during a late afternoon stop at the Roman Catholic Church in west suburban Norridge, where it came by every Monday to pick up the weekend collections.

It was the last stop of the day, so the truck would be loaded. The driver routinely switched on the dome light and stayed in the vehicle, thumbing through the day's receipts, while the messenger went into the rectory to pick up the money.

Peanuts scheduled the job for December 28. At that time of year it was already dark by 4:30 p.m. as he, DeLegge, LaJoy and D'Argento rang the buzzer at the door of the Divine Savior rectory.

"Do you think they'll let us in?" DeLegge asked.

"Are you kiddin'?" Peanuts scoffed. "The church is open to everybody. I hear someone comin' now."

As a priest appeared at the door, the four bandits pushed their way inside. They assured the startled cleric, "We ain't gonna hurt ya, father," as they bound and gagged him. Peanuts then went back out to the car to listen in on police calls while his partners remained in the rectory, waiting for the Brinks truck.

Less than ten minutes later the money wagon pulled up. As expected, the messenger went to the rectory to get the money while the driver remained in the truck, getting his reports in order. When he rang the buzzer, LaJoy opened the door and D'Argento yanked him inside. D'Argento and DeLegge tied the guard up with the priest, while LaJoy put on the Brinks uniform jacket and cap.

The trio decided to leave the church money behind. They did not want the curse of God on their souls.

Dressed as the messenger, with a money sack slung over his shoulder, LaJoy marched back out to the truck and tapped on the door. When the driver opened it to admit the man he mistook in the dark for his partner, Peanuts, DeLegge and D'Argento were right behind him. The surprised driver barely had time to toss the keys into a slot in the money drop in the rear of the truck before the bandits overpowered him.

Earlier in the day the thieves had made a key for the padlock to the gates at Acacia Park Cemetery, several blocks away. LaJoy, still wearing the Brinks uniform, got behind the wheel of the truck and drove to the cemetery on Irving Park Road. D'Argento followed in the get-away car.

On arriving at Acacia Park, they opened the gate and drove in, locking the gate behind them. They then drove the truck to a remote part of the cemetery, where they forced the lid off the money drop with a four-foot railroad pry bar.

"Shhhh. You're making too damned much noise," D'Argento cautioned, as Peanuts strained at the pry bar.

"We're in the middle of the goddam cemetery," Peanuts groaned. "Who's gonna hear us? Dead people?"

Once he got the lid off the cash drop, they scooped up all the money and put it into bushel baskets, which they loaded into the back end of their car. Then they let themselves out of the cemetery, locked the gate, and drove off, leaving the Brinks driver handcuffed to the steering wheel of his own truck.

They went about ten blocks, to the home of Frank Culotta Junior, whose father was a burglar friend of Peanuts. "You can't find a better house than this," Peanuts assured his partners. "Frank's old man, he's got a very good name among thieves."

They went to Culotta's basement den, where they divided up the loot and put it into pillow cases. There was more than $220,000 in currency, giving each man a good $55,000 for his evening's work. There was also between $8,000 and

$10,000 in loose change, which they let Culotta keep for his trouble.

The theft would not have been discovered until the following morning, except for the fact that the fleeing bandits had made the mistake of handcuffing the driver to the steering wheel. From that position he was able to lean on the truck's horn until some irritated neighbor called police, who found him in the cemetery.

By that time, of course, Peanuts and his buddies were back in the old neighborhood, celebrating. He had also begun dating again, now that Norma had given him the boot. He was especially fond of thirty-four-year-old Margaret "Sissy" Gorman, whose sister, Mary, used to date Butch.

Six weeks later Peanuts went back before Marovitz in federal court, to face the music for getting caught with those mailbox keys. He stood meekly before the bench, arrayed in a shiny silk suit, white on white shirt, and expensive alligator shoes, as his lawyer begged for probation. But Peanuts knew he was going to get socked, just by the way the judge opened the proceedings.

"I can find no extenuating circumstances that would justify granting any consideration of a plea for probation," Marovitz said. "The report I have shows he has no honest livelihood and earns his money by betting on various athletic events. He has filed no income tax returns, yet he lives well and travels extensively. His only employment record is for the years 1943 through 1945, when he was a machine operator in a plant making munitions. This he did apparently to gain deferment from military service."

Marovitz then went down Peanuts' litany of arrests, including the prison term in Tennessee, the life sentence in Florida, which was subsequently reversed, and his pending trial for those counterfeit ten dollar bills.

"The police and the Federal Bureau of Investigation report that Paul Walter Panczko is a professional criminal who shows no remorse about his way of life," the judge continued. "This court must weigh the rights of the defendant with those of society. We conclude that his character and reputation are below any acceptable standards."

With those words, Marovitz imposed the maximum fine of $500 and sentenced Peanuts to a maximum term of ten years in federal prison. Furthermore, the judge denied an appeal bond, and ordered the prisoner to begin serving his sentence immediately.

Peanuts would spend the next year behind bars before his lawyers could get the conviction reversed, on grounds that Judge Marovitz had permitted the jurors to go home overnight while deliberating their verdict.

While Peanuts was away, his two older brothers continued to do their best to keep the family name in headlines and on court dockets.

Pops even threatened to sue the owners of the Pacific Finance Company building on Wolfram Street, after police arrested him for attempted burglary when they found him in the entry way with a lock puller in his hands, and the mechanism for the door lock lying at his feet. "The tumbler fell on my toes," he complained, as he was led limping to the patrol wagon.

Shortly after that he was arrested for stealing three million trading stamps, which he tried to sell to neighborhood merchants at a discount. While Peanuts had dabbled in diamonds, Pops swiped paper stamps.

And even though he was now fifty years old, Pops proved he was somewhat of an athlete when the cops came by the house one cold November day and tried to bust his brother, Butch.

Someone had jotted down the license number of a car seen leaving the scene of a burglary of the Ban Sales Company on Irving Park Road, and the number checked out to Edward Panczko. He hadn't even bothered to use a stolen car with phony plates, like Peanuts always did.

Police went to where the brothers now lived with their mother on North Avers Avenue, and had no trouble locating the suspect car, since it was double parked. Butch ran out of the house and tried to drive away when he saw them coming, but they cut him off and attempted to place him under arrest.

Butch had other plans, and decided to take on half the police force. Seeing the melee from the front window, Pops ran out of the house, barefoot and in his undershirt, and dived headlong into the fray shouting, "Let my brudder alone!" It took the occupants of six squad cars and three patrol wagons to subdue the battling brothers. The only official casualty was Detective John DiMaggio, who claimed Pops kicked him in the leg with his bare foot.

Pops was charged with resisting arrest, interfering with a police officer, and battery of a police officer. Butch was booked for resisting arrest and drunken driving.

On March 15, 1966, Pops was sentenced to one year and a day in the Illinois State Penitentiary for possession of burglary tools and attempted bribery. The bribery charge came when he offered Policeman Casimer Golosinski forty-four watches, valued at $2,000, after he was arrested outside a jewelry store that had just been looted.

In a typical bit of Chicago reasoning, a jury had found him innocent of burglarizing the store.

Since he was going to jail for bribery and possession of burglar tools, however, all charges stemming from his battle with police were dropped.

Peanuts, meanwhile, was brought back from prison to face trial on the counterfeiting charges. The case was assigned to none other than Judge Abraham Lincoln Marovitz. In a show of extreme panic, his lawyers quickly got the case transferred to another judge. Unfortunately for Peanuts, the case was sent to Judge Bernard M. Decker, who had a reputation of being even tougher than Marovitz.

A jury found Peanuts guilty, and Decker sentenced him to fifteen years.

He was released from prison on the mailbox key case just in time to begin serving the new term. Decker, however, permitted him to remain free on $50,000 bond pending an appeal. The United States Court of Appeals upheld the conviction, and on January 18, 1967, Peanuts surrendered to the federal marshal's office.

Before he turned himself in, he and Sissy Gorman were married. He was 43, and she was 37. They spent the weekend at the swank Park Hyatt Hotel on North Michigan Avenue, courtesy of his bail bondsman, who picked up the tab. It was the least he could do for one of his all-time best customers.

It was Sissy's idea that they make it legal. "I'm on the way to prison for fifteen years," Peanuts protested. "You ain't gonna see me for a loooong time." "I don't care," Sissy said. "Let's get married."

So, what the hell? That's what they did.

CHAPTER 28

PEANUTS ON ICE; BUTCH DIES

Peanuts spent the first two months of his new married life in the federal penitentiary at Terre Haute. From there he was sent to Leavenworth, where he would remain until the fall of 1978.

It was not exactly a great honeymoon for Sissy, either. She was indicted for attempting to bribe a juror in the mailbox key trial. The juror, Sue Taylor, told authorities that Sissy offered her $500 to hold out for acquittal and force a hung jury.

Sissy was convicted, and sentenced to five years in prison. She served two years before being released on parole. Peanuts was also convicted in the bribery case, and Judge Bernard M. Decker added another fifteen years to his prison term.

While still in the pen, he was indicted for the two Brinks jobs. One of his own pals had squealed on him in order to cut a deal for a light sentence in connection with an unrelated arrest.

Things were starting to come apart for the Panczko brothers.

Another big batch of S&H Green Stamps disappeared, and Pops became the most logical suspect. FBI agent Robert

John Miller and two other agents went to the home of Pops' sister, Louise, with whom he lived, with a search warrant.

They did not find any trading stamps, but the visit was not a complete loss. During a search of the house, a disc-like contraption with key blanks and a puncher was discovered under Pops' bed. Pops, thinking the FBI men were going to seize his precious key-making machine as evidence, grabbed it and smashed it on the floor. Then he stood, smiling smugly at the federal men as if to say, "Haw, I outfoxed youse guys." The joke was on him, however.

"Pops, you just destroyed your own property," Miller laughed. "We weren't going to take your key puncher. Our warrant only says we can look for S&H Green Stamps. Well, adios."

It seemed that Pops couldn't do anything right any more.

He thought he had perfected the art of burglarizing clothing stores. He would pull the lock out of the front door, run in while the burglar alarm was clanging, grab several armloads of suits or coats off the racks, hangers and all, throw them in the car and be on his way before police arrived.

Then one night he broke into a men's clothing store, grabbed an armload of suits hanging on a rack, gave them a yank, and the damned rack tumbled over on top of him, suits and all. The merchant had gotten wise to him, and reversed every other coat hanger.

One morning, while Pops was in the press room at the Criminal Courts Building making coffee for the reporters, two FBI agents walked in and arrested him on a charge of using slugs in pay phones. The metal slugs, known as bagels because they had a hole in the middle, had also been turning up in stamp machines in Panczko's neighborhood, which was what brought the G-men in on the case.

What led directly to Pops, however, was the fact that pay phones throughout the Criminal Courts building were being stuffed with the bagels. Always generous, Pops had been passing them out to George Bieber and other criminal lawyers, a handful at a time, and the lawyers were making a lot of calls.

As the two federal agents led Pops away for questioning, he nonchalantly dipped his hand into his pocket and sprinkled a trail of slugs on the floor behind him as they walked, getting rid of all the evidence by the time they were out of the building.

The feds had already built a pretty solid case against him, however, in the form of 1,207 slugs retrieved from various vending machines. On July 10, 1967, he was convicted of fraud and sentenced to two years in prison. He served nineteen months at Sandstone in Minnesota, returned home, and went right back to work.

On his first week back on the streets Pops and Walter Jednyak stole a Phillip Morris cigarette salesman's car on Lower Wacker Drive. They drove over to a cigar store at Ashland Avenue and Halsted Street to dispose of the loot. As they were unloading the car, a squad car approached, and Jednyak took off. Pops continued stacking cartons of cigarettes on the sidewalk, knowing that the cigar store operator regularly paid off the neighborhood cops.

The squad car stopped alongside, and one of the cops asked, "Where'd you get them cigarettes?"

"Whaddya ya mean, where'd I get'em? I work for Phillip Morris," Pops declared.

"Do you know a Phillip Morris car has been stolen?" the cop asked.

"Yeah. I been keepin' my eyes open. My boss, he warned me."

"Let me see something that says you work for Phillip Morris," the cop ordered.

Pops was running out of words. He turned to the second cop, whom he recognized from one of his many previous arrests, and said, "Harry, tell dis guy who I am."

"This is Pops Panczko, the famous burglar," Harry explained. "You know, the Polish Robin Hood."

"It's going to cost you five hundred," the other cop said.

Pops looked pleadingly at Harry. "Okay, I'll give it to ya."

"You got it now?"

"No, I'll get it later. Harry knows I'm good."

"I want that typewriter in the back seat, too."

"Yeah, okay. Meet me at twelve o'clock at Chicago and Western."

Two hours later Pops showed up at Chicago and Western avenues, paid the cops $500 and gave them the typewriter. In the interim he had peddled the load of cigarettes for $300, so the morning was a $200 loss.

Shortly after that Pops had the misfortune of running into Jack Muller. The burly Muller, who was widely acclaimed as Chicago's most honest cop, was driving an unmarked police car in the 2900 block of Devon Avenue when he spotted Panczko admiring the display window of a men's clothing store.

Muller parked the car and walked over to where he was standing. "I do not think you are out walking for your health, Pops," he surmised.

"You're right," Pops agreed. "It's kinda smoggy. I'm looking for a Christmas present—a suede jacket if you must know. It's for my brother, Paul."

"Your brother's in Leavenworth," Muller reminded him. "I don't think he's going to need a suede jacket for several Christmases to come. Put your hands against the wall and spread your feet wide apart."

On searching Pops, Muller found a key ring containing master keys for just about every known make of auto. He thought this rather strange, since Pops did now own a car at the moment. "I'm placing you under arrest for possession of burglar tools."

"Can I talk to ya?" Pops asked.

"Sure."

"You can take dis and you let me take a bus," Pops said, handing Muller $200.

"I am also charging you with bribery," Muller added.

"Well," shrugged Pops. "It don't hurt to try. Some guys wind up in prison 'cause they don't try." Warming up to the subject, he continued, "You ask some guy in prison why he didn't try to bribe a cop, he'll tell ya, 'He didn't ask me.' So, I figured I'd ask ya."

While Pops was awaiting trial for trying to bribe Muller, Peanuts was brought back from Kansas to stand trial for hijacking the two Brinks trucks. Figuring he couldn't do worse than the thirty years he was already serving, he pleaded guilty to get it over with. He was sentenced to twelve years in the federal penitentiary, to run concurrently with his other terms.

Pops fared somewhat better when he went on trial. Judge Mel R. Jiganti declared a mistrial in Criminal Court after Muller, on the witness stand, grew overly enthusiastic and blurted out information about Panczko's past that was inadmissible.

Pops figured Muller had given him a raw deal. If he didn't want to take the money, at least he could have let him go. After being freed in court Pops went over to the Shakespeare district station to look for Muller's Cadillac. He was spotted by Captain William Hanhardt, who asked, "What the hell are you hanging around here for, Pops?"

"I'm lookin' for Muller's car," Pops replied. "I'm gonna stick a bomb under da hood."

"Get out of here before I lock you up," Hanhardt warned.

Hanhardt told Muller what had happened, and Muller telephoned Panczko. "Hey, Pops. You aren't really thinking of putting a bomb in my car, are you?"

"If I'm gonna put a bomb in your car, I ain't gonna tell ya," Pops replied.

For the next several weeks, until he figured it was all a mind game, Muller opened the hood and inspected the engine every time, before he started the car.

During the holiday season of 1973, brother Butch suffered the indignity of being arrested in a neighborhood discount store as, of all things, a shoplifter. Butch, reeking of Christmas spirits, was seen walking out of the Turn-Style Family Center on North Kostner Avenue decked out in a new coat, new hat, and a pair of gloves, while carrying two bottles of My Sin spray cologne and two boxes of fine cigars under his arm.

Gregory Pittatsis, the security manager, recalled that Butch had been wearing tattered trousers and a light jacket when he entered the store. He collared the non-paying customer in the parking lot and held him for police. Pops, who was currently free on bail for stealing a drug salesman's car, hurried over to the Shakespeare Avenue station and posted $100 bond for his brother.

In the early 1970s Peanuts was transferred to the federal maximum security prison at Marion, Illinois—the modern day Alcatraz. While there he learned that his oldest brother, John—the legit one, who had been like a father to him—lay dying of cancer in Cuneo Memorial Hospital. Peanuts petitioned prison authorities for permission to pay him one last visit.

"Sure," he was told. "If you pay for the trip and take a couple of guards with you."

They didn't know Paul Panczko. The same determination that had made him one of the nation's number one thieves caused him to agree to every stipulation prison authorities tried to put in his way.

He chartered a plane, and agreed to pay the salaries of two guards who volunteered to make the trip with him on their day off. Pops met the party at Palwaukee Airport in Wheeling, and drove them to the hospital.

"What the hell are you doing here?" John said when Peanuts walked into the room.

"John, I'm not here for my health," Peanuts told him. "You ain't got much time. You know, that, don't you?" Peanuts then reached into his pocket and dug out a letter he had received in prison, advising him that his brother was near death. Tears welled in John's eyes as he read it, and he gripped his kid brother's beefy hand.

After the hospital visit Pops took Peanuts and the two prison guards out for dinner and cocktails. He then drove them back to Palwaukee, and they flew back to Marion. A few days later Peanuts was notified that John had died.

The next brother to go was Butch, who died on March 14, 1978, at the age of 61. Pops, who was badly shaken by his brother's death, was stuck with the responsibility of making arrangements. The nearest Catholic church was Saint Philomena's, about six blocks from Butch's house, on North Kedvale Avenue.

"My brother, he was a real religious guy. He never ate meat on Friday, even after ya didn't have to anymore. He stuck to eatin' fish," he told the Rev. Charles Kelly. The priest reluctantly agreed to handle the services, and Pops gave him one hundred dollars.

For his sermon, he likened Butch to one of the two thieves who were crucified next to Jesus Christ on Calvary. He spoke hopefully of the thief who repented on the cross and asked Christ to remember him.

Before the casket was closed, Pops stepped forward and placed a metal cross on a chain around his dead brother's neck.

"My brother had dis cross around his neck because he believed it would take him to Heaven," Pops explained. "Well, I didn't want dis chain being ripped off him by anybody. I know how dese tings happen, so I took da chain off his neck myself. I just wanted to make sure it was on him when dey closed da casket."

Peanuts refused to return to Chicago for the services, because prison authorities told him he would have to wear handcuffs in church, whether he liked it or not.

The Chicago press covered Butch's funeral like he was a Hollywood celebrity. During his lifetime, Butch had been arrested seventy-seven times yet, thanks to George Bieber, he had served only ten days in jail and been fined a total of $113.

The *Miami Herald* called Butch "a giant in his field," and suggested that if there was ever a Hall of Fame for Burglars, he should certainly be in it.

Two months later Pops was again arrested for breaking into a clothing salesman's car. He arrived for trial carrying ten leather attache cases under his arm. Handing them to his lawyer he said, "Here, you can always use dese."

"Where'd you get them?"

"Dey fell off a delivery truck downstairs."

When he walked into court, and saw the array of clothing laid out as evidence against him, he nudged a bailiff in the ribs and said, "If ya see a coat in here dat ya like, let me know and I'll steal it for ya."

Pops' cockiness left him when a jury found him guilty, and Judge Robert L. Sklodowski sentenced him to six years in prison. "You'll see me again at my wake," he said glumly, as he was led from the courtroom by bailiffs.

With one burglar brother buried in St. Adalbert's Cemetery and the other two locked away in prison, it looked like Chicago would be safe from crime for the first time in nearly half a century. But not for long.

Peanuts, who had sat out the Viet Nam war, the riotous Democratic National Convention of 1968, and Watergate, was paroled in September of 1978. Prison authorities gave him $100 and a bus ticket, but when he walked out of the gates at 6:30 a.m., the bus for Chicago had already pulled out and another was not due until noon.

"I ain't hangin' around here no five-six hours," Peanuts fumed. He went to the airport and gave the whole hundred bucks to the pilot of a small plane to fly him to Chicago. "Crank it up and let's go," he ordered.

In his wallet was another $500 he had accumulated in his account during his long prison stay. As soon as the plane landed at Meigs Field he took a taxi downtown to the Palmer House where he splurged on a facial, shave, massage, manicure, shoe shine and a new wardrobe.

He paid $50 for a shirt that had only cost $15 when he went away.

Then he bought a big box of candy and a dozen roses and took a cab to the North Side to call on Mary Lou Frank, a pen-pal who had written to him in prison, but whom he had never met. The marriage to Sissy Gorman, while still on the books, had long been kaput.

Mary Lou took him to R.J. Grunt's. "What's that thing?" he asked, pointing wide-eyed at the salad bar. He had never seen one before. "What are you going to have?" Mary Lou asked him. "Jeez, I dunno. I'll have whatever you have," he said.

Peanuts then moved in with his sister, Lou, and bought himself a used 1975 Cadillac. On his first night out he was arrested for making an illegal left turn.

"What the hell are ya talkin' about?" he told the arresting officer. "There's a left turn sign, right there."

"Yeah, but didn't you see the slash running through it?"

The universal traffic sign system had been introduced during the thirteen years that Peanuts was in prison, and it was all foreign to him.

When he went to court, Bieber dropped a twenty-dollar bill in the bailiff's cigar box, and Peanuts' case was called first. The judge asked the arresting officer, "Was there a sign that actually said No Left Turn?"

"No, your honor. It was a red circle, with a turn arrow in the center, and a diagonal line running through it."

"Well, I'm afraid this gentleman hasn't caught up with the new system yet," the judge said. "Case dismissed."

Right after that Peanuts got some of the old gang together and they made a jewelry salesman in Mount Prospect. The jeweler, Ted Benowitz, was robbed of $110,000 worth of jewelry after displaying his items at a flea market.

The first suspect the police came up with was Peanuts. It was his M.O., and the physical description of one of the robbers fit him exactly. He was indignant.

"Somebody knows I'm on parole and they're trying to put the heat on me by doing something like this," he said.

The roof fell in on Peanuts on December 3, 1979, as he was about to get his hands on some money for some heavy Christmas shopping. He and four of his men were nabbed in the parking lot outside a Des Plaines bank as they were putting on their masks in preparation for going inside.

Peanuts was hailed into federal court as a parole violator, and sent back to prison, where he would spend another twenty-six months.

CHAPTER 29

POPS' LAST HURRAH

Back out on parole, Joseph "Pops" Panczko reached his 65th birthday on August 30, 1983. At this milestone in life when senior citizen status is officially attained, the dean of Chicago burglars could look back on a career that had earned him a nine-page arrest record festooned with more than 180 entries. But retirement was the farthest thing from his mind. Pops still had one good score left in his repertoire.

For weeks he and his partner, forty-one-year-old George Schnell, had been following Dennis Williams, a jewelry salesman from west suburban Naperville.

They were so busy keeping tabs on Williams that they never took time to take a really good look back over their own shoulders. If they had, they might have discovered that Central Intelligence Unit detectives from Chicago, directed by Commander John Auriemma, were shadowing the two of them.

Over decades of being outwitted by the Panczkos, the cops had learned a trick or two themselves. For this surveillance operation they were using six different tail cars, changing vehicles regularly so Pops would not notice the same one behind him and get wise.

The CIU cops were waiting when Williams came out of his house that morning, stopped for gas, and headed down the road in his 1982 Buick. Pops and Schnell were a few car lengths behind him in their 1978 Chevrolet. The CIU was behind Pops in an unmarked squad car.

"We're about five miles out of town, heading south," the tail car radioed to Auriemma. "Do you want us to stick with them?"

"No. Let 'em go," Auriemma said. "If the guy gets robbed, we'll hear about it—and we'll know who did it."

Just outside of Springfield, Williams pulled into a gas station, parked his car, and went to use the washroom. Schnell jumped into the car, using a key Pops had made earlier, and drove off.

With Pops right behind him, Schnell drove the salesman's car to a school yard several blocks away, where they opened the trunk and helped themselves to his jewelry samples, his suitcase full of clothes, and a bottle of vodka.

When Williams came out of the john and saw that his car was missing, he immediately notified the state police. As suspected, the call went out over the police radio network to be on the lookout for a 1982 Buick. As soon as Pops monitored the message he figured he was home free.

"Dey're lookin' for da wrong car," he chortled.

When Auriemma heard the stolen car broadcast back in Chicago, however, he knew exactly what had happened. His agents soon spotted Panczko's Chevrolet on Interstate Hwy. 55, about 100 miles southwest of Chicago, heading home. "Let 'em come," Auriemma advised his men. "We'll be waiting for 'em."

All of the toll booths were backed up except one when they pulled up to the first toll station on the Tri State-Tollway, after leaving I-55. There was only one car ahead of them, a 1978 maroon Chevrolet, as Panczko and Schnell pulled in behind it. Schnell, who was driving, had the thirty-five cents in his hand, ready to toss into the hopper, but the car ahead didn't move.

"What da hell's wrong wit' dat guy?" Pops said aloud. "Oh, oh. Shit!"

"What's the matter, Pops."

"Dat Chevy's got M license plates. It's a CIU car. Back up!"

It was too late, another car with license plates beginning with the letter "M" had pulled in behind them and blocked them in. Before Pops and Schnell could make a break for it they were surrounded by burly men in old clothes, waving guns. One CIU agent jumped onto their hood, leveled a shotgun at them through the windshield, and shouted, "Get out of the car."

Another agent yelled, "Get the ignition keys." One of them tossed him the keys. He walked around behind the car and opened the trunk. "Yea! I've got the jewelry case," he yelled. "Plus a bottle of vodka."

Panczko and Schnell were handcuffed and placed in separate cars, to be driven to police headquarters at Eleventh and State Streets. As the caravan headed toward town Pops turned to the CIU man sitting next to him and said, "Ya know what? Dis is my birthday. How 'bout givin' me a break."

"No shit! Today's your birthday?"

"Honest to God."

"Hey, guys. It's Pops' birthday," the agent laughed. "What can we do for him?"

As if on cue, one of the cops in the front seat reached for the microphone on the dash and announced, "Attention all cars: This is Pops' birthday."

Then he started to sing, joined by voices coming over the police radio from the other five cars. "Happy birthday to you. Happy birthday to you . . ."

Strange as it was, under the circumstances, it was the first birthday party Pops Panczko ever had. It took all the meanness he could muster to keep from crying.

When they reached police headquarters, some of the top brass was there, including Captain William Hanhardt and Captain John Hinchy, whom Pops had known since they were patrolmen.

"Take the cuffs off him. He's not going to run away," Handhardt ordered when Pops was brought into detective headquarters. Then, grabbing Panczko's right hand and pumping it up and down, Hanhardt smiled, "Happy birthday, you old son-of-a-bitch."

"How much did I get, Bill?" Pops asked. "I never even had a chance ta look it over."

"The jewelry? It was worth around two hundred thousand," Hanhardt said.

"Two hunnert grand? I tink dat woulda been da best score of my life."

Pops was then led to a squad room, where nearly fifty uniformed police officers and detectives had gathered to serenade him again with "Happy Birthday." After they had finished the song, someone yelled "Speech! Speech!"

Pops was really touched. "Ya know," he said, his voice quavering with emotion. "Dis is da first time in fifty years dat youse guys didn't beat me."

After being freed on bond Pops came down with a slight headache, and palmed a bottle of aspirin tablets at Walgreen's. As he was walking out the door a buzzer went off, and he was arrested for shoplifting. What an inglorious comedown— from one of the biggest thefts of his career to the chintziest.

In true Cook County fashion, the cases kicked around through the courts for nearly two years, until Pops went on trial before Judge Thomas Durkin on August 27, 1985. As the prosecution presented its evidence one of the CIU agents testified that the jewels were recovered from the back seat of Panczko's car after it was hemmed in at the toll booth.

"Dat's a lie!" Pops shouted angrily.

"Order. Order," responded Judge Durkin, rapping his gavel.

"I object," Pops argued. "I ain't dat stupid, dat I would put da stuff in da back seat for everybody to see. It was in da trunk."

"Your objection is noted," the judge smiled. "Let the record show that the defendant says the stolen jewelry was in the trunk."

George Bieber had died in 1981 at the age of seventy-six, forcing Pops to shop around for a new lawyer. He was now being represented by Joseph Stillo, who had never dealt with anyone like Panczko before. Putting his hand on his client's arm, Stillo whispered, "We don't have a chance to win this case. I think you should plead guilty."

So Pops did, and three days later—on his 67th birthday—Judge Durkin sentenced him to four years in prison. "I can do dat in my sleep," Pops winked at Stillo.

Today Pops and Peanuts are both back on the street, collecting Social Security, and through with crime forever—they say.

Aside from his government check that the mailman brings on the third of every month, Pops has no visible means of support. He lives with his older sister, Lou, and her husband, Frank, on Chicago's Northwest Side. In February of 1991 he was the guest speaker at a Chicago Crime Commission luncheon, where he demonstrated the uses of various burglar tools. He has also lectured to the Merry Gangsters Literary Society.

For awhile, Peanuts drove a Checker Cab on the streets of Chicago. One of his biggest customers was Doris "Dolly" Fischer, a North Side madam, who used him to pick up and deliver customers for her "escort service." They fell in love, were married, and Dolly retired from the business.

"I have changed my whole life since I met this woman," Peanuts said. "She turned my life around. She is my whole life, what I have left of my life."

Today Peanuts is in the federal government's protective witness program, and lectures to FBI recruits at Quantico, Virginia.

Pops and Peanuts do not talk to one another any more, and that's really quite sad. Peanuts, of course, has Dolly to keep his feet warm at night, but Pops has only his memories.

CHAPTER 30

ADVICE FOR JEWELRY SALESMEN

By Joseph "Pops" Panczko

When a fellow goes into a jewelry store with a suitcase, you figure he has to be in that store to show his line of merchandise. He opens the case up and starts to show the store owner his jewelry samples, hoping to write up an order.

Now, jewelry thieves work the streets in pairs. When they are on a shopping avenue, one will walk down one side of the street, and his partner will take the opposite side.

When they see someone inside a store with a case with wheels on it, that means the case is pretty heavy to carry. It could be full of gold rings.

Now, when we find one of these salesmen in the store, one of us would walk in and act like a customer, and ask the price of a certain watch. As the store owner waits on him, the jewelry thief looks over at the traveling salesman's line of jewels. By now they are usually laid out on the show case.

So, now that the thief has seen what the salesman has, he tells the store owner he might come back and buy that watch. He's got to think it over. Then he and his partner will wait for the salesman—sometimes a couple of hours—to finish his sale.

Then they follow him to his next stop. When he arrives there, he usually parks his car and goes into the jewelry store to see if the owner has time to look at his samples, because he can give him a good buy.

The store owner says, "Okay. I got no buyers in my store now, so I got some time to go through your line. Bring it in." So the salesman goes back to his car to get his sample cases. He looks, but he doesn't see his car. So he runs back to the store and tells the owner what happened. "My car was stolen with all the jewelry samples in the trunk!"

The store owner tells him, "There's the phone. Call the police." So he calls the police and the police right away put it on the air. They ask him over the phone, "What kind of car have you got?" He tells them the make and model of the car, what year it is, what color, and the license plate number.

So the police put out a bulletin on the air: "All cars be on the lookout for a 1993 Buick, license LU 1002, white top, black bottom. This car is loaded with jewelry, taken in the Fifteenth District."

While this being broadcast, two or three police cars are on the scene, investigating the case, asking the salesman questions—what he had, what was the value of the jewels, and so on.

After they are finished they drive him to the station to make a general investigation by plainclothes police. Now the police show the salesman pictures of known jewel thieves. They ask him, "Did you ever see any of these fellows at any time? Maybe in a restaurant while you were having lunch?" The salesman, he tells them, "No."

Two days later his car is found abandoned. The police fingerprint the car and call a tow truck to take it to the auto pound. They call the owner and he comes to get it. He has to pay for towing, plus a storage fee for every day it was there.

Then the salesman asks the policeman at the pound, "How did they steal my car and open the trunk without forcing anything or breaking the trunk open?" The policeman tells the salesman, "They had a copy of your key."

So now the salesman leaves the auto pound and heads for the locksmith. The locksmith tells him new locks will cost forty dollars for the door locks and trunk, and fifty dollars for the ignition. The salesman says, "I won't pay that much money." So he goes home.

Now the thieves know his car, and know that he carries good merchandise, because the fence gave them a good price for it. So, two months later they rob him again, with the same keys. They got his address from his license plates, and they wait by his house for him to come out in the morning with his suitcase of jewels.

It's early, and the stores on Michigan Avenue aren't open yet, so the salesman goes to a restaurant for a cup of coffee. When he comes out fifteen minutes later, his car is gone. It's the same thing all over again. When the police find his car and he claims it at the pound, the cop at the pound says, "Did you do what I told you?"

The salesman says, "No, the locksmith wanted ninety dollars to change the locks."

So the pound policeman says, "You didn't do as I told you. Well, you lost a hundred thousand dollars worth of jewels again. That's for being too cheap to invest ninety dollars." Plus it cost him right away fifteen to twenty dollars for a cab to get home when his car was stolen, and another towing fee and storage fee at the pound.

So now, after the horse is out of the barn, he changes his locks on the car. The next time the thieves spot him they stay with him all day until he makes another mistake, which he does.

He goes to a gas station. After traveling two hundred miles on his rounds, he has to fill his tank. Then he leaves the car at the gas pump and goes into the station to sign a credit card slip, which they all carry. As he opens the door and goes into the station, he hears a car start. He gives a little look and yells, "That's my car! They're stealing my car! Stop!"

But his car is going down the road at a high speed. He calls the police and tells them he's been made for the third time. "Who would ever think that they would steal a car out of a gas station with all these people pulling in for gas?" he says. Of course, that's the whole idea.

Now the thieves let this guy alone for about a year, because he starts being careful. After a year they check his house and find that he bought a new car. They look on the back of the car to see where he got it, call the dealer and tell him they are locksmiths and a customer lost his keys, and the dealer gives them the key numbers. Then they make a set of keys for the guy's new car.

By now the salesman has told himself, "I ain't gonna let them rob me no more. I'll take my suitcase full of rings with me at all times, no matter where I go."

So the thieves are on his tail again. They follow him for six hours. He takes the suitcase out of the trunk at every stop he makes. When he goes to lunch, he takes the jewelry with him. What are the thieves going to do? That's easy.

They tail the salesman to his next stop, where he parks his car, takes his suitcase of jewels, and goes into the store. I watch from across the street, and when I see him packing his merchandise back into the grip after he makes his sale, I give the high sign to my partner who has the car staked out.

My partner lets himself into the jeweler's car with the key we already made, and lays down on the front seat. When the jeweler gets to his car he heads right for the trunk, to stow his samples out of sight. The second the guy lying in the front seat hears the trunk lid slam shut, he starts up the car and drives off, leaving the salesman standing in the street with his keys in his hand.

This salesman has now been robbed four times, because he is dumb.

The word goes out among thieves that he's an easy make. Six weeks later a couple of guys drive by his house around 8 o'clock at night. His car isn't there. They call the house, but no one answers the phone. Then they ring the doorbell—again, nobody home. The salesman is out with his wife. So the thieves pry the door open, go in, and find his jewelry case in the bedroom closet.

Why do salesmen always hide their jewelry in the bedroom closet? The thieves don't touch anything else in the house. They aren't burglars, they are jewel thieves, and that's all they take.

But we aren't the only crooks. Let me tell you a true story. This is a good tip for cops and insurance investigators:

Once we followed a jewelry salesman to a store, and when he went in to see if the jeweler had time to talk to him, we jumped into his car and took off. As soon as we got out of sight of the store we opened his trunk and—guess what?—it was empty. No sample case. We were tricked!

It turned out that the salesman suspected he was being followed the previous afternoon, and he left his sample case in the jeweler's safe overnight. We stole an empty car! Now the salesman comes out of the store, sees his car is gone, and rushes back into the store.

"Why did you come back? Did you forget something?"

"Somebody stole my car. We've got to call the police."

"Wait a minute," the jeweler tells him. "When the police arrive, you tell them your sample case was in the car when it was stolen. I'll be your witness. I'll tell them you arrived to make a call to my store, which I been buying jewels off you for years, and somebody stole your car. When the police find your car there will be no sample case in it. The police will be good witnesses. The insurance company will pay, and nobody will know but the two of us. I'll give you a good price for your samples. Nobody will know."

And that's what happened. The next day we read in the paper that the jewelry salesman's car had been stolen with all his samples. So the salesman and the store owner beat the insurance company out of $100,000. They made out better than we would have in fencing the loot.

And people call me a crook!

CHAPTER 31

ANTI-CRIME TIPS FROM ONE WHO KNOWS

By Paul "Peanuts" Panczko

These days all the top burglars go all over the country. Now, how they know when you're not home is newspapers lying around, of course, mail out in front of your house, and the same lights on day and night.

Most of the very exclusive homes have alarms. No problem. They can be shut off with ordinary burglar tools. How you can tell when people are out, is you just ride by at night and you will see a small light, usually near the front door of the house. It is either red or yellow in color.

A red light means the alarm is on and the people are out. The yellow light means they, the home owners, want people to know they have an alarm. They have little emblems on the door. Some kids who see them will probably stay away, because these alarms are like direct to the police stations. But for a pro, they are no problem. If you know your business, these alarms are not difficult to deactivate.

What people should do when they set the alarm and go out is stick a piece of tape over the little light. So then, when burglars cruise by, they won't see it on in the darkness. If they do make the house, without knowing the alarm is there— boom!—the police will be right over.

If the cops are after you, the most important thing is being a good wheelman. You got to have a lot of driving experience, where you are being chased a lot. Anybody can't be a wheelman. I've seen guys at the Indianapolis 500. They are drivers, aren't they? Great drivers, right? Put them behind the wheel where a copper is shooting at you and he will lock up, freeze.

You can't be afraid. It's got to be in you. When you are being chased and getting shot at, it is different than just going around the track, around and around.

Those Indy 500 guys are probably greater drivers than I will ever be. But get them under pressure, police cars are chasing you and they got the intersections blocked off and shooting at you, and then let's see what they can do.

My souped-up 1940 Ford was fitted in the back with a piece of steel or armor plating about an inch thick—the kind of plating found on loading docks used to bridge the gap between the dock and the rear of a truck. In the Ford, the plating was placed right behind the rear seat, in front of the trunk.

My Ford could go eighty-ninety miles an hour inside half a block. I could be doing fifty or sixty in first gear before I slapped it into second.

When I'm chased, I got the advantage. I got the faster car. The copper, with his radio, he got that on me a little bit. But you never go straight. You got to go like one, two blocks left, one, two blocks right. That way, they can't radio a description of the streets you're going down because you keep changing streets. That way, they can't set up your capture. They can't lock you in.

Then we had special switches to control the lights. You see, when you are being chased, that is when you have the advantage. Like going sixty, seventy miles an hour down a side street, and two, three blocks ahead of them. Now you put on the brake and they don't see the brake lights because you switched them off. You whip around the corner and they go right by you. The switches were right on the dashboard. One switch would put out all the lights.

Now, as far as jail is concerned, there are three things prison officials must maintain or face riots: good food, generous visitation privileges with people on the outside, and no tampering with the mail. And, oh yes, I might mention a fourth—sex, you know, with those gal-boys.

I never voted in my life. My people were Democrats, so I am a Democrat. As far as politics, what I think of politics— what is politics? You know what politics is? You vote for people. Or, they will do this and do that. I don't care who gets in, it's all bullshit. They all look for the bottom line. They all make their own dollar, or get their own people in there. I think the late Richard J. Daley was one of the greatest mayors there ever was. He at least helped everybody. You know, fixed up the city. But he took care of his people. Politics is getting your friends in something. You are supposed to help your friends because they helped you get in. That's politics.

Me and Pops would be millionaires today if we had played it straight.

CHAPTER 32

KEEP YOUR NOSE CLEAN

By Pops Panczko

When I went to sign up for the Marines in World War II, they told me my teeth weren't even. If I had made it I would have been there until I retired, and probably would have had five kids. I would have been a sergeant or a colonel, if I wouldn't have been dead. I was young enough to teach me things.

Now that I've survived four shootings and long stretches in prison, and have reached my seventies, I'm old enough to teach others a few things. Young people should listen to me, because the cops always said I'm a good teacher.

I used to be a teacher in crime, wising up young punks on how not to get caught; how to profit by my mistakes. But no more. I'm ready to close the book on my life with that much-repeated statement: Crime doesn't pay.

All my life I stole for lawyers and police payoffs, and did all that time in the penitentiary, and got shot once in the head, once in the stomach, once in the chest and once in the back. The one in the head was the bad one. I was in a coma for over thirty days. My brains were out at one time. I ain't like I should be.

So, don't be a fool, kids. Quit now before it's too late. I wish you could see all the kids I saw while I was in the Graham Correctional Institute. Plus, there is Lincoln, which holds 1,500. Also Logan. All kids. And when they get filled up they send them to Graham.

So, wake up before it's too late. I mean it, kids.

Joliet prison has young kids. All mixed with lovers. Once you arrive in one of those places, you will never be a boy or a man. Most of the prisoners are street gang members from the worst parts of Chicago—Vice Lords and Kings and people like that. They will make a girl out of you the first day you are behind bars, and will force you to commit unspeakable sex acts.

I had a young fellow about thirty years old in my cell. Nice kid from a good home, with fine parents. The gang-bangers came to see him, and after that he was afraid to go out of the cell, even to the day room. He told me they had tried to rape him.

So think twice, kids, before you commit a crime. If you get away, your partner will beef on you later. Most of the young people I knew in prison were there because someone had told on them.

Let me tell you about one kid who came to Graham while I was there. He was sentenced from Wheaton, in Du Page County. He had gotten caught shoplifting in a store. Because he had a small record, the judge gave him thirteen years. Can you believe it? Thirteen Years!

Everything in stores today is wired up. An alarm is on. If you put something in your pocket and pass the cashier, an alarm goes off. I know all about that, because I was once caught with a bottle of aspirins in my pocket. Luckily, I had the money to pay for it, and the store people let me go after I gave them thirty dollars and talked them into giving me a break.

Was I happy! Never again will I take anything off the counter and put it into my pocket. Believe me. If you don't believe me, go into a Walgreen's and put something into your pocket. You'll never reach the outside door.

The only people crime does pay for are the guards in the penitentiaries. Because of crime, they have good jobs watching thieves and crooks. Without thieves and crooks, they would have no jobs. The government would have to close all the penitentiaries. So, those guys will be happy to see you. But—take my word for it—you won't be happy to see them.

Remember, you heard it from Pops.

EPILOGUE

Shortly after completing the research for this book, the authors were driving on Chicago's Northwest Side when a shiny blue car came up behind them and sounded its siren. The authors pulled over to let the car pass. Instead, it pulled alongside, siren still wailing, and stopped. Then its 75-year-old driver leaned over, rolled down the window on the passenger side, and flashed a toothy grin. It was Pops.

"Haw! Haw!" he laughed, and drove away.

INDEX

ADT Security, 94
Aberdeen Street, 116
Acacia Park Cemetery, 287
Accardo, Anthony J., 228
Accardo, Clarice, 228
Ace Key Shop, 5
Ace Lock Company, 122
Adamowski, State's Attorney
  Benjamin S., 209
Adams Street, 77, 99, 138, 148
Agerone, Rocco, 166
Agin, Stephen, wagonman, 212
Aitken, Captain Andrew, 229
Albany Park District station,
  102, 246
Alberto VO-5 hair cream, 22,
  224
Alcock, John, policeman, 138
Amelia Restaurant, 116, 129
American Lock Co., 25
Amlings Florists, 145
Andrew Jackson Hotel, 132
Archer Avenue, 103
Armitage Avenue, 62, 129, 165
Ashcraft, Judge Alan E., 128

Ashkanez Deli, 108
Ashland Avenue, 79, 111, 116,
  142, 295
Augusta Boulevard, 50
Auriemma, Commander John,
  303
Aurora, Illinois, 121
Austin Boulevard, 229
Avers Avenue, 289

Bad Lands, 28, 36
Baer, Moishe, 235
Bahamas, 275
Baker, Everett, 110, 128
Baltimore, Maryland, 249
Ban Sales Company, 289
Bananas, Johnny, 131
Barfield, Warden Joseph, 161
Barnes, Judge John P., 151
Barney's Market Club, 145, 167
Barsey, Herbert, 192, 195
Bates, Linn, 207
Baumann, Ed, 200
Bed Bug Row, 28
Behnke, Robert, 176

Bellwood, Illinois, 222
Bellows, Charlie, 195
Belmont Avenue, 148, 189
Benowitz, Ted, 301
Benton Harbor, Michigan, 126
Berg, Detective Raymond, 65
Bergstrom, Judge Burton, 211, 214
Bertonicini, Gugliemo, 139
Berwyn, Illinois, 84
Beverly Hills, 20, 233
Bicek, Judge Frank, 49, 103
Bieber, George, 103, 105, 108, 126, 135, 141, 145, 147, 165, 171, 178, 186, 195, 199, 206, 211, 213, 229, 271, 284, 294, 299, 301, 306
Bimmerlee, Sergeant Patrick, 216
Biscayne Boulevard, 273
Black, Francis, 144
Black Hole, 28
Blanton, Mary, 263
Bloodgood, Joseph, 207
Bonafede, Sam, 215
Boone, Warden Dan, 158
Boston, Massachusetts, 271
Boston Red Sox, 76
Bosworth-Devon Garage, 98
Bradshaw, Buddy, 278
Bragg, Johnny, 156
Bridewell, 59, 66, 91, 116, 140
Brinks, 24, 223, 226, 286, 297
Brodkin, Mike, 105, 136, 147, 151, 165, 195
Brooklyn, New York, 122
Broward County, Florida, 264
Brunk, I.W., 137
Bruns, Policeman Albert, 87
Brushy Mountain Prison, 157
Bughouse Square, 117
Burglary, Inc., 175
Busch, Harry J., 68, 187, 195

Bush, Eddie, 200, 202, 203
Byrne, Don, patrolman, 177
Byrnes, Daniel E., 168

California Avenue, 48, 94, 128, 168
California Boulevard, 209
Callaghan, George, 285
Camp McCoy, 53
Campagna, Ralph, 183, 188
Campbell Avenue, 171
Capone, Al, 86; whiskey, 32
Caracas, Venezuela, 278, 280
Carson Pirie Scott, 184
Cartin, James "Snuffy Ryan", 72
Casey, Cornelius, patrolman, 206
Central Avenue, 120, 142
Central Intelligence Unit (CIU), 12, 303
Cermak, Anton, 195
Champagne, Anthony, mob lawyer, 198
Checker Cab, 7, 307
Chicago American, 180, 200
Chicago Avenue, 100, 139, 173, 210, 216
Chicago Crime Commission, 104, 307
Chicago Cubs, 73
Chicago Daily Defender, 200
Chicago Daily News, 86, 200
Chicago Heights, Illinois, 268
Chicago Hilton and Towers, 169
Chicago Loop, 88, 112
Chicago & North Western station, 109
Chicago River, 48, 175
Chicago Sun-Times, 86, 200
Chicago Tribune, 86, 144, 179, 197, 200

Chicago White Sox, 74
Cicero Avenue, 72, 83, 145
Cicero, Illinois, 134
City News Bureau, 111, 200
Civella, Nick, mobster, 143
Civilian Conservation Corps (CCC), 45, 53
Clark Street, 74, 139, 148
Clark, William, detective, 174
Clarksville, Tennessee, 163, 222
Clay, Policeman Frank, 111
Clement, Tennessee Gov. Frank G., 155
Cleveland, Ohio, 145
Coffee Man, 54
Cohen, Marvin, 122
Cohn, Charlie, 195
Collins, Justice of the Peace Joseph R., 126
Comiskey Park, 74
Concord Restaurant, 90
Conley, Robert, 211
Cook County Morgue, 177
Cook, Edward, 257
Cook, Jesse, 200, 202, 203
Cooney, John, patrolman, 177
Cooper, William, detective, 175
Corbett, Detective Sgt. James, 99, 214
Cosellino, Ralph, 159
Cotton fields, 160
Cragin police district, 150
Crane Company, 72
Crane, George, 195
Crane Technical High School, 50
Crash gates, 23
Crawford Avenue, 245
Criminal Courts Building, 59, 91, 105, 112, 145, 179, 190, 195–204, 294
Cuba, 280

Culotta, Frank, 287
Cullen, T.J., jewelers, 183
Cullen, Thomas, 183
Cuneo Memorial Hospital, 298
Curry, Detective Al, 90
Cusack, Detective Frank, 90
Curtin, John, policeman, 192

D'Amato, John, 272
D'Antonio, James, 268, 284
D'Argento, Joe, 284, 286
Dakey, Lieutenant James, 138
Daley, Patrick, detective, 207
Daly, Patrick, detective, 170
Daly, Judge William V., 110, 128, 192, 206, 208
Damen Avenue, 144, 165
Dane County, Wisconsin, 207
Davis, Jacob, 132, 134
Dawson, Hanley, 4
De Biase, John, 131
Decker, Judge Bernard M., 290
De Grazio, Anthony, 228
DeLegge, Frank, 224, 271, 286
Democratic National Convention, 300
Desplaines Street, 44; police station, 128
Devine, Richard, 178, 186, 190, 211
Devon Avenue, 94, 296
Di Franzo, John, 129
Dieringer, Judge Henry, 190
Diets, Policeman Walter, 90
Dillinger, John, 62
DiMaggio, John, detective, 290
Divine Savior Rectory, 286
Division Street, 57, 62, 77, 142, 177, 191, 207
Doherty, James, 86
Dominican Republic, 280
Dougherty, Judge Charles S., 67, 91, 111, 138, 142

Drake Hotel, 91
Duffy, Ray, policeman, 138
Durkin, Judge Thomas, 306

East Chicago Avenue Police
    District, 2
Edens Plaza, 183, 189
Edison, Thomas, 10
Edwards, Jesse, 259
Egan, Edward, 199
Eighteenth District station, 216
Eisenhower Expressway, 115
Eleventh and State Streets, 305
Elmwood Park, 145
Elston Avenue, 67, 142, 190
English, Judge Robert, 208, 214
Erie Street, 62, 116
Evangalista, William, 215
Evanston Hospital, 185
Evanston, Illinois, 180

Fairfield Avenue, 210
Fantasies, Unlimited, 7
Federal Bureau of Investiga-
    tion, 120, 121, 148, 183, 254,
    263, 288, 294, 307
Fedore, George "Stogie", 228,
    242
Felony Court, 103, 138, 171, 196
Ficarotta, Vincent, 96, 137
Fillmore Street Station, 96
Fiore, Lena, 162
First Distributors, 95
Fischer, Dolly, 7, 307
Florio, Lou, 191
Flynn, Patrick, police sergeant,
    173
Foley, Peter M., policeman, 150
Foree, James, 200
Forest Park, Illinois, 180
Formfit Aluminum, 268
Forst, Frank, 65, 242
Fort Lauderdale, 257, 264

Fort Pillow, 159
Fort Sheridan, 45, 53
Foster Avenue, 168
Fox, Peter & Sons, 41, 82
Frank, Mary Lou, 300
Franklin Park, 226
Franklin Street, 77, 292
Freund, Otto, 87
Friedlander, Dan, 200
Fullerton Avenue, 77, 107
Fulton Street Market, 30, 32,
    41

Gaines, Lewis, 211
Garippo, Lou, 197
Gariti, Marty, 72, 152, 225
Garrett, Bill E., 200
Gary, Indiana, 137, 139
Gaughn, Thomas, detective,
    207
Geary, Judge Joseph, 166
Geraci, Vincent, 285
Giancana, Sam "Mooney",
    198, 200
Gilbert, Judge Charles, 136
Glazik, Henry, patrolman, 206
Glencoe, Illinois, 47
Glenview, Illinois, 185
Globe Beverage Co., 93
Glon, John, patrolman, 84
Goelz, Harry, policeman, 140
Gold Coast, 62, 91
Goldstein, Irving, 5
Golf Mill, 283
Golosinski, Casimer, police-
    man, 290
Gordon, Meyer, 120, 134
Gorman, Margaret "Sissy",
    288
Gowran, Clay, 200
Graf, Harold, policeman, 184
Grand Avenue, 72, 116
Grand jury, 202

Grant Park, 171
Grapp, Wesley G., 264
Gray, Chester, 109, 257
Griffin, Judge John J., 111
Grunt's, R.J., 300
Grygiel, Frank, 15, 50, 307;
    Louise, 15, 307; Richie, 15
Guinness Book of Records, 265
Gutknecht, John, 178
Guzik, Jacob "Greasy Thumb",
    86
Gypsy proverb, 71

Haiti, 280
Halsted Street, 97, 108, 242, 295
Hanhardt, William, detective,
    225, 297, 305
Harlem Avenue, 145
Harrington, Judge Cornelius J.,
    180
Harrison, Capt. Thomas, 116
Hasten, Judge Erwin J., 232
Havana, Cuba, 265
Hayes, Detective Roland, 79–81
Hell's Half Acre, 28
Heneghan, William, 206
Herd, Lawrence, 132
Hermitage, 132, 135, 152
Highwood, Ill., 47
Hilton Hotel, 109, 170
Hinchy, Captain John, 305
Holland Jewelers, 97
Hollywood, 233
Holmgren, Judge Elmer, 178
Holod, Thaddeus, 165
Holy Cross Hospital, 141
Holy Innocents Roman Catho-
    lic Church, 27
Holy Name Cathedral, 68
Hornstein, Irving, 236, 272
House of Correction, 59
Hoyne Avenue, 79
Humboldt Park, 27

Hunt, Robert, patrolman, 165
Huron Street, 116

Iacocca, Lee, 25
Igoe, Judge Michael L., 127
Illinois Bell Telephone Co., 112
Illinois Parole Board, 166
Illinois Secretary of State, 3,
    107, 241, 246
Illinois State Penitentiary, 68,
    128, 290
Illinois Supreme Court, 68, 215
Indiana State Penitentiary, 127
Internal Revenue Service, 112
Interstate Hwy. 55, 304
Iowa Street, 50, 93
Irvin, Gene, detective, 210
Irving Park Road, 111, 145
Irwen, Eugene, detective, 270

Jack's Men's Shop, 134
Jackson, Andrew, 136
Jaffe, Milton, 110
Janesville, Wis., 119
Jannick, William, policeman,
    171
Jednyak, Walter, 79, 97, 99,
    106, 116, 131, 137, 295
Jefferson Park police, 141
Jiganti, Judge Mel, 297
Johnson, Arthur "Fish", 42,
    62, 77, 129, 131
Johnson, Judge E.C., 17
Johnson, John Patrick, 257
Joliet, Illinois, 68, 122
Jordan, Michael, 22
Joy Club, 151
Juvenile Detention Center, 31,
    40, 48

Kaczmarek, Chester, 63
Kaczynski, Old Man, 30
Kalusa, Frank, patrolman, 165

Kansas City, 144
Karlov Avenue, 143
Katilus, Paul, policeman, 136
Kay, Richard, 257
Kearney, James, 268, 285
Kearney, John, 285
Kedzie Avenue, 63
Kelleher, James, detective, 175
Kelly, Reverend Charles, 299
Kelly, Donald, detective, 190
Kennedy family, 1
Kennedy, John, 258
Kennedy, President John F., 272
Kennelly, Mayor Martin, 170
King Solomon's Mines, 20, 275
Kleine, Henry, 98
Kluczynski, Judge Thomas, 141
Knoxville, Tennessee, 157
Koniecki, Dennis, 205, 212
Koniecki, Edward, 205, 208, 212, 214
Kupinski, Walter, 34, 55
Kush, George, detective, 170, 180, 207
Kysar, Dr. John E., 270

La Buy, Judge Walter J., 144
Labriola, Paul "Needle Nose", 86, 111
Lafayette elementary school, 37, 50
LaJoy, Mike, 224, 271, 286
Lake Michigan, 125
Lake Shore Drive, 111
Lake Street, 74, 97
Lakeshore Athletic Club, 107
Lambeth, Judge Douglas, 265
Landato, Frank, 210, 214
Lane, Clem, 86
Lang, Irving, 188
LaSalle Street, 88
Lawndale Avenue, 87, 120

Lawrence Police District, 172
Leavenworth Penitentiary, 128, 293
Legato, Tony, 227, 257
Leopold-Loeb, 197
Leoto, Sam, 65
Levee, 28
Lima, Ohio, 145
Lincoln Avenue, 225
Lindsay, Judge William J., 165, 197
Little Cheyenne, 28
Logan Boulevard, 143
Lohman, Joseph D., 166
Longdon, Rodney, policeman, 213
Los Angeles, 240
Loser, District Attorney General J. Carlton, 135
Luczak, Judge Edward, 140
Lurie, Max, 141
Luzon, 141
Lynch, Lieutenant James, 175

Mackey, Lieutenant Thomas, 140
Madison Street, 72
Madison, Wisconsin, 207
Madsen, Elmer "Whitey", 63, 129
Mafia, 69
Magner, John, police sergeant, 171
Malitz, Marvin, 66
Mandel Brothers Department Store, 175
Mandel-Lear Building, 175, 189
Manhattan, 254
Mannheim Road, 272, 283
Manufacturers' National Bank, 143
Maplewood Avenue, 151

Mardi Gras, 132
Marines, U.S., 55, 191
Marion, Illinois, 298
Marko, Walter, 71, 119, 152
Marmaduke, Virginia, 86
Marovitz, Judge Abraham Lincoln, 206, 285, 290
Marshall Field's, 112
Martin, Hans, 189
Martin, Vincent, detective, 175
Maryland, 249
Maxwell Street, 25, 34
McCormick, Patrolman John, 135
McGarr, Judge Frank J., 269
McGarr, Michael, 269, 285
McNally, Lt. Eugene, 98
McSwain, George, FBI chief, 148
Meade Avenue, 148
Meigs Field, Chicago, 126, 300
Melrose Park, 144, 268
Melvina Avenue, 146
Memphis, Tennessee, 159
Mendola, Donna, 96, 138
Mendola, Guy "Lover Boy", 74, 84, 96, 113, 121, 131, 133, 137, 222, 237, 240, 253, 268, 284
Merchandise Mart, 1, 167, 215
Mercury convertible, 78
Merry Gangsters Literary Society, 307
Meyer, Edward, 143
Miami, 278
Miami Beach, 257
Miami Herald, 278, 299
Michigan Avenue, 91, 139, 170, 175, 291
Michigan State trooper, 124
Miller, Robert John, 294
Milwaukee Avenue, 20, 65, 77, 237

Milwaukee Road, 29
Miner, Judge Julius H., 68, 186, 188
Minneapolis-St. Paul, 227
Minnesota, 227
Mister Grand's, 11
Moll, Richard, 213
Moloney, Thomas J., policeman, 150
Moody, Betty Jane, 263
Mosel's Clothing Store, 139
Moss, LeRoy, 128
Mount Prospect, Illinois, 301
Muller, Jack, policeman, 296
Municipal Court, 140
Murphy, Captain Thomas, 206
Murray, James, 140, 145, 222
My Sin, 297

Nadherny, Louis J., 177
Naperville, Illinois, 303
Narcotics Court, 201
Nashville Jewelers' Association, 136
Nashville, Tennessee, 20, 132, 151, 221
Nassau, 275
National Currency Exchange, 140
National Jewelry Fair, 170
National Tea Company, 185, 269
Nelson, Judge Benjamin, 270
Neil, W.S., prison warden, 154
Neilsen's Restaurant, 145
Ness, Eliot, 263
Neurauter, Lieutenant John, 190
New Orleans, 132
New York Motor Vehicle Department, 122
Newark, New Jersey, 253
Newport Avenue, 148

Nick the Greek, 11
Niles, Illinois, 283
Nobel Park, 28, 40
Norman, Jack, 136
Norridge, Illinois, 286
North Avenue, 95, 108, 136, 139, 193
North Shore train, 47
Norwegian-American Hospital, 66

Oak Park, Ill., 62, 222
Oakdale Avenue, 113
Ochs, Martin "The Ox", 110
O'Connell, Judge Harold P., 171, 173, 192
O'Connor, Timothy J., police commissioner, 151, 166
Ogden Avenue, 72, 97
O'Hara, Detective Donald, 99, 102
O'Hare International Airport, 271
O'Malley, Patrolman Raymond, 135
O'Neill, Sergeant James, 175
Ohlin, Carl, 115
Olson, Harold, detective, 175
Oriental Theatre, 88
Orkowski, Al, 101
Orleans Street, 167, 216
Orloski, Eddie, 90
Ortman, Marguerite, 180
Oswald, Lee Harvey, 273
Owens, Detective Sgt. William, 99

Pacific Finance Company, 289
Palm Beach, 258
Palmer House, 300
Palwaukee Airport, 298
Palzen, Frank, 142
Panczko, Adeline, 221

Panczko, Edward "Butch", birth, 27; bladder problem, 118; bribe arrest, 206; burglar, 19, 96; CCCs, 45; cement mixer theft, 189; currency exchange, 145; death, 298; fights Detective Hayes, 80; fights detective Kelly, 190; fights cops, 289; flees to Fox Lake, 80; jewelry heist, 88; Mandel-Lear job, 175; mopery, 87; murder charge, 178; "Sissy" Gorman, 288; shot, 140, 173; takes over, 165; trading stamps, 269; whiskey theft, 116, 128
Panczko, Eva, 27, 42, 50, 100
Panczko, Frank, 27, 152, 221
Panczko, John, 27, 45, 151, 298
Panczko, Joseph "Pops", advice from, 309; birth, 27; birthday bust, 305; bribes cops, 219, 243; burglar, 19; CCC, 47, 53; car shot up, 217; car stolen, 216; coffee man, 10; contempt of court, 214; dognapping, 109, 168; Edens Plaza job, 183; first date, 67; first press notice, 57; fur job, 84, 228; furniture job, 172; jewelry heists, 82, 88, 94, 121, 207, 290; kills pedestrian, 66; last hurrah, 303; Merchandise Mart caper, 6; onion hijack, 210; press room, 201; run over, 85; parole, 166; poodle theft, 108; Pops nickname, 93; prison, 68, 81; Saint Joseph, Michigan, 125; "screwdrive" trial, 205; shot, 40, 90, 116, 184; Thanksgiving, 54; Vandalia, 233

Panczko, Lauretta, 78, 132, 134, 147, 151

Panczko, Louise, 27, 40, 50, 66, 79, 83, 100, 141, 162, 168, 294, 301

Panczko, Norma, 222, 225, 284

Panczko, Paul "Peanuts", anti-crime tips, 315; baseball games, 74; birth, 27; Brinks jobs, 286; burglar, 9, 19, 116; cab driver, 7; CCCs, 53; currency heist, 143; fur jobs, 84; Hollywood, 233; jewelry heists, 83, 88, 96, 110, 128, 145, 223, 239, 249; King Solomon's Mines, 275; meets Lauretta, 78; murder arrest, 284; Nashville caper, 132; meets Norma, 222; Parker Pen caper, 119; perfecting the van, 24; Pompano Beach, 257; San Juan, 274; Sears caper, 226; shakedown victim, 144; shootout, 142; takes over, 71; Tennessee State Prison, 153; released, 221; truck stops, 223

Panczko, Paulette, 146, 151

Panczko, Peter, 27, 45, 48, 82

Panos, James, 190

Panozzo, Louie, 100, 169

Park Hyatt Hotel, 291

Parker Pens, 22, 119–121, 144

Parole officer, 93, 106

Paulina Street, 138

Pearl Harbor, 66

Pennsylvania, 178

Petacque, Lieutenant Ralph, 171

Peterson, Virgil, 104

Petros, Tennessee, 157

Pettler, Robert, detective, 210

Phillip Morris, 295

Pinkerton Detective Agency, 63, 83

Pittasis, Gregory, 298

Pittsburgh, Pennsylvania, 132

Pittsfield Building, 180

Plastic face masks, 24

Polack Bruno, 145, 152, 225, 286

Pompano Beach, 257

Port Huron, Michigan, 124

Portman, Morris, 66

Principe, Daniel, patrolman, 268

Prisonaires, The, 156

Pseris, James, 116

Pulawski, old lady, 30

Pumpernickel's, 262

Quantico, Virginia, 307

Racine Avenue, 36; station, 66, 102, 206; court, 111

Ragen, Warden Joseph, 82

Raguse, Arthur, policeman, 173

Railway Express Agency, 115, 127, 253

Randolph Street, 88, 167

Ration board thefts, 72, 73

Ravenswood Hospital, 142

Regan, Jack, 216

Rice, Detective Max, 99

Ricky's restaurant, 191

Robart, Policeman Edward, 111

Rockwell Street, 41, 66, 251

Rodi's Boatyard, 203

Rogers Park District police, 98

Rollins, Lawrence, 285

Roman Catholic Church, 286

Roosevelt, Franklin D., 45

Roosevelt Road, 31, 96, 137

Rossi, Joe, 240, 253

Royer, Detective Murray, 96

Runyon, Damon, 195

Rusty, 168
Ryan, Judge Daniel, 201
Ryan, James "Snuffy", 72, 152, 225
Ryan, Kevin, detective, 193

S & H Green Stamps, 293
Saint Adalbert's Cemetery, 300
Saint Charles, 37, 49
Saint Hedwig's Church, 79
Saint Joseph, Michigan, 124; Herald-Press, 125
Saint Philomena's Roman Catholic Church, 299
Salato, Pete, 93
San Francisco, 240
San Juan, Puerto Rico, 274
Sandstone, Minnesota, 295
Sbarbaro, Judge John, 68
Schnell, George, 303
School Street, 146
Schultz, Edward G., 180
Schultz, Walter, policeman, 144
Scislo, Charles, 129
Scordo, Bruno, 139, 145
Screwdrive trial, 211
Sears, Roebuck & Company, 226, 283
Severinghaus, Weiler and Heager, 67
Sexton, Charlie, 223
Shaker Heights, Ohio, 145
Shakespeare District Station, 129, 165, 173, 191, 297
Shoshone, Idaho, 53
Sinatra, Frank, 203
Sklodowski, Judge Robert L., 300
Skokie, Illinois, 236
Skokie Lagoons, 47
Smicklas, Detective Emil, 128, 138

Social Security, 15
South State Street Court, 110
South Water Street, 90
Sparta, Wis., 53
Sponges, 77
Springfield, Illinois, 304
Stahlman, Sergeant Richard, 117
Starzyk, Adolph, 57, 63
State Prison Farm, Vandalia, 232
State Street, 88
Stateville Penitentiary, 82, 91, 144, 232
Steel shutters, 23
Stellato, Anthony, patrolman, 268
Sterczek, Stanley, 41
Stevens Hotel, 22, 169
Stillo, Joseph, 307
Storm, Peter, policeman, 173
Stratton, Governor William G., 215
Sullivan, Judge Mason S., 128
Summerdale Police District, 171
Sunbeam shavers, 222
Sun Valley, 53
Superior Court, 139, 215
Superior Street, 93, 100, 170, 217
Sweeney, Russell, detective, 175
Sylvester, Lawrence, 89, 96, 242
Szymanski, Skeets, 143

Tank traps, 22
Tarkington, Dr. Joseph, 183, 186
Tarnove, Joseph, 259
Taylor, Leonard, jeweler, 258
Taylor, Sue, 293

Tennessee State Penitentiary, 136, 152–163
Terre Haute, Indiana, 128, 293
Three Minute Gang, 75, 84, 120, 129, 139, 239
Thirty-Fourth District station, 68
Thompson, Illinois Governor James, 197
Thompson, Wisconsin Governor Vernon, 207
Thumb, prison guard, 160
Tobin, Joseph, 188
Togel sisters, Florence, Vera and Wanda, 87
Tomaras, Steve, 75, 87, 96, 103, 110, 116, 136, 139, 152, 179, 233
Tomasczek, Gerald, 16
Tomasello, Albert, 176
Trading stamps, 269
Treasure Island Motel, 257, 262
Tri-State Tollway, 304
Triner, Fred, policeman, 140
Turner, James, policeman, 138
Turn-Style Family Center, 297
Twenty-Sixth and Cal, 195

U.S. Court of Appeals, 151, 290
U.S. District Court, 151
U.S. Highway 30, 122
U.S. Highway 41, 133
U.S. Post Office, 268
U.S. Secret Service, 284
U.S. Weather Bureau, 137
University of Minnesota, 227

Valente, Joe, 166
Van Nuys, California, 235
Vansclow, Patrolman Herbert, 57
Varon, Joe, 264

Wabansia Avenue, 142, 173
Wacker Drive, 90, 23
Walgreen Drugs, 7, 306
Walsh, Patrolman Lester, 57
Walther Memorial Hospital, 140
Walton Street, 66
Warrenville, Ohio, 207
Washington Senators, 74
Washington Square, 117
Washtenaw Avenue, 57
Water Street, 176
Watergate, 300
Waveland Avenue, 147
Webb, Detective Dwight, 65
Weber, Maurice, 127
Weiss, Judge George B., 136
Weiss, Hymie, 68
Western Avenue, 65, 77, 95, 100, 219
Wheeling, Illinois, 298
White Castle, 10
Whiteside, Chief Edwin, 184
Williams, Dennis, 303
Williams, Ted, 76
Wilmette, Illinois, 87, 183
Wilshire Boulevard, 233
Winston Plaza, 226
Woltman, George, 200
Wood Street, 173, 205
Woods, Nyland, policeman, 138
Works Progress Administration (WPA), 45
World War II, 72, 184
Wright, George, 197, 200, 202
Wright Junior College, 149
Wrigley Field, 74

Yellow Cabs, 91

Zilligen, Terrence, 283

SPECIAL THANKS

The authors are grateful to Panczko victims Dan Byrnes and Walter Sterczek, Chicago Police Commander Kenneth Curin, former FBI agents John K. Chadwick, Robert John Miller and Thomas J. Green, and W.S. Neil, retired deputy warden of the Tennessee State Penitentiary, for sharing their frustrations with us.

In several instances in this book, where the Panczko brothers clearly identify police officers whom they said accepted bribes from them, or when they detail activities of fellow criminals who are still active, the authors exercised the discretion of giving the subjects assumed names out of consideration for their own well-being.

OTHER BOOKS
BY THE AUTHORS

Chicago Heist
Getting Away With Murder
Murder Next Door
Teresita, the Voice from the Grave

Also by Ed Baumann:
Step Into My Parlor, The Chilling Story of Serial Killer
   Jeffrey Dahmer
Chicago Originals with Kenan Heise

ABOUT THE AUTHORS

Between them, Edward Baumann and John O'Brien have covered every major crime in Chicago and the Middle-West in the past four decades. As crime reporters they have covered the Panczko brothers so often that they are on a first-name basis with one another.

Baumann, a native of Kenosha, Wisconsin, served with the Army Air Corps in the South Pacific during World War II. He worked as a reporter or editor for the Waukegan News-Sun, Chicago Daily News, Chicago's American, Chicago Today and The Chicago Tribune, before turning to free-lancing in 1988. He is past president of the Chicago Press Club, former chairman of the Chicago Press Veterans Association, a director of the Chicago Newspaper Reporters Association, and a member of the Midwest Chapter of the Mystery Writers of America, Milwaukee Press Club and Merry Gangsters Literary Society. In 1988 his peers honored him as Chicago Press Veteran of the Year.

O'Brien, who was born in Chicago, served with the U.S. Marine Corps before becoming a reporter for The Chicago Tribune. He has done in-depth stories on criminal justice in Michigan and California, exposes on child abuse in Texas and political dirty tricks in North Dakota, covered the late Mob chief Tony Accardo in Florida, and joined investigators in tracking down three suspects in a fortune in stolen cash all the way to the British West Indies. He once helped arrest a probation officer for taking a bribe from a probationer. In 1989 he shared the Tribune's Edward Scott Beck award for investigative reporting. He is currently one of three authors of the On The Law column, appearing weekly in The Tribune.

BESTSELLING TRUE CRIME TITLES

Teresita
The voice from the grave
Ed Baumann and John O'Brien
ISBN 0-929387-67-8 ● 318 pages
6" x 9" ● illustrated ● $19.95 cloth

Murder Next Door
How police tracked down 18 brutal killers
Ed Baumann and John O'Brien
ISBN 0-929387-61-9 ● 328 pages
6" x 9" ● illustrated ● $19.95 cloth

Getting Away with Murder
57 unsolved murders with
reward information
Ed Baumann and John O'Brien
ISBN 0-929387-51-1 ● 385 pages
6" x 9" ● illustrated ● $19.95 cloth

Step Into My Parlor
The chilling story of serial killer
Jeffrey Dahmer
Ed Baumann
ISBN 0-929387-64-3 ● 305 pages
6" x 9" ● illustrated ● $19.95 cloth

William Heirens: His Day In Court
Did an innocent teen-ager confess
to three shocking murders?
Dolores Kennedy
ISBN 0-929387-50-3 ● 408 pages
6" x 9" ● illustrated ● $19.95 cloth

On a Killing Day
The bizarre story and trial of the first female serial
killer, Aileen "Lee" Wuornos
Dolores Kennedy
ISBN 0-929387-75-9 ● 290 pages
6" x 9" ● illustrated ● $19.95 cloth

160 east Illinois street
chicago, illinois 60611

Toll Free
1●800●225●3775